APPLETONS' POPULAR LIBRARY

OF THE BEST AUTHORS.

THE CONFESSIONS OF FITZ-BOODLE;

AND

SOME PASSAGES IN THE LIFE OF MAJOR GAHAGAN.

THE

CONFESSIONS OF FITZ-BOODLE;

AND

SOME PASSAGES

IN THE

LIFE OF MAJOR GAHAGAN.

BY

W. M. THACKERAY.

AUTHOR OF "PENDENNIS," "THE LUCK OF BARRY LYNDON,"
"THE BOOK OF SNOBS," "MEN'S WIVES," ETC.

NEW-YORK:
D. APPLETON & COMPANY, 200 BROADWAY.
M.DCCC.LII.

PUBLISHER'S ADVERTISEMENT.

THE "CONFESSIONS OF FITZ-BOODLE" are printed from *Fraser's Magazine* for the year 1842, and "SOME PASSAGES IN THE LIFE OF MAJOR GAHAGAN," from the London edition, of the year 1841.

NEW YORK, NOVEMBER, 1852.

CONTENTS.

CONFESSIONS OF FITZ-BOODLE.

SOME PASSAGES IN THE LIFE OF MAJOR GAHAGAN.

FITZ-BOODLE'S CONFESSIONS.

PREFACE.

GEORGE FITZ-BOODLE, ESQUIRE, TO OLIVER YORKE, ESQUIRE.

Omnium Club, May 20, 1842.

DEAR SIR,—I have always been considered the third-best whist-player in Europe, and (though never betting more than five pounds) have for many years past added considerably to my yearly income by my skill in the game, until the commencement of the present season, when a French gentleman, Monsieur Lalouette, was admitted to the club where I usually play. His skill and reputation were so great, that no men of the club were inclined to play against us two of a side; and the consequence has been, that we have been in a manner pitted against one another. By a strange turn of luck (for I cannot admit the idea of his superiority), Fortune, since the Frenchman's arrival, has been almost constantly against me, and I have lost two-and-thirty nights in the course of a couple of score of nights' play.

Every body knows that I am a poor man; and so much has Lalouette's luck drained my finances, that only last week I was obliged to give him that famous grey cob on which you have seen me riding in the Park (I can't afford a thorough-bred, and hate a cocktail),—I was, I say, forced to give him up my cob in exchange for four ponies which I owed him. Thus, as I never walk, being a heavy man whom nobody cares to mount, my time hangs heavily on my hands; and as I hate home, or that apology for it—a bachelor's lodgings, and as I have nothing earthly to do now until I can afford to purchase another horse, I spend my time in sauntering from one club to another, passing many rather listless hours in them before the men come in.

You will say, Why not take to backgammon, or *écarté*, or amuse yourself with a book? Sir (putting out of the question the fact that I do not play upon credit), I make a point never to play before candles are lighted; and as for books, I must candidly confess to you I am not a reading man. 'Twas but the other day that some one recommended me to read your Magazine after dinner, saying it contained an exceedingly witty article upon—I forget what—I give you my honour, sir, that I took up the work at six, meaning to amuse myself till seven, when Lord Trumpington's dinner was to come off, and egad! in two minutes I fell asleep, and never woke till midnight. Nobody ever thought of looking for me in the library, where nobody ever goes; and so ravenously hungry was I, that I was obliged to walk off to Crockford's for supper.

What is it that makes you literary persons so stupid? I have met various individuals in society who I was told were writers of books, and that sort of thing, and expecting rather to be amused by their conversation, have invariably found them dull to a degree, and as for information, without a particle of it. Sir, I actually asked one of these fellows, "What was the nick to seven?" and he stared in my face, and said he didn't know. He was hugely overdressed in satin, rings, chains, and so forth; and at the beginning of dinner was disposed to be rather talkative and pert; but my little sally silenced *him* I promise you, and got up a good laugh at his expense, too. "Leave George alone," said little Lord Cinqbars, "I warrant he'll be a match for any of you literary fellows." Cinqbars is no great wiseacre; but, indeed, it requires no great wiseacre to know *that.*

What is the simple deduction to be drawn from this truth? Why this,—that a man to be amusing and well-informed, has no need of books at all, and had much better go to the world and to men for his knowledge. There was Ulysses, now, the Greek fellow engaged in the Trojan war, as I dare say you know; well, he was the cleverest man possible, and how? from having seen men and cities, their manners noted and their realms surveyed, to be sure: so have I—I have been in every capital, and can order a dinner in every language in Europe.

My notion, then, is this. I have a great deal of spare time on my hands, and as I am told you pay a handsome sum to persons writing for you, I will furnish you occasionally with some of my views upon men and things; occasional histories of my acquaintance, which I think may amuse you; personal narratives of my own; essays, and what not. I am told that I do not spell correctly. This, of course, I don't know; but you will remember that Richelieu and Marlborough could not spell, and, egad! I am an honest man, and desire to be no better than they. I know that it is the matter, and not the manner, which is of importance. Have the goodness, then, to let one of your understrappers correct the spelling and the grammar of my papers; and you can give him a few shillings in my name for his trouble.

Begging you to accept the assurance of my high consideration, I am, sir,

Your obedient servant,

George Savage Fitz-Boodle.

P. S. By the way, I have said in my letter that I found *all* literary persons vulgar and dull. Permit me to contradict this with regard to yourself. I met you once at Blackwall, I think it was, and really did not remark anything offensive in your accent or appearance.

FITZ-BOODLE'S CONFESSIONS.

Before commencing the series of moral disquisitions, &c., which I intend, the reader may as well know who I am, and what my past course of life has been. To say that I am a Fitz-Boodle is to say at once that I am a gentleman. Our family has held the estate of Boodle ever since the reign of Henry II.; and it is out of no ill-will to my elder brother, or unnatural desire for his death, but only because the estate is a very good one, that I wish heartily it was mine: I would say as much of Chatsworth or Eaton Hall.

I am not, in the first place, what is called a ladies' man, having contracted an irrepressible habit of smoking after dinner, which has obliged me to give up a great deal of the dear creatures' society; nor can I go much to country-houses for the same reason. Say what they will, ladies do not like you to smoke in their bed-rooms; their silly little noses scent out the odour upon the chintz, weeks after you have left them. Sir John has been caught coming to bed particularly merry and redolent of cigar smoke. Young George, from Eton, was absolutely found in the little green-house puffing an Havanna; and when discovered, they both lay the blame upon Fitz-Boodle. "It was Mr. Fitz-Boodle, mamma," says George, "who offered me the cigar, and I did not like to refuse him." "That rascal Fitz seduced us, my dear," says Sir John, "and kept us laughing until past midnight." Her ladyship instantly sets me down as a person to be avoided. "George," whispers she to her boy, "promise me, on your honour, when you go to town, not to know that man." And when she enters the breakfast room for prayers, the first greeting is a peculiar expression of countenance and inhaling of breath, by which my lady indicates the presence of some exceedingly disagreeable odour in the room. She makes you the faintest of courtesys, and regards you, if not with a "flashing eye," as in the novels, at least with a "distended nostril." During the whole of the service, her heart is filled with the blackest gall towards you; and she is thinking about the best means of getting you out of the house.

What is this smoking that it should be considered a crime? I believe in my heart that women are jealous of it, as of a rival. They speak of it as of some secret, awful vice that seizes upon a man, and makes him a Pariah from genteel society. I would lay a guinea that many a lady who has just been kind enough to read the above lines lays down the book, after this confession of mine that I am a smoker, and says, "Oh, the vulgar wretch!" and passes on to something else.

The fact is, that the cigar *is* a rival to the ladies, and their conqueror, too. In the chief pipe-smoking nations they are kept in subjection. While the chief, Little White Belt, smokes, the women are silent in his wigwam; while Mahomet Ben Jawbrakine causes volumes of odorous incense of Latakia to play round his beard, the women of the harem do not disturb his meditations, but only add to the delight of them by tinkling on a dulcimer and dancing before him. When Professor Strumpff, of Göttingen, takes down No. 13 from the wall, with a picture of Beatrice Cenci upon it, and which holds a pound of canaster, the Frau Professorin knows that for two hours Hermann is engaged, and takes up her stockings, and knits in quiet. The constitution of French society has been quite changed within the last twelve years; an ancient and respectable dynasty has been overthrown; an aristocracy which Napoleon could never master has disappeared: and from what cause? I do not hesitate to say,—*from the habit of smoking*. Ask any man whether, five years before the revolution of July, if you wanted a cigar at Paris, they did not bring you a roll of tobacco with a straw in it? Now, the whole city smokes; society is changed; and be sure of this, ladies, a similar combat is going on in this country at present between cigar-smoking and you. Do you suppose you will conquer? Look over the wide world, and see that your adversary has overcome it. Germany has been puffing for threescore years; France smokes to a man. Do you think you can keep the enemy out of England? Pshaw! look at his progress. Ask the club-houses, Have they smoking rooms, or not? Are they not obliged to yield to the general want of the age, in spite of the resistance of the old women on the committees? I, for my part, do not despair to see a bishop lolling out of the Athenæum with a cheroot in his mouth, or, at any rate, a pipe stuck in his shovel-hat.

But as in all great causes and in promulgating of new and illustrious theories, their first propounders and exponents are generally the victims of their enthusiasm, of course the first preachers of smoking have been martyrs too; and George Fitz-Boodle is one. The first gasman was ruined; the inventor of steam-engine printing became a pauper. I began to smoke in days when the task was one of some danger, and paid the penalty of my crime. I was flogged most fiercely for my first cigar; for being asked to dine one Sunday evening with a half-pay colonel of dragoons (the gallant, simple, humorous Shortcut—Heaven bless him!—I have had many a guinea from him who had so few), he insisted upon my smoking in his room at the Salopian, and the consequence was, that I became so violently ill as to be reported intoxicated upon my return to Slaughter-house School, where I was a boarder, and I was whipped the next morning for my peccadillo. At Christ Church, one of our tutors was the celebrated lamented Otto Rose, who would have been a bishop under the present government, had not an immoderate indulgence in water-gruel cut short his elegant and useful career. He was a good man, a pretty scholar and poet (the episode upon the discovery of eau de Cologne, in his prize-poem on "The Rhine," was considered a masterpiece of art, though I am not much of a judge myself upon such matters), and he was as remarkable for his fondness for a tuft as for his nervous antipathy to tobacco. As ill-luck would have it, my rooms (in Tom Quad) were exactly under his; and I was grown by this time to be a confirmed smoker. I was a baronet's son (we are of James's first creation), and I do believe our tutor could have pardoned any crime in the world but this. He had seen me in a tandem, and at that moment was seized with a violent fit of sneezing sternutatory paroxysm, he called it), at the conclusion of which I was a mile down the Woodstock Road. He had seen me in pink, as we used to call it, swaggering in the open sunshine across a grass-plat in the court; but spied out opportunely a servitor, one Todhunter by name, who was going to morning chapel with his shoe-string untied, and forthwith sprung towards that unfortunate person, to set him an imposition. Every thing, in fact, but tobacco he could forgive. Why did cursed fortune bring him into the rooms over mine? The odour of the cigars made his gentle spirit quite furious; and one luckless morning, when I was standing before my "oak," and chanced to puff a great *bouffée* of Varinas into his face, he forgot his respect for my family altogether (I was the second son, and my brother a sickly creature *then*,—he is now sixteen stone in weight, and has a half-score of children); gave me a severe lecture, to which I replied rather hotly, as was my wont. And then came demand for an apology; refusal on my part; appeal to the dean; convocation; and rustication of George Edward Fitz-Boodle.

My father had taken a second wife (of the noble house of Flintskinner), and Lady Fitz-Boodle detested smoking, as a woman of her high principles should. She had an entire mastery over the worthy old gentleman, and thought I was a sort of demon of wickedness. The old man went to his grave with some similar notion,—Heaven help him! and left me but the wretched twelve thousand pounds secured to me on my poor mother's property.

In the army, my luck was much the same. I joined the ———th lancers, Lieut.-Col. Lord Martingale, in the year 1817. I only did duty with the regiment for three months. We were quartered at Cork, where I found the Irish doodheen and tobacco the pleasantest smoking possible; and was found by his lordship one day upon stable duty, smoking the shortest, dearest, little, dumpy clay-pipe in the world.

"Cornet Fitz-Boodle," said my lord, in a towering passion, "from what blackguard did you get that pipe?"

I omit the oaths which garnished invariably his lordship's conversation.

"I got it, my lord," said I, "from one Terence Mullins, a jingle-driver, with a packet of his peculiar tobacco. You sometimes smoke Turkish, I believe; do try this. Isn't it good?" And in the simplest way in the world I puffed a volume into his face. "I see you like it," said I, so coolly, that the men, and I do believe the horses, burst out laughing.

He started back—choking almost, and recovered himself only to vent such a storm of oaths and curses, that I was compelled to request Capt. Rawdon (the captain on duty) to take note of his lordship's words; and unluckily could not help adding a question which settled my business. "You were good enough," I said, "to ask me, my lord, from what blackguard I got my pipe; might I ask from what blackguard you learned your language?"

This was quite enough. Had I said "from what

gentleman did your lordship learn your language?" the point would have been quite as good, and my lord Martingale would have suffered in my place: as it was, I was so strongly recommended to sell out by his Royal Highness the Commander-in-chief, that being of a good-natured disposition, never knowing how to refuse a friend, I at once threw up my hopes of military distinction, and retired into civil life.

My lord was kind enough to meet me afterwards, in a field in the Glaumire Road, where he put a ball into my leg. This I returned to him some years later with about twenty-three others—black ones—when he came to be balloted for at a club of which I have the honour to be a member.

Thus by the indulgence of a simple and harmless propensity,—of a propensity which can inflict an injury upon no person or thing except the coat and the person of him who indulges in it,—of a custom honoured and observed in almost all the nations of the world,—of a custom which far from leading a man into any wickedness or dissipation to which youth is subject, but, on the contrary, begets only benevolent silence and thoughtful good-humoured observation, I found at the age of twenty all my prospects in life destroyed. I cared not for woman in those days; the calm smoker has a sweet companion in his pipe: I did not drink immoderately of wine; for though a friend to trifling potations, to excessively strong drinks tobacco is abhorrent; I never thought of gambling, for the lover of the pipe has no need of such excitement; but I was considered a monster of dissipation in my family, and bade fair to come to ruin.

"Look at George," my mother-in-law said to the genteel and correct young Flintskinners; "he entered the world with every prospect in life, and see in what an abyss of degradation his fatal habits have plunged him! At school he was flogged and disgraced, he was disgraced and rusticated at the university, he was disgraced and expelled from the army. He might have had the living of Boodle (her ladyship gave it to one of her nephews), but he would not take his degree; his papa would have purchased him a troop—nay, a lieutenant-colonelcy some day, but for his fatal excesses. And now as long as my dear husband will listen to the voice of a wife who adores him—never, never shall he spend a shilling upon so worthless a young man. He has a small income from his mother (I cannot but think that the first Lady Fitz-Boodle was a weak and misguided person); let him live upon his mean pittance as he can, and I heartily pray we may not hear of him in gaol!"

My brother, after he came to the estate, married the ninth daughter of our neighbour, Sir John Spreadeagle; and Boodle Hall has seen a new little Fitz-Boodle with every succeeding spring. The dowager retired to Scotland with a large jointure and a wondrous heap of savings. Lady Fitz is a good creature, but she thinks me something diabolical, trembles when she sees me, and gathers all her children about her, rushes into the nursery whenever I pay that little seminary a visit, and actually slapped poor little Frank's ears one day when I was teaching him to ride upon the back of a Newfoundland dog.

"George," said my brother to me the last time I paid

him a visit to the old hall, "don't be angry, my dear fellow, but Maria is in a—hum—in a delicate situation, expecting her—hum—(the eleventh)—and do you know you frighten her? It was but yesterday you met her in the Rookery, you were smoking that enormous German pipe, and when she came in she had an hysterical seizure, and Drench says that in her situation it's dangerous; and I say, George, if you go to town you'll find a couple of hundred at your banker's;" and with this the poor fellow shook me by the hand, and called for a fresh bottle of claret.

Since then he told me, with many hesitations, that my room at Boodle Hall had been made into a second nursery. I see my sister-in-law in London twice or thrice in the season, and the little people, who have almost forgotten to call me Uncle George.

It's hard, too, for I am a lonely man, after all, and my heart yearns to them. The other day I smuggled a couple of them into my chambers, and had a little feast of cream and strawberries to welcome them. But it had like to have cost the nurserymaid (a Swiss girl that Fitz-Boodle hired somewhere in his travels) her place. My step-mamma, who happened to be in town, came flying down in her chariot, pounced upon the poor thing and the children in the midst of the entertainment; and when I asked her, with rather a bad grace to be sure, to take a chair and a share of the feast,—

"Mr. Fitz-Boodle," said she, "I am not accustomed to sit down in a place that smells of tobacco like an ale-house—an ale-house inhabited by a *serpent*, sir! A *serpent!* do you understand me? who carries his poison into his brother's own house, and purshues his eenfamous designs before his brother's own children. Put on Miss Maria's bonnet this instant. Mamsell, ontondy-voo ? *Metty le bonny à mamsell ;* and I shall take care, mamsell, that you return to Switzerland to-morrow. I've no doubt you are a relation of Courvoisier : *oui, oui, Courvoisier ; vous comprenny ?* and you shall certainly be sent back to your friends."

With this speech, and with the children and their maid sobbing before her, my lady retired ; but for once my sister-in-law was on my side, not liking the meddlement of the elder lady.

I know, then, that from indulging in that simple habit of smoking, I have gained among the ladies a dreadful reputation. I see that they look coolly upon me, and darkly at their husbands when they arrive at home in my company. Men, I observe, in consequence, ask me to dine much oftener at the club, or the Star and Garter at Richmond, or at Lovegrove's, than in their own houses ; and with this sort of arrangement I am fain to acquiesce ; for, as I said before, I am of an easy temper, and can at any rate take my cigar-case out after dinner at Blackwall, when my lady or the duchess are not by. I know, of course, the best *men* in town ; and as for ladies' society, not having it (for I will have none of your pseudo-ladies, such as sometimes honour bachelors' parties,—actresses, couturières, opera-dancers, and so forth)—as for ladies' society, I say, I cry pish ! 't is not worth the trouble of the complimenting, and the bother of pumps and black silk stockings.

Let any man remember what ladies' society was when he had an opportunity of seeing them among themselves, as What-d'ye-call'em does in Thesmophoriazu—(I beg pardon, I was on the verge of a classical allusion, which I abominate)—I mean at that period of his life when the intellect is pretty acute, though the body is small—namely, when a young gentleman is about eleven years of age, dining at his father's table during the holydays, and is requested by his papa to quit the dinner-table when the ladies retire from it.

Corbleu! I recollect their whole talk as well as if it had been whispered but yesterday; and can see, after a long dinner, the yellow summer sun throwing long shadows over the lawn before the dining-room windows, my poor mother and her company of ladies, sailing away to the music-room in old Boodle Hall. The Countess Dawdley was the great Lady in our county,—a portly lady who used to love crimson satin in those days, and birds of paradise. She was flaxen-haired, and tho Regent once said she resembled one of King Charles's beauties.

When Sir John Todcaster used to begin his famous story of the exciseman (I shall not tell it here, for very good reasons), my poor mother used to turn to Lady Dawdley, and give that mystic signal at which all females rise from their chairs. Tufthunt the curate would spring from his seat, and be sure to be the first to open the door for the retreating ladies; and my brother Tom and I, though remaining stoutly in our places, were speedily ejected from them by the governor's invariable remark, "Tom and George, if you have had *quite* enough of wine, you had better go and join your mamma." Yonder she marches, Heaven bless her! through the old oak hall (how long the shadows of the antlers are on the wainscot, and the armour of Rollo Fitz-Boodle looks in the sunset as if it were emblazoned with rubies)—yonder she marches, stately and tall in her invariable pearl-coloured tabinet, followed by Lady Dawdley, blazing like a flamingo; next comes Lady Emily Tufthunt (she was Lady Emily Skinflinter), who will not for all the world take precedence of rich, vulgar, kind, good-humoured Mrs. *Colonel* Grogwater, as she would be called, with a yellow little husband from Madras, who first taught me to drink sangaree. He was a new arrival in our county, but paid nobly to the hounds, and occupied hospitably a house which was always famous for its hospitality—Sievely Hall (poor Bob Cullender ran through seven thousand a-year before he was thirty years old). Once when I was a lad, Colonel Grogwater gave me two gold mohurs out of his desk for whist-markers, and I'm sorry to say I ran up from Eton and sold them both for seventy-three shillings at a shop in Cornhill. But to return to the ladies who are all this while kept waiting in the hall, and to their usual conversation after dinner.

Can any man forget how miserably flat it was? Five matrons sit on sofas and talk in a subdued voice:—

First lady (mysteriously). "My dear Lady Dawdley, do tell me about poor Susan Tuckett."

Second lady. "All three children are perfectly well, and I assure you as fine babies as I ever saw in my life. I made her give them Daffy's Elixir the first day; and it was the greatest mercy that I had some of Frederick's baby-clothes by me; for you know I had provided Susan with sets for one only, and really——"

Third lady. "Of course one couldn't; and for my

part I think your ladyship is a great deal too kind to these people. A little gardener's boy dressed in Lord Dawdley's frocks, indeed! I recollect that one at his christening had the sweetest lace in the world!"

Fourth lady. "What do you think of this, ma'am—Lady Emily, I mean? I have just had it from Howell and James:—gipure, they call it. Isn't it an odd name for lace? And they charge me upon my conscience, four guineas a yard!"

Third lady. "My mother, when she came to Skinflinter, had lace upon her robe that cost sixty guineas a yard, ma'am! 'T was sent from Malines direct by our relation, the Count d'Araignay."

Fourth Lady (*aside*). "I thought she would not let the evening pass without talking of her Malines lace and her Count d'Araignay. Odious people! they don't spare their backs, but they pinch their ——"

Here Tom upsets a coffee-cup over his white jean trousers, and another young gentleman bursts into a laugh, saying, "By Jove, that's a good 'un!"

"George, my dear," says mamma, "had not you and your young friend better go into the garden? But mind, no fruit, or Dr. Glauber must be called in again immediately!" and we all go, and in ten minutes I and my brother are fighting in the stables.

If instead of listening to the matrons and their discourse, we had taken the opportunity of attending to the conversation of the misses, we should have heard matter not a whit more interesting.

First Miss. "They were all three in blue crape; you never saw any thing so odious. And I know for a certainty that they wore those dresses at Gúttlebury at the archery-ball, and I daresay they had them in town."

Second Miss. "Don't you think Jemima decidedly crooked? And those fair complexions they freckle so, that really Miss Blanch ought to be called Miss Brown."

Third Miss. "He, he, he!"

Fourth Miss. "Don't you think Blanch is a pretty name?"

First Miss. "La! do you think so, dear? Why, it's my second name!"

Second Miss. "Then I'm sure Captain Travers thinks it a *beautiful* name!"

Third Miss. "He, he, he!"

Fourth Miss. "What was he telling you at dinner that seemed to interest you so?"

First Miss. "O law, nothing!—that is, yes! Charles—that is, Captain Travers, is a sweet poet, and was reciting to me some lines that he had composed upon a faded violet:—

'The odour from the flower is gone,
That like thy ——'

like thy something, I forget what it was; but his lines are sweet, and so original too! I wish that horrid Sir John Todhunter had not begun his story of the exciseman, for Lady Fitz-Boodle always quits the table when he begins."

Third Miss. "Do you like those tufts that gentlemen wear sometimes on their chins?"

Second Miss. "Nonsense, Mary!"

Third Miss. "Well, I only asked, Jane. Frank

thinks, you know, that he shall very soon have one, and puts bear's-grease on his chin every night."

Second Miss. "Mary, nonsense!"

Third Miss. "Well, only ask him. You know he came to our dressing-room last night and took the pomatum away; and he says that when boys go to Oxford they always ——"

First Miss. "Oh, heavens! have you heard the news about the Lancers? Charles—that is, Captain Travers, told it me!"

Second Miss. "Law! they won't go away before the ball, I hope!"

First Miss. "No, but on the 15th they are to shave their mustachios! He says that Lord Tufto is in a perfect fury about it!"

Second Miss. "And poor George Beardmore, too!" &c.

Here Tom upsets the coffee over his trousers, and the conversations end. I can recollect a dozen such, and ask any man of sense whether such talk amuses him?

Try again to speak to a young lady while you are dancing—what we call in this country—a quadrille. What nonsense do you invariably give and receive in return! No, I am a woman-scorner, and don't care to own it. I hate young ladies! Have I not been in love with several, and has any one of them ever treated me decently? I hate married women! Do they not hate me? and, simply because I smoke, try to draw their husbands away from my society? I hate dowagers! Have I not cause? Does not every dowager in London point to George Fitz-Boodle as to a dissolute wretch whom young and old should avoid?

And yet do not imagine that I have not loved. I have, and madly, many, many times! I am but eight-and-thirty,* not past the age of passion, and may very likely end by running off with an heiress—or a cook-maid (for who knows what strange freaks Love may choose to play in his own particular person? and I hold a man to be a mean creature who calculates about checking any such sacred impulse as lawful love)—I say, though despising the sex in general for their conduct to me, I know of particular persons belonging to it who are worthy of all respect and esteem, and as such I beg leave to point out the particular young lady who is perusing these lines. Do not, dear madam, then imagine that if I knew you, I should be disposed to sneer at you. Ah, no! Fitz-Boodle's bosom has tenderer sentiments than from his way of life you would fancy, and stern by rule is only too soft by practice. Shall I whisper to you the story of one or two of my attachments? All terminating fatally (not in death, but in disappointment, which, as it occurred, I used to imagine a thousand times more bitter than death, but from which one recovers somehow more readily than from the other-named complaint)—all, I say, terminating wretchedly to myself, as if some fatality pursued my desire to become a domestic character.

My first love—no, let us pass *that* over. Sweet one! thy name shall profane no hireling page. Sweet, sweet memory! Ah, ladies; those delicate hearts of yours have too felt the throb;—and between that last *ob* in the word throb and the words now written, I have

* He is five-and-forty if he is a day old.—O. Y.

passed a delicious period of perhaps an hour, perhaps a minute, I know not how long, thinking of that holy first love and of her who inspired it. How clearly every single incident of the passion is remembered by me! and yet 'twas long, long since; I was but a child then—a child at school—and, if the truth must be told L—ra R–ggl–s (I would not write her whole name to be made one of the Marquess of Hertford's executors) was a woman full thirteen years older than myself; at the period of which I write, she must have been at least five-and-twenty. She and her mother used to sell tarts, hard-bake, lollipops, and other such simple comestibles, on Wednesdays and Saturdays (half-holidays) at a private school where I received the first rudiments of a classical education. I used to go and sit before her tray for hours, but I do not think the poor girl ever supposed any motive led me so constantly to her little stall beyond a vulgar longing for her tarts and her ginger-beer. Yes, even at that early period my actions were misrepresented, and the fatality which has oppressed my whole life began to show itself,—the purest passion was misinterpreted by her and my schoolfellows, and they thought I was actuated by simple gluttony. They nicknamed me Alicompayne.

Well, be it so. Laugh at early passion ye who will; a high-born boy madly in love with a lowly ginger-beer girl! She married afterwards, took the name of Latter, and now keeps with her old husband a turnpike, through which I often ride; but I can recollect her bright and rosy of a sunny summer afternoon, her red cheeks shaded by a battered straw bonnet, her tarts and ginger-beer upon a neat white cloth before her, mending blue worsted stockings until the young gentlemen should interrupt her by coming to buy.

Many persons will call this description low; I do not envy them their gentility, and have always observed through life (as, to be sure, every other *gentleman* has observed as well as myself) that it is your *parvenu* who stickles most for what he calls the genteel, and has the most squeamish abhorrence for what is frank and natural. Let us pass at once, however, as all the world must be pleased, to a recital of an affair which occurred in the very best circles of society as they are called, viz., my next unfortunate attachment.

It did not occur for several years after that simple and platonic passion just described, for though they may talk of youth as the season of romance, it has always appeared to me that there are no beings in the world so entirely unromantic and selfish as certain young English gentlemen from the age of fifteen to twenty. The oldest Lovelace about town is scarcely more hard-hearted and scornful than they; they ape all sorts of selfishness and *rouerie;* they aim at excelling at cricket, at billiards, at rowing, and drinking, and set more store by a red coat and a neat pair of top-boots than by any other glory. A young fellow staggers into college-chapel of a morning, and communicates to all his friends that he was "*so cut* last night," with the greatest possible pride. He makes a joke of having sisters and a kind mother at home who loves him; and if he speaks of his father, it is with a knowing sneer to say that he has a tailor's and a horse-dealer's bill that will surprise "the old governor." He would be ashamed of being in love. I, in common with my kind, had these affectations, and my perpetual custom of smoking added not a little to my reputation as an accomplished *roué*. What came of this custom in the army and at college, the reader has already heard. Alas! in life it went no better with me, and many pretty chances I had went off in that accursed smoke.

After quitting the army in the abrupt manner stated, I passed some short time at home, and was tolerated by my mother-in-law, because I had formed an attachment to a young lady of good connexions and with a considerable fortune, which was really very nearly becoming mine. Mary M'Alister was the only daughter of Colonel M'Alister, late of the Blues, and Lady Susan his wife. Her ladyship was no more; and, indeed, of no family compared to ours (which has refused a peerage any time these two hundred years), but being an earl's daughter and a Scotch woman, Lady Emily Fitz-Boodle did not fail to consider her highly. Lady Susan was daughter of the late Admiral Earl of Marlingspike and Baron Plumduff. The colonel, Miss M'Alister's father, had a good estate, of which his daughter was the heiress, and as I fished her out of the water upon a pleasure-party, and swam with her to shore, we became naturally intimate, and Colonel M'Alister forgot, on account of the service rendered to him, the dreadful reputation for profligacy which I enjoyed in the county.

Well, to cut a long story short, which is told here merely for the moral at the end of it, I should have been Fitz-Boodle M'Alister at this minute most probably, and master of four thousand a-year, but for the fatal cigar-box. I bear Mary no malice in saying that she was a high-spirited little girl, loving, before all things, her own way; nay, perhaps, do not from long habit and indulgence in tobacco-smoking appreciate the delicacy of female organisations which were oftentimes most painfully affected by it. She was a keen-sighted little person, and soon found that the world had belied poor George Fitz-Boodle, who, instead of being the cunning monster people supposed him to be, was a simple, reckless, good-humoured, honest fellow, marvellously addicted to smoking, idleness, and telling the truth. She called me Orson, and I was happy enough on the 14th February, in the year 18— (it's of no consequence), to send her such a pretty little copy of verses about Orson and *Valentine*, in which the rude habits of the savage man were shown to be overcome by the polished graces of his kind and brilliant conqueror, that she was fairly overcome, and said to me, "George Fitz-Boodle, if you give up smoking for a year I will marry you."

I swore I would, of course, and went home and flung four pounds of Hudson's cigars, two meerschaum pipes that had cost me ten guineas at the establishment of Mr. Gattie at Oxford, a tobacco-bag that Lady Fitz-Boodle had given me *before* her marriage with my father (it was the only present that I ever had from her or any member of the Skinflinter family), and some choice packets of Varinas and Syrian, into the lake in Boodle Park. The weapon amongst them all which I most regretted was—will it be believed?—the little black doodheen which had been the cause of the quarrel between Lord Martingale and me. However, it went along with the others. I would not allow my groom to have so much as a cigar, lest I should be tempted hereafter; and the consequence was that a few days after many fat carps and tenches in the lake (I must confess 'twas no bigger than a pond) nibbled at the tobacco, and came floating on their backs on the top of the water quite intoxicated. My conversion made some noise in the county, being emphasised as it were by this fact of the fish. I can't tell you with what pangs I kept my resolution; but keep it I did for some time.

With so much beauty and wealth, Mary M'Alister had of course many suitors, and among them was the young Lord Dawdley, whose mamma has previously been described in her gown of red satin. As I used to thrash Dawdley at school, I thrashed him in after life in love, and he put up with his disappointment pretty well, and came after a while and shook hands with me, telling me of the bets that there were in the county where the whole story was known, for and against me. For the fact is, as I must own, that Mary M'Alister, the queerest, frankest of women, made no secret of the agreement, or the cause of it.

"I did not care a penny for Orson," she said, "but he would go on writing me such dear pretty verses that at last I couldn't help saying yes. But if he breaks his promise to me, I declare, upon my honour, I'll break mine, and nobody's heart will be broken either."

This was the perfect fact, as I must confess, and I declare that it was only because she amused me and delighted me, and provoked me and made me laugh very much, and because, no doubt, she was very rich, that I had any attachment for her.

"For Heaven's sake, George," my father said to me,

as I quitted home to follow my beloved to London, "remember that you are a younger brother and have a lovely girl and four thousand a-year within a year's reach of you. Smoke as much as you like, my boy, after marriage," added the old gentleman, knowingly (as if *he*, honest soul, after his second marriage, dared drink an extra pint of wine without my lady's permission!) "but eschew the tobacco-shops till then."

I went to London resolving to act upon the paternal advice, and oh! how I longed for the day when I should be married, vowing in my secret soul that I would light a cigar as I walked out of St. George's Hanover Square.

Well, I came to London, and so carefully avoided smoking that I would not even go into Hudson's shop to pay his bill, and as smoking was not the fashion then among young men as (thank Heaven!) it is now, I had not many temptations from my friends' examples in my clubs or elsewhere; only little Dawdley began to smoke as if to spite me. He had never done so before, but confessed—the rascal!—that he enjoyed a cigar now, if it were but to mortify me. But I took to other and more dangerous excitements, and upon the nights when not in attendance upon Mary M'Alister, might be found in very dangerous proximity to a polished mahogany table, round which claret-bottles circulated a great deal too often, or, worse still, to a table covered with green cloth and ornamented with a couple of wax-candles and a couple of packs of cards, and four gentlemen playing the enticing game of whist. Likewise, I came to carry a snuff-box, and to consume in secret huge quantities of rappee.

For ladies' society I was even then disinclined, hating and despising small-talk, and dancing, and hot routs, and vulgar scrambles for suppers. I never could understand the pleasure of acting the part of lackey to a dowager, and standing behind her chair, or bustling through the crowd for her carriage. I always found an opera too long by two acts, and have repeatedly fallen asleep in the presence of Mary M'Alister herself, sitting at the back of the box shaded by the huge beret of her old aunt, Lady Betty Plumduff; and many a time has Dawdley, with Miss M'Alister on his arm, wakened me up at the close of the entertainment in time to offer my hand to Lady Betty, and lead the ladies to their carriage. If I attended her occasionally to any ball or party of pleasure, I went, it must be confessed, with clumsy, ill-disguised, ill-humour. Good Heavens! have I often and often thought in the midst of a song, or the very thick of a ball-room, can people prefer this to a book and a sofa, and a dear, dear cigar-box, from thy stores, O charming Mariana Woodville! Deprived of my favourite plant, I grew sick in mind and body, moody, sarcastic, and discontented.

Such a state of things could not long continue, nor could Miss M'Alister continue to have much attachment for such a sullen, ill-conditioned creature as I then was. She used to make me wild with her wit and her sarcasm, nor have I ever possessed the readiness to parry or reply to those fine points of woman's wit, and she treated me the more mercilessly as she saw that I could not resist her.

Well; the polite reader must remember a great fête that was given at B—— House, some years back, in honour of his Highness the Hereditary Prince of Kalbsbraten-Pumpernickel, who was then in London on a visit to his illustrious relatives. It was a fancy ball, and the poems of Scott being at that time all the fashion, Mary was to appear in the character of the "Lady of the Lake," old M'Alister making a very tall and severe-looking harper; Dawdley, a most insignificant Fitzjames; and your humble servant a stalwart and manly Roderick Dhu. We were to meet at B—— House, at twelve o'clock, and as I had no fancy to drive through the town in my cab dressed in a kilt and philibeg, I agreed to take a seat in Dawdley's carriage, and to dress at his house in May Fair. At eleven I left a very pleasant bachelors' party, growling to quit them and the honest, jovial claret bottle, in order to scrape and cut capers like a harlequin from the theatre. When I arrived at Dawdley's, I mounted to a dressing-room, and began to array myself in my cursed costume.

The art of costuming was by no means so well understood in those days as it has been since, and mine was out of all correctness. I was made to sport an enormous plume of black ostrich feathers, such as never was worn by any Highland chief, and had a huge tiger-skin sporran to dangle like an apron before innumerable yards of plaid petticoat. The Tartan cloak was outrageously hot and voluminous: it was the dog-days, and all these things I was condemned to wear in the midst of a crowd of a thousand people!

Dawdley sent up word as I was dressing, that his dress had not arrived, and he took my cab, and drove off in a rage to his tailor.

There was no hurry, I thought, to make a fool of

myself; so having put on a pair of plaid trews, and very neat pumps with shoe-buckles, my courage failed me as to the rest of the dress, and taking down one of his dressing-gowns, I went down-stairs to the study, to wait until he should arrive.

The windows of the pretty room were open, and a snug sofa, with innumerable cushions, drawn towards one of them. A great tranquil moon was staring into the chamber, in which stood, amidst books and all sorts of bachelors' lumber, a silver tray with a couple of tall Venice glasses, and a bottle of Maraschino bound with straw. I can see now the twinkle of the liquor in the moonshine, as I poured it into the glass; and I swallowed two or three little cups of it, for my spirits were downcast. Close to the tray of Maraschino stood—must I say it?—a box, a mere box of cedar, bound rudely together with pink paper, branded with the name of "HUDSON" on the side, and bearing on the cover the arms of Spain. I thought I would just take up the box, and look in it.

Ah, Heaven! there they were—a hundred and fifty of them, in calm, comfortable rows, lovingly side by side, they lay with the great moon shining down upon them—thin at the tip, full in the waist, elegantly round and full, a little spot here and there shining upon them—beauty-spots upon the cheek of Silva. The house was quite quiet. Dawdley always smoked in his room;—I had not smoked for four months and eleven days.

* * * * *

When Lord Dawdley came into the study, he did not make any remarks; and, oh, how easy my heart felt! He was dressed in his green and boots, after Westall's picture, correctly.

"It's time to be off, George," said he; "they told me you were dressed long ago. Come up, my man, and get ready."

I rushed up into the dressing-room, and madly dashed my head and arms into a pool of eau de Cologne. I drank, I believe, a tumbler-full of it. I called for my clothes, and, strange to say, they were gone. My servant brought them, however, saying that he had put them away—making some stupid excuse. I put them on not heeding them much, for I was half tipsy with the excitement of the ci—, of the smo——, of what had taken place in Dawdley's study, and with the Maraschino and the eau de Cologne I had drunk.

"What a fine odour of lavender-water!" said Dawdley, as we rode in the carriage.

I put my head out of the window and shrieked out a laugh; but made no other reply.

"What's the joke, George?" said Dawdley; "did I say any thing witty?"

"No," cried I, yelling still more wildly; "nothing more witty than usual."

"Don't be severe, George," said he, with a mortified air; and we drove on to B—— House.

* * * * *

There must have been something strange and wild in my appearance, and these awful black plumes, as I passed through the crowd; for I observed people looking and making a strange nasal noise (it is called sniffing, and for which I have no other more delicate term), and making way as I pushed on; but I moved forward very fiercely, for the wine, the Maraschino, the eau de Cologne, and the—the excitement had rendered me almost wild; and at length I arrived at the place where my lovely Lady of the Lake and her Harper stood. How beautiful she looked,—all eyes were upon her as she stood blushing. When she saw me, however, her countenance assumed an appearance of alarm. "Good heavens, George!" she said, stretching her hand to me; "what makes you look so wild and pale?" I advanced, and was going to take her hand, when she dropped it with a scream.

"Ah—ah—ah!" she said; "Mr. Fitz-Boodle, you've been smoking!"

There was an immense laugh from four hundred people round about us, and the scoundrelly Dawdley joined in the yell. I rushed furiously out, and as I passed hurtled over the fat Hereditary Prince of Kalbsbreton-Pumpernickel.

"Es nicht hier ungeheuer stark von Tabak!" I heard his highness say, as I madly flung myself through the aides-de-camp.

The next day Mary M'Alister, in a note full of the most odious good sense and sarcasm, reminded me of our agreement; said that she was quite convinced that we were not by any means fitted for one another, and begged me to consider myself henceforth quite free. The little wretch had the impertinence to send me a dozen boxes of cigars, which, she said, would console me for my lost love; as she was perfectly certain that I was not mercenary, and that I loved tobacco better than any woman in the world.

I believe she was right, though I have never to this

day been able to pardon the scoundrelly stratagem by which Dawdley robbed me of a wife and won one himself. As I was lying on his sofa, looking at the moon and lost in a thousand happy contemplations, Lord Dawdley, returning from the tailor's, saw me smoking at my leisure. On entering his dressing-room, a horrible treacherous thought struck him. "I must not betray my friend," said he; "but in love all is fair, and he shall betray himself." There were my tartans, my cursed feathers, my tiger-skin sporran, upon the sofa.

He called up my groom; he made the rascal put on all my clothes, and, giving him a guinea and four cigars, bade him lock himself into the little pantry and smoke them *without taking the clothes off*. John did so, and was very ill in consequence, and so when I came to B—— House, my clothes were redolent of tobacco, and I lost lovely Mary M'Alister.

I am godfather to one of Lady Dawdley's boys, and hers is the only house where I am allowed to smoke unmolested; but I have never been able to admire Dawdley, a sly *sournois*, spiritless, lily-livered fellow, that took his name off all his clubs the year he married.

"I am sick of this squeamish English world," said I, in bitter scorn, as I sat in my lonely lodgings smoking Mary M'Alister's cigars: "a curse upon their affectations of propriety and silly obedience to the dictates of whimpering woman! I will away to some other country where thought is free, and honest men have their way. I will have no more of your rose-water passion, or cringing drawing-room tenderness. Pshaw! is George Fitz-Boodle to be bound up in the scented ringlets of a woman, or made to fetch and carry her reticule? No, I will go where woman shall obey and not command me. I will be a Sheikh, and my wife shall cook my couscous, and dance before me, and light my narghilé. I will be a painted savage spearing the fish, and striking the deer, and my wife shall sing my great actions to me as I smoke my calumet in my lodge. Away! land of dowagers and milk-sops, Fitz-Boodle disowns you; he will wander to some other clime, where man is respected, and woman takes her proper rank in the creation, as the pretty smiling slave she would be."

I received at this time, in an abrupt enclosure from my father, 120*l.*, being a quarter's income, and a polite intimation from Lady Fitz-Boodle, that as I had disappointed every one of my parents' expectations (*she* my parent! faugh!), I must never look to the slightest pecuniary aid from them. Such a sum would not enable me to travel across the Atlantic or to the shores of the Red Sea, as was my first intention; I determined, therefore, to visit a country where, if woman was still too foolishly worshipped, at least smoking was tolerated, and took my departure at the Tower Stairs for Rotterdam and the Rhine.

There were no incidents of the voyage worth recounting, nor am I so absurd as to attempt to give the reader an account of Holland or any other country. This memoir is purely personal: and relates rather to what I suffered than to what I saw. Not a word then about Cologne and the eleven thousand British virgins, whom a storm drove into that port, and who were condemned, as I am pleased to think, to a most merited death. Ah, Mary M'Alister! in my rage and fury I wished that there had been eleven thousand and one spinsters so destroyed. Ah! Minna Löwe, Jewess as thou wert, thou meritedst no better a fate than that which overtook those Christian damsels.

Minna Löwe was the daughter of Moses Löwe, banker at Bonn. I passed through the town last year, fifteen years after the event I am about to relate, and heard that Moses was imprisoned for forgery and fraudulent bankruptcy. He merited the punishment which the merciful Prussian law inflicted on him.

Minna was the most beautiful creature that my eyes ever lighted on. Sneer not, ye Christian maidens; but the fact was so. I saw her for the first time seated at a window covered with golden vine-leaves, with grapes just turning to purple, and tendrils twisting in the most fantastical arabesques. The leaves cast a pretty chequered shadow over her sweet face, and the simple, thin, white muslin gown in which she was dressed. She had bare white arms, and a blue riband confined her little waist. She was knitting, as all German women do, whether of the Jewish sort or otherwise; and in the shadow of the room sat her sister Emma, a powerful woman with a powerful voice. Emma was at the piano, singing, "Herz mein herz warum so trau-au-rig,"—singing much out of tune.

I had come to change one of Coutts's circulars at Löwe's bank, and was looking for the door of the caisse.

"*Links, mein herr!*" said Minna Löwe, making the gentlest inclination with her pretty little head; and blushing ever so little, and raising up tenderly a pair of heavy blue eyes, and then dropping them again, overcome by the sight of the stranger. And no wonder, I was a sight worth contemplating then,—I had golden hair which fell gracefully over my shoulders, and a slim waist (where are you now, slim waist and golden hair?), and a pair of brown mustachies that curled gracefully under a firm Roman nose, and a tuft to my chin that could not but vanquish *any* woman. "Links, mein herr," said lovely Minna Löwe.

That little word *links* dropped upon my wounded soul like balm. There is nothing in *links;* it is not a pretty word. Minna Löwe simply told me to turn to the left, when I was debating between that side and its opposite, in order to find the cash-room door. Any other person might have said *links* (or *rechts* for that matter), and would not have made the slightest impression upon me; but Minna's full red lips, as they let slip the monosyllable, wore a smile so tender, and uttered it with such inconceivable sweetness, that I was overcome at once. "Sweet bell!" I could have said, "tinkle that dulcet note for ever,—links, chinks, linx! I love the chime. It soothes and blesses me." All this I could have said, and much more, had I had my senses about me, and had I been a proficient in the German language; but I could not speak, both from ignorance and emotion. I blushed, stuttered, took off my cap, made an immensely foolish bow, and began forthwith fumbling at the door-handle.

The reason why I have introduced the name of this siren is to shew that if tobacco in a former unlucky instance has proved my enemy, in the present case it was my firmest friend. I, the descendant of the Norman Fitz-Boodle, the relative of kings and emperors, might, but for tobacco, have married the daughter of Moses Löwe, the Jew forger and convict of Bonn. I would have done it; for I hold the man a slave who calculates in love, and who thinks about prudence when his heart is in question. Men marry their cook-maids, and the world looks down upon them. *Ne sit ancillæ amor pudori!* I exclaimed with a notorious poet, if you heartily and entirely love your cook-maid, you are a fool and a coward not to wed her. What more can you want than to have your heart filled up? Can a duchess do more? You talk of the difference of rank and the decencies of society. Away, sir! love is divine, and knows not your paltry, worldly calculations. It is not love you worship, O heartless, silly calculator! it is the interest of thirty thousand pounds in the three per cents, and the blessing of a genteel mother-in-law in Harley Street, and the ineffable joy of snug dinners, and a butler behind your chair. Fool! love is eternal, butlers and mothers-in-law are perishable: you have but the enjoyment of your three per cents for forty years: and *then*, what do they avail you? But if you believe that she whom you choose, and to whom your heart clings, is to be your soul's companion, not now merely, but for *ever and ever;* then what a paltry item of money or time has deterred you from your happiness, what a miserable penny-wise economist you have been!

And here, if, as a man of the world, I might be allowed to give advice to fathers and mothers of families, it would be this: young men fall in love with people of a lower rank, and they are not strong enough to resist the dread of disinheritance, or of the world's scorn, or of the cursed tyrant gentility, and dare not marry the woman they love above all. But if prudence is strong, passion is strong too, and principle is not, and women (Heaven keep them!) are weak. We all know what happens then. Prudent papas and mammas say, "George will sow his wild oats soon, he will be tired of that odious woman one day, and we'll get a good marriage for him: meanwhile it is best to hush the matter up and pretend to know nothing about it." But suppose George does the only honest thing in his power, and marries the woman he loves above all; *then* what a cry you have from parents and guardians, what shrieks from aunts and sisters, what excommunications and disinheriting! "What a weak fool George is!" say his male friends in the clubs; and no hand of sympathy is held out to poor *Mrs.* George, who is never forgiven, but shunned like a plague, and sneered at by a relentless pharisaical world until death sets her free. As long as she is *unmarried*, avoid her if you will; but as soon as she is married, go! be kind to her, and comfort her, and pardon and forget, if you can! And lest some charitable people should declare that I am setting up here an apology for vice, let me here, and by way of precaution, flatly contradict them, and declare that I only would offer a *plea for marriage*.

But where has Minna Löwe been left during this page of disquisition? Blushing under the vine-leaves positively, whilst I was thanking my stars that she never became Mrs. George Fitz-Boodle. And yet who knows what thou mightst have become, Minna, had such a lot fallen to thee? She was too pretty and innocent-looking to have been by nature that artful, intriguing huzzy that education made her, and that my experience found her. The case was simply this, not a romantical one by any means.

* * * * * * * *

At this very juncture, perhaps, it will be as well to pause, and leave the world to wait for a month until it learns the result of the loves of Minna Löwe and George Fitz-Boodle. I have other tales still more interesting in store; and though I have never written a line until now, I doubt not before long to have excited such a vast sympathy in my favour, that I shall become as popular as the oldest (I mean the handsomest and most popular) literary characters of this or any other age or country. Artists and print-publishers, desirous of taking my portrait, may as well, therefore, begin sending in their proposals to Mr. Nickisson; nor shall I so much look to a high remuneration for sitting (egad! it is a frightful operation), as to a clever and skilful painter, who must likewise be a decently bred and companionable person.

Nor is it merely upon matters relating to myself (for egotism I hate, and the reader will remark that there is scarcely a single "I" in the foregoing pages) that I propose to speak. Next month, for instance (besides the continuation of my own and other people's memoirs), I shall acquaint the public with a discovery which is intensely interesting to all fathers of families: I have in my eye *three new professions* which a gentleman may follow with credit and profit, which are to this day unknown, and which, in the present difficult times, cannot fail to be eagerly seized upon.

Before submitting them to public competition, I will treat privately with parents and guardians, or with young men of good education and address; such only will suit.

G. S. F. B.

PROFESSIONS BY GEORGE FITZ-BOODLE.

BEING APPEALS TO THE UNEMPLOYED YOUNGER SONS OF THE NOBILITY.

FIRST PROFESSION.

THE fair and honest proposition which I put forth at the end of my last (and first) appeal to the British public, and in which I offered to communicate privately with parents and guardians relative to three new and lucrative professions which I had discovered, has, I find from the publisher, elicited not one single inquiry from those personages, who I can't but think are very little careful of their children's welfare to allow such a chance to be thrown away. It is not for myself I speak, as my conscience proudly tells me; for though I actually gave up Ascot in order to be in the way should any father of a family be inclined to treat with me regarding my discoveries, yet I am grieved, not on my own account, but on theirs, and for the wretched penny-wise policy that has held them back.

That they must feel an interest in my announcement is unquestionable. Look at the way in which the public prints of all parties have noticed my appearance in the character of a literary man! Putting aside my personal narrative, look at the offer I made to the nation, —a choice of no less than three new professions! Suppose I had invented as many new kinds of butcher's meat; does any one pretend that the world, tired as it is of the perpetual recurrence of beef, mutton, veal, cold beef, cold veal, cold mutton, hashed ditto, would not have jumped eagerly at the delighful intelligence that their old, stale, stupid meals were about to be varied at last?

Of course people would have come forward. I should have had deputations from Mr. Gibletts and the fashionable butchers of this world; petitions would have poured in from Whitechapel salesmen; the speculators panting to know the discovery; the cautious with stock in hand eager to bribe me to silence and prevent the certain depreciation of the goods which they already possessed. I should have dealt with them, not greedily or rapaciously, but on honest principles of fair barter. "Gentlemen," I should have said, or rather, "Gents," which affectionate diminutive is, I am given to understand, at present much in use among commercial persons, "Gents, my researches, my genius, or my good fortune, have brought me to the valuable discovery about which you are come to treat. Will you purchase it outright, or will you give the discoverer an honest share of the profits resulting from your speculation? My position in the world puts *me* out of the power of executing the vast plan I have formed, but 'twill be a certain fortune to him who engages in it; and why should not I, too, participate in that fortune?"

Such would have been my manner of dealing with the world, too, with regard to my discovery of the new professions. Does not the world want new professions? Are there not thousands of well-educated men panting, struggling, pushing, starving, in the old ones? Grim tenants of chambers looking out for attorneys who never come?—wretched physicians practising the stale joke of being called out of church until people no longer think fit even to laugh or to pity? Are there not hoary-headed midshipmen, antique ensigns growing mouldy upon fifty years' half-pay? Nay, are there not men who would pay any thing to be employed rather than remain idle? But such is the glut of professionals, the horrible cut-throat competition among them, that there is no chance for one in a thousand, be he ever so willing, or brave, or clever: in the great ocean of life he makes a few strokes, and puffs, and sputters, and sinks, and the innumerable waves overwhelm him and he is heard of no more.

Walking to my banker's t'other day—and I pledge my sacred honour this story is true—I met a young fellow whom I had known *attaché* to an embassy abroad, a young man of tolerable parts, unwearied patience, with some fortune, too, and, moreover, allied to a noble Whig family, whose interest had procured him his appointment to the legation at Krahwinkel, where I knew him. He remained for ten years a diplomatic character; he was the working-man of the legation: he sent over the most diffuse translations of the German papers for the use of the Foreign Secretary; he signed passports with most astonishing ardour; he exiled himself for ten long years in a wretched German town, dancing attendance at court-balls and paying no end of money for uniforms. And for what? At the end of the ten years—during which period of labour he never received a single shilling from the government which employed him (rascally spendthrifts of a government, *va!*),—he was offered the paid *attachéship* to the court of H. M. the king of the Mosquito Islands, and refused that appointment a week before the Whig ministry retired. Then he knew that there was no further chance for him, and incontinently quitted the diplomatic service for ever, and I have no doubt will sell his uniform a bargain. The government had *him* a bargain certainly, nor is he by any means the first person who has been sold at that price.

Well, my worthy friend met me in the street and informed me of these facts with a smiling countenance, —which I thought a master-piece of diplomacy. Fortune had been belabouring and kicking him for ten whole years, and here he was grinning in my face: could Monsieur de Talleyrand have acted better? "I have given up diplomacy," said Protocol, quite simply and good-humouredly, "for between you and me, my good fellow, it's a very slow profession; sure perhaps, but slow. But though I gained no actual pecuniary remuneration in the service, I have learned all the languages in Europe, which will be invaluable to me in my new profession—the mercantile one—in which directly I looked out for a post. I found one."

"What! and a good pay?" said I.

"Why, no; that's absurd, you know. No young men, strangers to business, are paid much to speak of. Besides, I don't look to a paltry clerk's pay. Some day, when thoroughly acquainted with the business (I shall learn it in about seven years), I shall go into a good house with my capital and become junior partner."

"And meanwhile?"

"Meanwhile I conduct the foreign correspondence of the eminent house of Jam, Ram, and Johnson; and very heavy it is, I can tell you. From nine till six every day, except foreign post days, and then from nine till eleven; dirty dark court to sit; snobs to talk to,—great change, as you may fancy."

"And you do all this for nothing?"

"I do it to learn the business;" and so saying Protocol gave me a knowing nod and went his way.

Good Heavens! I thought, and is this a true story? Are there hundreds of young men in a similar situation at the present day, giving away the best years of their youth for the sake of a mere windy hope of something in old age, and dying before they come to the goal? In seven years he hopes to have a business, and then to have the pleasure of risking his money? He will be admitted into some great house as a particular favour, and three months after the house will fail. Has it not happened to a thousand of our acquaintance? I thought I would run after him and tell him about the new professions that I have invented.

"Oh! ay! those you wrote about in *Fraser's Magazine.* Egad! George, Necessity makes strange fellows of us all. Who would ever have thought of you *spelling*, much more writing?"

"Never mind that. Will you, if I tell you of a new profession, that with a little cleverness and instruction from me, you may bring to a most successful end—will you, I say, make me a fair return?"

"My dear creature," replied young Protocol, "what nonsense you talk! I saw that very humbug in the Magazine. You say you have made a great discovery—very good; you puff your discovery—very right; you ask money for it—nothing can be more reasonable· and then you say that you intend to make your discovery public in the next number of the Magazine. Do you think I will be such a fool as to give you money for a thing which I can have next month for nothing? Good-by, George my boy; the *next* discovery you make I'll tell you how to get a better price for it;" and with this the fellow walked off, looking supremely knowing and clever.

This tale of the person I have called Protocol is not told without a purpose, you may be sure. In the first place, it shews what are the reasons that nobody has made application to me concerning the new professions, namely, because I have passed my word to make them known in this Magazine, which persons may have for the purchasing, stealing, borrowing, or hiring, and, therefore, they will never think of applying personally to me. And, secondly, his story proves also my assertion, viz. that all professions are most cruelly crowded at present, and that men will make the most absurd outlay and sacrifices for the smallest chance of success at some future period. Well, then, I will be a benefactor to my race, if I cannot be to one single member of it, whom I love better than most men. What I have discovered I will make known; there shall be no shilly-shallying work here, no circumlocution, no bottle-conjuring business. But oh! I wish for all our sakes that I had had an opportunity to impart the secret to one or two persons only; for, after all, but one or two can live in the manner I would suggest. And when the discovery is made known, I am sure ten thousand will try. The rascals! I can see their brass plates gleaming over scores of doors. Competition will ruin my professions, as it has all others.

It must be premised that the two first professions are intended for gentlemen, and gentlemen only—men of birth and education. No others could support the parts which they will be called upon to play.

And, likewise, it must be honestly confessed that these professions have, to a certain degree, been exercised before. Do not cry out at this and say it is no discovery! I say it *is* a discovery. It is a discovery, if I shew you—a gentleman—a profession which you may exercise without derogation or loss of standing, with certain profit, nay, possibly with honour, and of which until the reading of this present page, you never thought but as of a calling beneath your rank and quite below your reach. Sir, I do not mean to say that I create a profession. I cannot create gold; but if, when discovered, I find the means of putting it in your pocket, do I or do I not deserve credit?

I see you sneer contemptuously when I mention to you the word AUCTIONEER. "Is this all," you say, "that this fellow brags and prates about? An auctioneer forsooth! he might as well have 'invented' chimney-sweeping?"

No such thing. A little boy of seven, be he ever so low of birth, can do this as well as you. Do you suppose that little stolen Master Montague made a better sweeper than the lowest-bred chummy that yearly commemorates his release? No, sir. And he might have been ever so much a genius or a gentleman, and not have been able to make his trade respectable.

But all such trades as can be rendered decent the aristocracy has adopted one by one. At first they followed their profession of arms, flouting all others as unworthy, and thinking it ungentlemanlike to know how to read or write. They did not go into the church in very early days till the money to be got from the church was strong enough to tempt them. It is but of later years that they have condescended to go to the bar, and since the same time only that we see some of them following trades. I know an English lord's son who is, or was, a wine-merchant (he may have been a bankrupt for what I know). As for bankers, several partners in banking-houses have four balls to their coronets, and I have no doubt that another sort of banking, viz. that practised by gentlemen who lend small sums of money upon deposited securities, will be one day followed by the noble order, so that they may have four balls on their coronets and carriages, and three in front of their shops.

Yes, the nobles come peoplewards as the people, on the other hand, rise and mingle with the nobles. With the *plebs*, of course, Fitz-Boodle, in whose veins flows the blood of a thousand kings, can have nothing to do; but, watching the progress of the world, 'tis impossible to deny that the good old days for our race are passed away. We want money still as much as ever we did; but we cannot go down from our castles with horse and sword and waylay fat merchants—no, no, confounded new policemen and the assize-courts prevent that. Younger brothers cannot be pages to noble houses, as of old they were, serving gentle dames without disgrace, handing my lord's rose-water to wash, or holding his stirrup as he mounted for the chase. A page, forsooth! A pretty figure would George Fitz-Boodle, or any other man of fashion cut, in a jacket covered with sugar-loafed buttons and handing in penny-post notes on a silver tray. The *plebs* have robbed us of *that* trade among others, nor, I confess, do I much grudge them their *trouvaille*. Neither can we collect together a few scores of free lances, like honest Hugh Calverly in the Black Prince's time, or brave Harry Butler of Wallenstein's dragoons, and serve this or that prince, Peter the Cruel or Henry of Trastamare, Gustavus or the Emperor, at our leisure; or, in default of service, fight and rob on our own gallant account, as the good gentlemen of old did. Alas! no. In South America or Texas, perhaps, a man might have a chance that way; but in the ancient world no man can fight except in the king's service (and a mighty bad service that is too), and the lowest European sovereign, were it Baldomero Espartero himself, would think nothing of seizing the best born Condottiere chief that ever drew sword and shooting him down like the vulgarest deserter.

What, then, is to be done? We must discover fresh fields of enterprise—of peaceable and commercial enterprise in a peaceful and commercial age. I say, then, that the auctioneer's pulpit has never yet been ascended by a scion of the aristocracy, and am prepared to prove that they might scale it, and do so with dignity and profit.

For the auctioneer's pulpit is just the peculiar place where a man of social refinement, of elegant wit, of polite perceptions, can bring his wit, his eloquence, his taste, and his experience of life, most delightfully into play. It is not like the bar, where the better and higher qualities of a man of fashion find no room for exercise. In defending John Jorrocks in an action of trespass, for cutting down a stick in Sam Snooks's field, what powers of mind do you require?—powers of mind, that is, which Mr. Serjeant Snorter, a butcher's son with a great loud voice, a sizer at Cambridge, a wrangler, and so forth, does not possess as well as yourself? Snorter has never been in decent society in his life. He thinks the bar-mess the most fashionable assemblage in Europe, and the jokes of "grand day" the *ne plus ultra* of wit. Snorter lives near Russell Square, eats beef and Yorkshire-pudding, is a judge of port-wine, is in all social respects your inferior. Well, it is ten to one but in the case of Snooks *v.* Jorrocks, before mentioned, he will be a better advocate than you; he knows the law of the case entirely, and better probably than you. He can speak long, loud, to the point, grammatically—more grammatically than you, no doubt, will condescend to do. In the case of Snooks *v.* Jorrocks he is all that can be desired. And so about dry disputes, respecting real property, he knows the law; and, beyond this, has no more need to be a gentleman than my body-servant has—who, by the way, from constant intercourse with the best society, *is* almost a gentleman. But this is apart from the question.

Now, in the matter of auctioneering, this, I apprehend, is not the case, and assert that a high-bred gentleman, with good powers of mind and speech, must, in such a profession, make a fortune. I do not mean in all auctioneering matters. I do not mean that such a person should be called upon to sell the good-will of a public-house, or discourse about the value of the beer-barrels, or bar with pewter fittings, or the beauty of a trade doing a stroke of so many hogsheads a week. I do not ask a gentleman to go down and sell pigs, ploughs, and cart-horses, at Stoke Pogis; or to enlarge at the Auction Rooms, Wapping, upon the beauty of the Lively Sally, schooner. These articles of commerce or use can be better appreciated by persons in a different rank of life to his.

But there are a thousand cases in which a gentleman only can do justice to the sale of objects which the necessity or convenience of the genteel world may require to change hands. All articles, properly called, of taste should be put under his charge. Pictures,—he is a travelled man, has seen and judged the best galleries of Europe, and can speak of them as a common person cannot. For, mark you, you must have the confidence of your society, you must be able to be familiar with them, to plant a happy *mot* in a graceful manner, to appeal to my lord or the duchess in such a modest, easy, pleasant way as that her grace should not be hurt by your allusion to her—nay, amused (like the rest of the company) by the manner in which it was done.

What is more disgusting than the familiarity of a snob? What more loathsome than the swaggering quackery of some present holders of the hammer? There was a late sale, for instance, which made some noise in the world (I mean the late Lord Gimcrack's at Dilberry Hill). Ah! what an opportunity was lost there! I declare solemnly that I believe, but for the absurd quackery and braggadocio of the advertisements, much more money would have been bid; people were kept away by the vulgar trumpeting of the auctioneer, and could not help thinking the things were worthless that were so outrageously lauded.

They say that sort of Bartholomew-fair advocacy (in which people are invited to an entertainment by the medium of a hoarse yelling beef-eater, twenty-four drums, and a jack-pudding turning head over heels) is absolutely necessary to excite the public attention. What an error! I say that the refined individual so accosted is more likely to close his ears, and, shuddering, run away from the booth. Poor Horace Waddlepoodle! to think that thy gentle accumulation of *bricabrac* should have passed away in such a manner! by means of a man who brings down a butterfly with a blunderbuss, and talks of a pin's head through a speaking trumpet! Why, the auctioneer's very voice was enough to crack the Sèvres porcelain and blow the lace into annihilation. Let it be remembered that I speak of the gentleman in his public character merely, meaning to insinuate nothing more than I would by stating that Lord Brougham speaks with a northern accent, or that the voice of Mr. Sheil is sometimes unpleasantly shrill.

Now the character I have formed to myself of a great auctioneer is this. I fancy him a man of first-rate and irreproachable birth and fashion. I fancy his person so agreeable that it must be a pleasure for ladies to behold and tailors to dress it. As a private man he must move in the very best society, which will flock round his pulpit when he mounts it in his public calling. It will be a privilege for vulgar people to attend the hall where he lectures; and they will consider it an honour to be allowed to pay their money for articles, the value of which is stamped by his high recommendation. Nor can such a person be a mere fribble, or any loose hanger-on of fashion imagine he may assume the character. The gentleman-auctioneer must be an artist above all, adoring his profession; and adoring it, what must he not know? He must have a good knowledge of the history and language of all nations; not the knowledge of the mere critical scholar, but of the lively and elegant man of the world. He will not commit the gross blunders of pronunciation that untravelled Englishmen perpetrate; he will not degrade his subject by coarse eulogy, or sicken his audience with vulgar banter. He will know where to apply praise and wit properly; he will have the tact only acquired in good society, and know where a joke is in place, and how far a compliment may go. He will not outrageously and indiscriminately laud all objects committed to his charge, for he knows the value of praise; that diamonds, could we have them by the bushel, would be used as coals; that, above all, he has a character of sincerity to support; that he is not merely the advocate of the person who employs him, but that the public is his client too, who honours him and confides in him. Ask him to sell a copy of Raffaelle for an original; a trumpery modern Brussels counterfeit for real old Mechlin; some common French forged crockery for the old delightful, delicate, Dresden china, and he will quit you with scorn, or order his servant to shew you the door of his study.

Study, by the way,—no, "study" is a vulgar word; every word is vulgar which a man uses to give the world an exaggerated notion of himself or his condition. When the wretched bagman, brought up to give evidence before Judge Coltman, was asked what his trade was, and replied that "he represented the house of Dobson and Hobson," he shewed himself to be a vulgar, mean-souled wretch, and was most properly reprimanded by his lordship. To be a bagman is to be humble, but not of necessity vulgar. Pomposity is vulgar, to ape a higher rank than your own is vulgar, for an ensign of militia to call himself captain is vulgar, or for a bagman to style himself the "representative" of Dobson and Hobson. The honest auctioneer, then, will not call his room his study; but his "private room," or his office, or whatever may be the phrase commonly used among auctioneers.

He will not for the same reason call himself (as once in a momentary feeling of pride and enthusiasm for the profession I thought he should)—he will not call himself "an advocate," but an auctioneer. There is no need to attempt to awe people by big titles, let each man bear his own name without shame. And a very gentlemanlike and agreeable, though exceptional position (for it is clear that there cannot be more than two of the class), may the auctioneer occupy.

He must not sacrifice his honesty, then, either for his own sake or his clients' in any way, nor tell fibs about himself or them. He is by no means called upon to draw the long bow in their behalf; all that his office obliges him to do—and let us hope his disposition will lead him to do it also—is to take a favourable, kindly, philanthropic view of the world; to say what can fairly be said by a good-natured and ingenious man in praise of any article for which he is desirous to awaken public sympathy. And how readily and pleasantly may this be done! I will take upon myself, for instance, to write an eulogium upon So-and-so's last novel, which shall be every word of it true; and which work, though to some discontented spirits it might appear dull, may be shewn to be really amusing and instructive,—nay, *is* amusing and instructive to those who have the art of discovering where those precious qualities lie.

An auctioneer should have the organ of truth large; of imagination and comparison, considerable; of wit, great; of benevolence excessively large.

And how happy might such a man be and cause others to be! He should go through the world laughing, merry, observant, kind-hearted. He should love everything in the world, because his profession regards everything. With books of lighter literature (for I do not recommend the genteel auctioneer to meddle with heavy antiquarian and philological works) he should be elegantly conversant, being able to give a neat history of the author, a pretty sparkling kind criticism of the work, and an appropriate eulogium upon the binding, which would make those people read who never read before; or buy, at least, which is his first consideration. Of pictures we have already spoken. Of china, of jewellery, of gold-headed canes, valuable arms, picturesque antiquities, with what eloquent *entraînement* might he not speak! He feels every one of these things in his heart. He has all the tastes of all the fashionable world. Dr. Meyrick cannot be more enthusiastic about an old suit of armour than he; Sir Harris Nicolas not more eloquent regarding the gallant times in which it was worn, and the brave histories connected with it. He takes up a pearl necklace with as much delight as any beauty who was sighing to wear it round her own snowy throat, and hugs a china monster with as much joy as the oldest duchess could do. Nor must he affect these things; he must feel them. He is a glass in which all the tastes of fashion are reflected. He must be every one of the characters to whom he addresses himself—a genteel Goethe or Shakespeare, a fashionable world-spirit.

How can a man be all this and not be a gentleman; and not have had an education in the midst of the best company—an insight into their most delicate feelings, and wants, and usages? The pulpit oratory of such a man would be invaluable, people would flock to listen to him from far and near. He might out of a single tea-cup cause streams of world-philosophy to flow, which would be drunk in by grateful thousands; and draw out of an old pincushion points of wit, morals, and experience, that would make a nation wise.

Look round, examine THE ANNALS OF AUCTIONS, as Mr. Robins remarks, and (with every respect for him and his brethren) say, is there in the profession SUCH A MAN? Do we want such a man? Is such a man likely or not likely to make an immense fortune? Can we get such a man except out of the very best society, and among the most favoured there?

Every body answers "No!" I knew you would

answer no. And now, gentlemen who have laughed at my pretension to discover a profession, say, have I not? I have laid my finger upon the spot where the social deficit exists. I have shown that we labour under a want; and when the world wants, do we not know that A MAN WILL STEP FORTH to fill the vacant space that Fate has left for him? Pass we now to the

SECOND PROFESSION.

This profession, too, is a great, lofty, and exceptional one, and discovered by me considering these things, and deeply musing upon the necessities of society. Nor let honourable gentlemen imagine that I am enabled to offer them in this profession, more than any other, a promise of what is called future glory, deathless fame, and so forth. All that I say is, that I can put young men in the way of making a comfortable livelihood, and leaving behind them, not a name, but, what is better, a decent maintenance to their children. Fitz-Boodle is as good a name as any in England. General Fitz-Boodle, who, in Marlborough's time, and in conjunction with the famous Van Slaap, beat the French in the famous action of Vischzouchee, near Mardyk, in Holland, on the 14th of February, 1709, is promised an immortality upon his tomb in Westminster Abbey; but he died of apoplexy, deucedly in debt, two years afterwards: and what after that is the use of a name?

No, no; the age of chivalry is passed. Take the twenty-four first men who come into the club, and ask who they are, and how they made their money?

There's Woolsey-Sackville, his father was lord-chancellor, and sat on the woolsack, whence he took his title; his grandfather dealt in coal-sacks, and not in woolsacks,—small coal-sacks, dribbling out little supplies of black diamonds to the poor. Yonder comes Frank Leveson, in a huge broad-brimmed hat, his short cuffs turned up to his elbows. Leveson is as gentlemanly a fellow as the world contains, and if he has a fault, is perhaps too finikin. Well, you fancy him related to the Sutherland family: nor, indeed, does honest Frank deny it; but, *entre nous*, my good sir, his father was an attorney, and his grandfather a bailiff in Chancery Lane, bearing a name still older than that of Leveson, namely, Levy. So it is that this confounded equality grows and grows, and has laid the good old nobility by the heels. Look at that venerable Sir Charles Kitely, of Kitely Park; he is interested about the Ashantees, and has just come from Exeter Hall. Kitely discounted bills in the City in the year 1787, and gained his baronetcy by a loan to the French princes. All these points of history are perfectly well known; and do you fancy the world cares? Psha! Profession is no disgrace to a man; be what you like, provided you succeed. If Mr. Fauntleroy could come to life with a million of money, you and I would dine with him; you know we would: for why should we be better than our neighbours?

Put, then, out of your head the idea that this or that profession is unworthy of you: take any that may bring you profit, and thank him that puts you in the way of being rich.

The profession I would urge (upon a person duly qualified to undertake it) has, I confess, at the first glance, something ridiculous about it; and will not appear to young ladies so romantic as the calling of a gallant soldier blazing with glory, gold lace, and vermilion coats; or a dear delightful clergyman, with a sweet blue eye, and a pocket handkerchief scented charmingly with lavender-water. The profession I allude to *will*, I own, be to young women disagreeable, to sober men trivial, to great, stupid moralists unworthy.

But mark my words for it, that in the religious world (I have once or twice, by mistake no doubt, had the honour of dining in "serious" houses, and can vouch for the fact, that the dinners there are of excellent quality), in the serious world, in the great mercantile world, among the legal community (notorious feeders), in every house in town (except some half-a-dozen which can afford to do without such aid), the man I propose might speedily render himself indispensable.

Does the reader now begin to take? Have I hinted enough for him that he may see with eagle glance the immense beauty of the profession I am about to unfold to him? We have all seen Gunter and Chevet; Fregoso, on the Puerta del Sol (a relation of the ex-minister Calomarde), is a good purveyor enough for the benighted olla-eaters of Madrid; nor have I any fault to find with Guimard, a Frenchman, who has lately set up on the Piazza d'Espagna, at Naples, where he furnishes people with decent food. It has given me pleasure, too, in walking about London—in the Strand, in Oxford Street, and elsewhere, to see fournisseurs and comestible merchants newly set up. Messrs. Morell have good articles in their warehouses; Fortnum and Mason are known to most of my readers.

But what is not known, what is wanted, what is languished for in England is *a dinner-master*,—a gentleman who is not a provider of meat or wine, like the parties before named,—who can have no earthly interest in the price of troufled turkeys or dry champagne beyond that legitimate interest which he may feel for his client, and which leads him to see that the latter is not cheated by his tradesman. For the dinner-giver is almost naturally an ignorant man. How in mercy's name can Mr. Sergeant Snorter, who is all day at Westminster, or in chambers, know possibly the mysteries, the delicacy, of dinner-giving? How can Alderman Pogson know any thing beyond the fact that venison is good with currant-jelly, and that he likes lots of green fat with his turtle? Snorter knows law, Pogson is acquainted with the state of the tallow-market; but what should he know of eating, like you and me, who have given up our time to it? (I say *me* only familiarly, for I have only reached so far in the science as to know that I know nothing.) But men there are, gifted individuals, who have spent years of deep thought—not merely intervals of labour, but hours of study every day—over the gormandising science,*—who, like alchemists, have let their fortunes go, guinea by guinea, into the all-devouring pot,—who, ruined as they sometimes are, never get a guinea by chance but they will have a plate of peas in May with it, or a little feast of ortolans,

* The publisher has referred me to an essay in this Magazine upon the subject of eating in Paris, by a person of the name of Tidmarsh, who may be a very worthy man for aught I know to the contrary; but has, with permission be it spoken, shown the most lamentable vulgarity and ignorance in his writing. As for Nimrod's "Cibaria," the barbarity of them is quite amazing.—G. F. B.

or a piece of Glo'ster salmon, or one more flask from their favourite claret-bin.

It is not the ruined gastronomist that I would advise a person to select as his *table-master;* for the opportunities of peculation would be too great in a position of such confidence—such complete abandonment of one man to another. A ruined man would be making bargains with the tradesmen. They would offer to cash bills for him, or send him opportune presents of wine, which he could convert into money, or bribe him in one way or another. Let this be done, and the profession of table-master is ruined. Snorter and Pogson may almost as well order their own dinners, as be at the mercy of a "gastronomic agent" whose faith is not beyond all question.

A vulgar mind, in reply to these remarks regarding the gastronomic ignorance of Snorter and Pogson, might say, "True, these gentlemen know nothing of household economy, being occupied with other more important business elsewhere. But what are their wives about? Lady Pogson in Harley Street has nothing earthly to do but to mind her poodle, and her mantua-makers' and house-keeper's bills. Mrs. Snorter in Bedford Place, when she has taken her drive in the Park with the young ladies, may surely have time to attend to her husband's guests and preside over the preparations of his kitchen, as she does worthily at his hospitable mahogany." To this I answer, that a man who expects a woman to understand the philosophy of dinner-giving, shews the strongest evidence of a low mind. He is unjust towards that lovely and delicate creature, woman, to suppose that she heartily understands and carès for what she eats and drinks. No; taken as a rule, women have no real appetites. They are children in the gormandising way; loving sugar, sops, tarts, trifles, apricot-creams, and such gewgaws. They would take a sip of Malmsey, and would drink currant-wine just as happily, if that accursed liquor were presented to them by the butler. Did you ever know a woman who could lay her fair hand upon her gentle heart and say on her conscience that she preferred dry sillery to sparkling champagne? Such a phenomenon does not exist. They are not made for eating and drinking; or, if they make a pretence to it, become downright odious. Nor can they, I am sure, witness the preparations of a really great repast without a certain jealousy. They grudge spending money (ask guards, coachmen, inn-waiters, whether this be not the case). They will give their all, Heaven bless them! to serve a son, a grandson, or a dear relative, but they have not the heart to pay for small things magnificently. They are jealous of good dinners, and no wonder. I have shewn in a former discourse how they are jealous of smoking, and other personal enjoyments of the male. I say, then, that Lady Pogson or Mrs. Snorter can never conduct their husbands' table properly. Fancy either of them consenting to allow a calf to be stewed down into gravy for one dish, or a dozen hares to be sacrificed to a single *purée* of game, or the best Madeira to be used for a sauce, or half-a-dozen champagne to boil a ham in. They will be for bringing a bottle of Marsala in place of the old particular, or for having the ham cooked in water. But of these matters—of kitchen philosophy —I have no practical or theoretic knowledge; and must beg pardon if, only understanding the goodness of a dish when cooked, I may have unconsciously made some blunder regarding the preparation.

Let it, then, be set down as an axiom, without further trouble of demonstration, that a woman is a bad dinner-caterer; either too great and simple for it, or too mean —I don't know which it is; and gentlemen accordingly as they admire or contemn the sex, may settle that matter their own way. In brief, the mental constitution of lovely woman is such that she cannot give a great dinner. It must be done by a man. It can't be done by an ordinary man, because he does not understand it. Vain fool! and he sends off to the pastry-cook in Great Russell Street or Baker Street, he lays on a couple of extra waiters (green-grocers in the neighbourhood), he makes a great pother with his butler in the cellar, and fancies he has done the business.

Bon Dieu! Who has not been at those dinners?—those monstrous exhibitions of the pastry-cook's art? Who does not know those made-dishes with the universal sauce to each, fricandeaux, sweet-breads, damp dumpy cutlets, &c., seasoned with the compound of grease, onions, bad port wine, cayenne-pepper, currie-powder (Warren's blacking, for what I know, but the taste is always the same)—there they lie in the old corner-dishes, the poor wiry Moselle and sparkling Burgundy in the ice-coolers, and the old story of white and brown soup, turbot, little smelts, boiled turkey, saddle of mutton, and so forth? "Try a little of that fricandeau," says Mrs. Snorter, with a kind smile; "you'll find it, I think, very nice;" be sure it has come in a green tray from Great Russell Street. "Mr. Fitz-Boodle, you have been in Germany," cries Snorter, knowingly; "taste the hock, and tell me what you think of *that*."

How should he know better, poor benighted creature; or she, dear good soul that she is? If they would have a leg of mutton, and an apple pudding, and a glass of sherry and port (or simple brandy and water called by its own name) after dinner, all would be very well; but they must shine, they must dine as their neighbours. There is no difference (as I have heard an excellent observer of human nature remark, the man who I don't care to own first opened my eyes to cookery)—there is no difference in the style of dinners in London; people with five hundred a-year treat you exactly as those of five thousand. They *will* have their Moselle or Hock, their fatal side-dishes brought in the green trays from the pastry-cooks.

Well, there is no harm done; not as regards the dinner-givers at least, though the dinner-eaters may have to suffer somewhat; it only shows that the former are hospitably inclined, and wish to do the very best in their power,—good honest fellows! If they do wrong, how can they help it? they know no better.

And now, is it not as clear as the sun at noon-day, that A WANT exists in London for a superintendent of the table—a gastronomic agent—a dinner-master, as I have called him before? A man of such a profession would be a metropolitan benefit; hundreds of thousands of people of the respectable sort, people in white waistcoats, would thank him daily. Calculate how many dinners are given in the City of London, and calculate the numbers of benedictions that "the Agency" might win.

And as no doubt the observant man of the world has remarked, that the freeborn Englishman of the respectable class is, of all others, the most slavish and truckling to a Lord; that there is no fly-blown peer but he is pleased to have him at his table, proud beyond measure to call him by his surname (without the lordly prefix); and that of those lords whom he does not know, he yet (the free-born Englishman) takes care to have their pedigrees and ages by heart from his world-bible, the peerage: as this is an indisputable fact, and as it is in this particular class of Britons that our agent must look to find clients, I need not say it is necessary that the agent should be as high-born as possible, and that he should be able to tack, if possible, an honourable or some other handle to his respectable name. He must have it on his card

The Honourable George Gormand Guttleton, Apician Chambers, Pall Mall.

Or,

Sir Augustus Carver Cramley Cramley, Amphytrionic Council Office, Swallow Street.

Or in some such neat way, Gothic letters on a large handsome crockery-ware card, with possibly a gilt coat of arms and supporters, or the blood-red hand of baronetcy duly displayed; depend on it plenty of guineas will fall in it, and that Guttleton's supporters will support him comfortably enough.

For this profession is not like that of the auctioneer, which I take to be a far more noble one, because more varied and more truthful: but in the Agency case, a little humbug at least is necessary. A man cannot be a successful agent by the mere force of his simple merit or genius in eating and drinking. He must of necessity impose upon the vulgar to a certain degree. He must be of that rank which will lead them naturally to respect him, otherwise they might be led to jeer at his profession; but let a noble exercise it, and bless your soul, all the court-guide is dumb!

He will then give out in a manly and somewhat pompous address what has before been mentioned, namely, that he has seen the fatal way in which the hospitality of England has been perverted hitherto, *accaparéd* by a few cooks with green trays. (He must use a good deal of French in his language, for that is considered very gentlemanlike by vulgar people.) He will take a set of chambers in Carlton Gardens, which will be richly though severely furnished, and the door of which will be opened by a French valet (he *must* be a Frenchman, remember), who will say, on letting Mr. Snorter or Sir Benjamin Pogson in, that "*Milor* is at home." Pogson will then be shown into a library furnished with massive book-cases containing all the works on cookery and wines (the titles of them) in all the known languages in the world. Any books, of course, will do, as you will have them handsomely bound, and keep them under plate glass. On a side-table will be little sample-bottles of wines, a few troufles on a white porcelain saucer, a prodigious strawberry or two, perhaps, at the time when such fruit costs much money. On the library will be busts marked UDE, CARÊME, BÉCHAMEL, in marble (never mind what heads of course); and, perhaps, on the clock should be a figure of the Prince of Condé's cook killing himself because the fish had not arrived in time; there may be a wreath of *immortels* on the figure to give it a more decidedly Frenchified air. The walls will be of a dark rich paper, hung round with neat gilt frames containing plans of *menus* of various great dinners, those of Cambacérès, Napoleon, Louis XIV., Louis XVIII., Heliogabalus, if you like, each signed by the respective cook.

After the stranger has looked about him at these things, which he does not understand in the least, especially the troufles which look like dirty potatoes, you will make your appearance, dressed in a dark dress with one handsome enormous gold chain, and one large diamond ring; a gold snuff-box, of course, which you will thrust into the visitor's paw before saying a word. You will be yourself a portly grave man, with your hair a little bald and grey. In fact, in this as in all other professions, you had best try to look as like Canning as you can.

When Pogson has done sneezing with the snuff, you will say to him, "Take a *fauteuil;* I have the honour of addressing Mr. Pogson, I believe?" And then you will explain to him your system.

This, of course, must vary with every person you address. But let us lay down a few of the heads of a plan which may be useful, or may be modified infinitely or may be cast aside altogether just as circumstances dictate. After all *I* am not going to turn gastronomic agent, and speak only for the benefit perhaps of the very person who is reading this.

SYNOPSIS OF THE GASTRONOMIC AGENCY OF THE HONOURABLE GEORGE GUTTLETON.

The Gastronomic Agent having traversed Europe, and dined with the best society of the world, has been led naturally, as a patriot, to turn his thought homeward, and cannot but deplore the lamentable ignorance regarding gastronomy displayed in a country for which Nature has done almost every thing.

But it is ever singularly thus. Inherent ignorance belongs to man, and The Agent, in his Continental travels, has always remarked, that the countries most fertile in themselves were invariably worse tilled than those more barren. The Italians and the Spaniards leave their fields to Nature, as we leave our vegetables, fish, and meat. And, Heavens! what richness do we fling away,—what dormant qualities in our dishes do we disregard,—what glorious gastronomic crops (if The Agent may be permitted the expression), what glorious gastronomic crops do we sacrifice, allowing our goodly meats and fishes to lie fallow! "Chance," it is said by an ingenious historian, who, having been long a secretary in the East India House, must certainly have had access to the best information upon Eastern matters, "Chance," it is said by Mr. Charles Lamb, "which burnt down a Chinaman's house, with a litter of sucking pigs that were unable to escape from the interior, discovered to the world the excellence of ROAST PIG." Gunpowder, we know, was invented by a similar fortuity. [The reader will observe that my style in the supposed character of a Gastronomic Agent is purposely pompous and loud.] So, 'tis said, was printing,—so glass. We should have drunk our wine poisoned with the villanous odour of the borachio, had not some Eastern merchants, lighting their fires in the desert, marked the strange composition which now glitters on our sideboard, and holds the costly produce of our vines.

We have spoken of the natural riches of a country. Let the reader think but for one moment of the gastronomic wealth of our country of England, and he will be lost in thankful amazement as he watches the astonishing riches poured out upon us from Nature's bounteous cornucopia! Look at our fisheries!—the trout and salmon tossing in our brawling streams; the white and full breasted turbot struggling in the mariner's net; the purple lobster lured by hopes of greed into his basket-prison, which he quits only for the red ordeal of the pot. Look at white-bait, great Heavens!—look at white-bait, and a thousand frisking, glittering, silvery things beside, which the nymphs of our native streams bear kindly to the deities of our kitchens—our kitchens such as they are.

And though it may be said, that other countries produce the freckle-backed salmon and the dark broad-shouldered turbot; though trout frequent many a stream besides those of England, and lobsters sprawl on other sands but ours; yet, let it be remembered, that OUR NATIVE COUNTRY possesses those altogether, while other lands only know them separately; that, above all,

WHITE-BAIT is peculiarly our country's,—OUR CITY'S own! Blessings and eternal praises be on it, and, of course, on brown bread and butter! And the Briton should further remember, with honest pride and thankfulness, the situation of his capital, of London: the lordly turtle floats from the sea into the stream, and from the stream to the city; the rapid fleets of all the world, *se donnent rendezvous*, in the docks of our silver Thames; the produce of our coasts and provincial cities, east and west, is borne to us on the swift lines of lightning railroads. In a word,—and no man but one who, like The Agent, has travelled Europe over, can appreciate the gift—there is no city on earth's surface so WELL SUPPLIED WITH FISH as London!

With respect to our meats, all praise is supererogatory. Ask the wretched hunter of *chevreuil*, the poor devourer of *rehbraten*, what they think of the noble English haunch, that, after bounding in the Park of Knole or Windsor, exposes its magnificent flank upon some broad silver platter at our tables? It is enough to say of foreign venison, that *they are obliged to lard it*. Away! ours is the palm of roast; whether of the crisp mutton that crops the thymy herbage of our downs, or the noble ox who revels on lush Althorpian oil-cakes. What game is like to ours? Mans excels us in poultry, 'tis true, but 'tis only in merry England that the partridge has a flavour, that the turkey can almost *se passer de truffes*, that the jolly juicy goose can be eaten as he deserves.

Our vegetables, moreover, surpass all comment; Art (by the means of glass) has wrung fruit out of the bosom of Nature, such as she grants to no other clime.

And if we have no vineyards on our hills, we have gold to purchase their best produce. Nature, and enterprise that masters Nature, have done every thing for our land.

But, with all these prodigious riches in our power, is it not painful to reflect how absurdly we employ them? Can we say that we are in the habit of DINING WELL? Alas, no! and The Agent, roaming o'er foreign lands, and seeing how, with small means and great ingenuity and perseverance, great ends were effected, comes back sadly to his own country, whose wealth he sees absurdly wasted, whose energies are misdirected, and whose vast capabilities are allowed to lie idle. * * * [Here should follow what I have only hinted at previously, a vivid and terrible picture of the degradation of our table.] * * * O, for a master spirit, to give an impetus to the land, to see its great power directed in the right way, and its wealth not squandered or hidden, but nobly put out to interest and spent!

The Agent dares not hope to win that proud station —to be the destroyer of a barbarous system wallowing in abusive prodigality—to become a dietetic reformer—the Luther of the table.

But convinced of the wrongs which exist, he will do his humble endeavour to set them right, and to those who know that they are ignorant (and this is a vast step to knowledge) he offers his counsels, his active co-operation, his frank and kindly sympathy. The Agent's qualifications are these:—

1. He is of one of the best families in England, and has in himself, or through his ancestors, been accustomed to good living for centuries. In the reign of

Henry V., his maternal great-great-grandfather, Roger de Gotylton [*the name may be varied, of course, or the king's reign, or the dish invented*], was the first who discovered the method of roasting a peacock whole, with its tail-feathers displayed; and the dish was served to the two kings at Rouen. Sir Walter Cramley, in Elizabeth's reign, produced before her majesty, when at Killingworth Castle, mackerel with the famous *gooseberry sauce*, &c.

2. He has, through life, devoted himself to no other study than that of the table; and has visited to that end the courts of all the monarchs of Europe: taking the receipts of the cooks, with whom he lives on terms of intimate friendship, often at an enormous expense to himself.

3. He has the same acquaintance with all the vintages of the Continent; having passed the autumn of 1811 (the comet year) on the great Weinberg of Johannisberg; being employed similarly at Bordeaux, in 1836; at Oporto, in 1822; and at Xeres de la Frontera, with his excellent friends, Duff, Gordon, and Co., the year after. He travelled to India and back in company with fourteen pipes of Madeira (on board of the Samuel Snob, East Indiaman, Captain Scuttler), and spent the vintage season in the island, with unlimited powers of observation granted to him by the great houses there.

4. He has attended Mr. Groves of Charing Cross, and Mr. Giblett of Bond Street, in a course of purchases of fish and meat; and is able at a glance to recognise the age of mutton, the primeness of beef, the firmness and freshness of fish of all kinds.

5. He has visited the Parks, the grouse-manors, and the principal gardens of England, in a similar professional point of view.

The Agent then, through his subordinates, engages to provide gentlemen who are about to give dinner-parties—

1. With cooks to dress the dinners; a list of which gentlemen he has by him, and will recommend none who are not worthy of the strictest confidence.

2. With a *menu* for the table, according to the price which the Amphitryon chooses to incur.

3. He will, through correspondences with the various fournisseurs of the metropolis, provide them with viands, fruit, wine, &c., sending to Paris, if need be, where he has a regular correspondence with Messrs. Chevet.

4. He has a list of dexterous table-waiters (all answering to the name of John for fear of mistakes, the butler's name to be settled according to pleasure), and would strongly recommend that the servants of the house should be locked in the back-kitchen or servants' hall during the time that the dinner takes place.

5. He will receive and examine all the accounts of the fournisseurs,—of course pledging his honour as a gentleman not to receive one shilling of paltry gratification from the tradesmen he employs, but to see that their bills are more moderate, and their goods of better quality, than they would provide to any person of less experience than himself.

6. His fee for superintending a dinner will be five guineas: and The Agent entreats his clients to trust

entirely to him and his subordinates for the arrangement of the repast,—*not to think* of inserting dishes of their own invention, or producing wine from their own cellars, as he engages to have it brought in the best order, and fit for immediate drinking. Should the Amphitryon, however, desire some particular dish or wine, he must consult The Agent, in the first case by writing, in the second, by sending a sample to The Agent's chambers. For it is manifest that the whole complexion of a dinner may be altered by the insertion of a single dish; and, therefore, parties will do well to mention their wishes on the first interview with The Agent. He cannot be called upon to recompose his bill of fare, except at great risk to the *ensemble* of the dinner and enormous inconvenience to himself.

7. The Agent will be at home for consultation from ten o'clock until two,—earlier, if gentlemen who are engaged at early hours in the City desire to have an interview; and be it remembered that a *personal interview* is always the best: for it is greatly necessary to know not only the number but the character of the guests whom the Amphitryon proposes to entertain,—whether they are fond of any particular wine or dish, what is their state of health, rank, style, profession, &c.

8. At two o'clock, he will commence his rounds; for as the metropolis is wide, it is clear that he must be early in the field in some districts. From 2 to 3, he will be in Russell Square and the neighbourhood; 3 to 3¾, Harley Street, Portland Place, Cavendish Square, and the environs; 3¾ to 4¼, Portman Square, Gloucester Place, Baker Street, &c.; 4¼ to 5, the new dis-

trict about Hyde Park Terrace; 5 to 5¾ St. John's Wood and the Regent's Park. He will be in Grosvenor Square by 6, and in Belgrave Square, Pimlico, and its vicinity, by 7. Parties there are requested not to dine until 8 o'clock; and The Agent, once for all, peremptorily announces that he will NOT go to the palace, where it is utterly impossible to serve a good dinner.

TO TRADESMEN.

Every Monday evening during the season the Gastronomic Agent proposes to give a series of trial-dinners, to which the principal gourmands of the metropolis, and a few of The Agent's most respectable clients, will be invited. Covers will be laid for *ten* at nine o'clock precisely. And as The Agent does not propose to exact a single shilling of profit from their bills, and as his recommendation will be of infinite value to them, the tradesmen he employs will furnish the weekly dinner gratis. Cooks will attend (who have acknowledged characters) upon the same terms. To save trouble, a book will be kept where butchers, poulterers, fishmongers, &c., may inscribe their names in order, taking it by turns to supply the trial-table. Wine merchants will naturally compete every week promiscuously, sending what they consider their best samples, and leaving with the hall-porter tickets of the prices. Confectionery to be done out of the house. Fruiterers, market-men, as butchers and poulterers. The Agent's *maître d'hôtel* will give a receipt to each individual for the articles he produces; and let all remember that The Agent is a *very keen judge*, and woe betide those who serve him or his clients ill!

GEORGE GORMAND GUTTLETON.

Carlton Gardens, June 10, 1842.

Here I have sketched out the heads of such an address as I conceive a gastronomic agent might put forth; and appeal pretty confidently to the British public regarding its merits and my own discovery. If this be not a profession—a new one—a feasible one—a lucrative one,—I don't know what is. Say that a man attends but fifteen dinners daily, that is seventy-five guineas, or five hundred and fifty pounds weekly, or fourteen thousand three hundred pounds for a season of six months: and how many of our younger sons have such a capital even? Let, then, some unemployed gentleman with the requisite qualifications come forward. It will not be necessary that he should have done all that is stated in the prospectus; but, at any rate, let him *say* he has: there can't be much harm in an innocent fib of that sort; for the gastronomic agent must be a sort of dinner-pope, whose opinions cannot be supposed to err.

And as he really will be an excellent judge of eating and drinking, and will bring his whole mind to bear upon the question, and will speedily acquire an experience which no person out of the profession can possibly have; and as, moreover, he will be an honourable man, not practising upon his client in any way, or demanding sixpence beyond his just fee, the world will gain vastly by the coming forward of such a person,—gain in good dinners, and absolutely save money; for what is five guineas for a dinner of sixteen? The sum may be *gaspillé* by a cook-wench, or by one of those abominable before-named pastry-cooks, with their green trays.

If any man take up the business, he will invite me, of course, to the Monday dinners. Or does ingratitude go so far as that a man should forget the author of his good fortune? I believe it does. Turn we away from the sickening theme, and let us say a few words regarding my

THIRD PROFESSION.

The last profession is one in all respects inferior to the two preceding—is merely temporary, whereas they are for life; but has this advantage, that it may be exercised by the vulgarest man in Europe, and requires not the least previous experience or education.

It is better, unluckily, for a foreigner than an Englishman; but the latter may easily adopt it, if he have any American relations, or if he choose to call himself a citizen of the great republic. In fact, this profession simply consists in being *a foreigner*.

You may be ever so illiterate and low-bred, and you are all the better for the profession. Your worst social qualities will stand you in stead. You should, to practise properly, be curious, talkative, abominably impudent, and forward. You should never be rebuffed because people turn their backs on you, but should attack them again and again; and, depend upon it, that if you are determined to know a man, he will end, out of mere weariness, by admitting you to his acquaintance.

Sáy that you have met a person once at a *café*, or tavern, and that you do not know one single Englishman in the world (except the tradesmen in the nameless quarter where you were born) but this, some young fellow from college probably, who is spending his vacation abroad. Well, you know *this* man, and it is enough. Ask him at once for letters of introduction: say that you are a young American (for I presume the reader is an Englishman, and this character he can therefore assume more readily than any other) wishing to travel, and ask him for letters to his family in England. He hums and ha's, and says he will send them. Nonsense! call the waiter to bring pens, ink, and paper; lay them laughingly before your friend; say that now is the best time, and almost certainly you will have the letters. He can't abuse you in the notes, because you are looking over his shoulder. The two or three first men upon whom you make the attempt may say that you may go to the deuce, and threaten to kick you out of the room;—but 'tis against the chances, this sort of ferocity. Men are rather soft than spirited; and if they *be* spirited, you have only to wait until you find a soft one.

It will be as well, perhaps, while making the demand upon your friend in the *café*, to produce a series of letters directed to the Marquess of L——e, the Duke of D——, Mr. R—— the poet, Mr. C. K——, the eminent actor now retired, and other distinguished literary or fashionable persons, saying that your friends in America have already supplied you with these, but that you want chiefly introductions to *private families*, to see "*the homes of England*;" and as Englishmen respect lords (see remarks in Profession II.), most likely your young *café* acquaintance will be dazzled by the sight of these addresses, and will give you letters the more willingly, saying to himself, "Who knows, egad, but that this American may get my sisters to L—— House?" One way or the other, you will be sure to end by having a letter—a real letter; and as for those you have written, why, upon my honour, I do not think that you can do better than present some of them on the chance; for the Duke and the Marquess receive so many people at their houses, that they cannot be expected to remember all their names. Write, then, bravely at once—

To his Grace the Duke of Dorsetshire, K. G. London.

Twenty-one Street, Boston, May 1842.

My dear Duke,—In the friendly hospitality which you exercised towards me on my last visit to London, I am fain to hope that you looked somewhat to my character as an individual, as well as to my quality as a citizen of the greatest country in the world: I, for my part, have always retained the warmest regard for you, and shall be happy to see you any time you come our way.

Assuming, I am sure justifiably, that your repeated assurances of regard were sincere (for I do not consider you as false, as I found the rest of the English nobility), I send, to be under your special protection whilst in London, my dear young friend, Nahum Hodge, distinguished among us as a patriot and a poet; in the first of which capacities he burned several farm-houses in Canada last fall, and, in the latter, has produced his celebrated work, "The Bellowings of the Buffalo," printed at Buffalo, New York, by Messrs. Bowie and Cutler, and which are far superior to any poems ever produced in the old country. Relying upon our acquaintance, I have put down your name, my dear Duke, as a subscriber for six copies, and will beg you to hand over to my young friend Nahum twelve dollars—the price.

He is a modest, retiring young man, as most of our young republicans are, and will want to be urged and pushed forward into good society. This, my dear fellow, I am sure you will do for me. Ask him as often as you can to dinner, and present him at the best houses you can in London. I have written to the Marquess of Sandown, reminding him of our acquaintance, and saying that you will vouch for the respectability of young Nahum, who will take the liberty of leaving his card at Sandown House. I do not wish that he should be presented at your court; for I conceive that a republican ought not to sanctify by his presence any exhibition so degrading as that of the English *levée.*

Nahum Hodge will call on you at breakfast-time; I have told him that is the best hour to find yourself and the dear Duchess at home. Give my love to her and the children, and believe me, my dear friend,

Your Lordship's most faithful Servant,

EBENEZER BROWN.

Such a letter as this will pretty surely get you admission to his Grace; and of course you will be left to your own resources to make yourself comfortable in the house. Do not be rebuffed if the porter says, "Not at home;" say, "You liveried varlet and slave! do you pretend to lie in the face of a free-born American republican? Take in that note, do you hear, or I'll whop you like one of my niggers!" Those fat, overfed men, who loll in porters' chairs, are generally timid, and your card will be sure to be received.

While a servant has gone up-stairs with it, walk into the library at once,* look at all the papers, the seals, the books on the table, the addresses of all the letters, examine the pictures, and shout out, "Here, you fat porter, come and tell me who these tarnation people are!" The man will respectfully come to you; and whatever be your fate with the family up-stairs—whether the Duke says he cannot see you, or that he knows nothing of you, at least you will have had an insight into his house and pictures, and may note down every thing you see.

It is not probable he will say he knows nothing of you. He is too polite and kind-hearted for that,—nay, possibly, may recall to his mind that he once *did* receive an American by the name of Brown. If he only says he cannot see you, of course you will call again till he does; and be sure that the porter will never dare to shut the door on you.

You will call and call so often, that he will end by inviting you to a party. Meanwhile, you will have had your evenings pretty well filled by invitations from the sisters of your friend whom you met in the *café* at Paris,—agreeable girls—say their name is Smith, and they live in Montague Place, or near Blackheath. Be

* Of course you will select a house that is not *entre cour et jardin.*

sure you tell them all that you know of the Duke of Dorsetshire, that you have been with his Grace that morning, and so on; and not only good old Mr. Smith, but all his circle, will take care to invite you to as many dinners as you can possibly devour.

Your conduct at these repasts will be perfectly simple. Keep your eyes open, and do pretty much as you see other people do; but never acknowledge you are in fault if any one presumes to blame you. Eat peas with your knife; and if gently taken to task about this habit by Smith (a worthy man, who takes an interest in his "son's friend,") say, "Well, General Jackson eats peas with *his* knife: and I a'n't proud. I guess General Jackson can whop any Englishman." Say this sort of thing simply and unaffectedly, and you will be sure not to be pestered as to your mode of conveying your food to your mouth.

Take care at dinner not to admire any thing; on the contrary, if they bring you madeira, say, "La bless you, taste *our* madeira! My father's got some that he gave fifty dollars a bottle for; this here ain't fit to bile for puddns." If there are ducks, ask every body if they have tasted canvass-back ducks; oysters, say the New York oyster will feed six men; turtle, prefer terrapin, and so on.

And don't fancy that because you are insolent and disagreeable, people will be shy of you in this country. Sir, they like to be bullied in England, as to be bullies when abroad. They like a man to sneer at their dinners; it argues that you are in the habit of getting better. I have known the lowest-bred men imaginable pass for fine fellows by following this simple rule.

Remember through life that a man will always rather submit to insolence than resist it.

Let this be your guide, then, in your commerce with all ranks. You will dine, of course, with your friends about Russell Square and Greenwich, until such time as you get a fair entry into the houses of greater people (by the way, you will find these much more shy of dinners and more profuse with their tea-parties than your humbler entertainers). But if you don't dine with them, you must keep up your credit in the other quarter of the town—*make believe* to dine with them. You can get a dinner for eightpence on those days, and figure in the evening party afterwards.

At the great parties, make up to that part of the room where the distinguished people are—not the great men of the land, but the wits, mark you—and begin talking with them at once; they will all respect you in their hearts, as they respect themselves, for being at such a grand house as that of his Grace the Duke of Dorsetshire.

The wits will, after a little, take you to the Wits' Club, the Muffinæum, where you will enter gratis as a distinguished foreigner. You can breakfast there for a shilling, have the run of the letter-paper, and will, of course, take care to date your letters from thence.

Mind, then, once put your foot into a great house, and your fortune in society is easily made. You have but to attack, people will rather yield than resist. I once knew a Kentucky man, who, hearing the Marquess of Carum Gorum talking of the likelihood of grouse that year, interposed, " My lord, it must be a wonderful sight for a stranger to see a grand meeting of the aris tocrats of England in the heathery hills of Scotia. What would I not give to behold such an exhibition?" The marquess smiled, shrugged, and said, "Well, sir, if you come north, you must give me a day;" and then turned on his heel. This was in March: on the fourteenth of August Kentuck appeared with a new shooting jacket and a double-barrelled gun, got on credit, and stayed a fortnight at Mull House.

At last, he sent in a letter, before breakfast on Sabbath morning, to Lord Carum Gorum, saying, that he knew he was trespassing beyond all measure upon his lordship's patience, but that he was a stranger in the land, his remittances from America had somehow been delayed, and the fact was, that there he was, waterlogged till they came.

Lord Carum Gorum inclosed him a ten-pound note in an envelope, with a notification that a gig would be ready for him after service: and Kentuck passed a very agreeable fortnight in Edinburgh, and published in the "Buffalo's Hump" a brilliant account of his stay at the noble lord's castle.

Then, again, if you see a famous beauty, praise every one of her points outrageously in your letter to the Buffalo's Hump," as

ON THE LADY EMILY X——

Who left dancing and came and talked to the poet at the déjeûné at C—— Lodge.

Beneath the gold acacia buds
My gentle Nora sits and broods,
Far, far away in Boston woods,
My gentle Nora!

I see the tear-drop in her e'e,
Her bosom's heaving tenderly;
I know—I know she thinks of me,
My darling Nora!

And where am I? My love, whilst thou
Sitt'st sad beneath the acacia bough,
Where pearl's on neck, and wreath on brow,
I stand, my Nora!

'Mid carcanet and coronet,
Where joy-lamps shine and flowers are set—
Where Englaad's chivalry are met,
Behold me, Nora!

In this strange scene of revelry,
Amidst this gorgeous chivalry,
A form I saw, was like to thee,
My love—my Nora!

She paused amidst her converse glad;
The lady saw that I was sad,
She pitied the poor lonely lad,—
Dost love her, Nora?

In sooth, she is a lovely dame,
A lip of red, an eye of flame,
And clustering golden locks, the same
As thine, dear Nora!

Her glance is softer than the dawn's,
Her foot is lighter than the fawn's,
Her breast is whiter than the swan's,
Or thine, my Nora!

Oh, gentle breast to pity me!
Oh, lovely Ladye Emily!
Till death—till death I'll think of thee—
Of thee and Nora!

This sort of thing addressed to a thin shrivelled person of five-and-forty (and I declare it is as easy to write such verses as to smoke a cigar) will be sure to have its effect; and in this way you may live a couple of years in England very fashionably and well. By impudence you may go from one great house to another—by impudence you may get credit with all the fashionable tradesmen in London—by impudence you may find a publisher for your tour; and if with all this impudence you cannot manage to pick up a few guineas by the way, you are not the man I take you for.

And this is my last *profession.* In concluding the sketch of which, it is of course not necessary for me to say that the little character I have drawn out is not taken from any particular individual. No, on my honour, far from it; it is, rather, an agreeable compound of many individuals, whom it has been our fortune to see here; and as for the story about the Marquess of Carum Gorum, it is, like the noble marquess himself, a fiction. It is a possibility, that is all—an embodiment of a good and feasible way of rising money. Perhaps gentlemen in America, where our periodicals are printed regularly, as I am given to understand, may find the speculation worth their while; and accordingly it is recommended to the republican press.

To the discriminating press of this country how shall I express my obligations for the unanimous applause which hailed my first appearance? It is the more wonderful, as I pledge my sacred word, I never wrote a document before much longer than a laundress's bill, or the acceptance of an invitation to dinner. But enough of this egotism; thanks for praise conferred sound like vanity; gratitude is hard to speak of, and at present it swells the full heart of

GEORGE SAVAGE FITZ-BOODLE.

P.S.—My memoirs, and other interesting works, will appear next month, the length necessary to a discussion of the promised "Professions" having precluded the possibility of their insertion in the present Number. They are of thrilling interest.

MISS LÖWE.

It has twice been my lot to leave Minna Löwe under the vine-leaves; on one occasion to break off into a dissertation about marriage, which, to my surprise, nobody has pronounced to be immoral; and, secondly, Minna was obliged to give place to that great essay on professions which appeared in July, and which enables me, as the *Kelso Warder* observes, "to take my place among the proudest and wisest of England's literary men." This praise is, to be sure, rather qualified; and I beg leave to say once more that I am *not* a literary character in the least, but simply a younger brother of a good house wanting money.

Well, twice has Minna Löwe been left. I was very nearly being off from her in the above sentence, but luckily paused in time; for if anything were to occur in this paragraph, calling me away from her yet a third time, I should think it a solemn warning to discontinue her history, which is, I confess, neither very romantic in its details, nor very creditable to myself.

Let us take her where we left her in the June number of this Magazine, gazing through a sunny cluster of vine-leaves upon a young and handsome stranger, of noble face and exquisite proportions, who was trying to find the door of her father's bank. That entrance being through her amiable directions discovered, I entered and found Messrs. Moses and Solomon Löwe in the counting-house, Herr Solomon being the son of Moses, and head clerk or partner in the business. That I was cheated in my little matter of exchange stands to reason. A Jew banker (or such as I have had the honour to know) cannot forego the privilege of cheating; no, if it be but for a shilling. What do I say,—a shilling?—a penny! He will cheat you, in the first place, in the exchanging your note; he will then cheat you in giving gold for your silver; and though very likely he will invite you to a splendid repast afterwards that shall have cost him a score of thalers to procure, he will have had the satisfaction of robbing you of your *groschen*, as no doubt he would rob his own father or son.

Herr Moses Löwe must have been a very sharp Israelite, indeed, to rob Herr Solomon, or *vice versâ*. The poor fellows are both in prison for a matter of forgery, as I heard last year when passing through Bonn; and I confess it was not without a little palpitation of the heart (it is a sausage-merchant's now) that I went and took one look at the house where I had first beheld the bright eyes of Minna Löwe.

For let them say as they will, that woman whom a man has once loved *cannot* be the same to him as another. Whenever one of my passions comes into a room, my cheeks flush,—my knees tremble,—I look at her with pleased tenderness and (for the objects of my adoration do not once in forty times know their good fortune) with melancholy secret wonder. There they are, the same women, and yet not the same; it is the same nose and eyes, if you will, but not the same looks; the same voice, but not the same sweet words as of old. The figure moves, and looks, and talks to you; you know how dear and how different its speech and actions once were; 'tis the hall with all the lights put out and the garlands dead (as I have said in one of my poems). Did you ever have a pocket-book that once contained five thousand pounds? Did you ever look at that pocket-book with the money lying in it? Do you remember how you respected and admired that pocket-book, investing it with a secret awe, imagining it had a superiority to other pocket-books? I have such a pocket-book; I keep it now, and often look at it rather tenderly. It cannot be as other portfolios to me. I remember that it once held five thousand pounds.

Thus it is with love. I have empty pocket-books scattered all over Europe of this kind; and I always go and look at them just for a moment, and the spirit flies back to days gone by, kind eyes look at me as of yore, and echoes of old gentle voices fall tenderly upon the ear. Away! to the true heart the past *never* is past —and some day when Death has cleared our dull faculties, and past and future shall be rolled into one, we shall * * * * *

Well, you were quite right, my good sir, to interrupt me. I can't help it, I am too apt to grow sentimental, and always on the most absurd pretexts. I never know when the fit will come on me, or *à-propos* of what. I never was so jolly in my whole life as one day coming home from a funeral; and once went to a masked ball at Paris, the gaiety of which made me so profoundly miserable, that, egad! I wept like Xerxes (wasn't that the fellow's name?) and was sick—sick at heart. This premised, permit me, my friend, to indulge in sentiment *à-propos* of Minna Löwe; for, *corbleu!* for three weeks, at least, I adored the wench; and could give any person curious that way a complete psychological history of the passion's rise, progress, and decay;—decay, indeed! why do I say decay? A man does not "decay" when he tumbles down a well, but drowns there; so is love choked sometimes by abrupt conclusions, falls down wells, and oh! the dismal truth at the bottom of them!

"If, my lord," said Herr Moses, counting out the gold fredericks to me, "you intend to shtay in our town, I hope my daughtersh and I vill have shometimesh de pleashure of your high vell-born shoshiety?"

"The town is a most delightful one, Mr. Löwe," answered I. "I am myself an Oxford man, and exceedingly interested about—ahem—about the Byzantine historians, of which I see the University is producing an edition; and I shall make, I think, a considerable stay." Heaven bless us! 'twas Miss Minna's eyes that had done the business. But for them I should have slept at Coblentz that very night; where, by the way, the Hôtel de la Poste is one of the very best inns in Europe.

A friend had accompanied me to Bonn,—a jolly dragoon, who was quite versed in the German language, having spent some time in the Austrian service before he joined us; or in the "Awthtwian thervith," as he would call it, with a double-distilled gentility of accent very difficult to be acquired out of Regent Street. We had quarrelled already thrice on the passage from England—viz., at Rotterdam, at Cologne, and once here; so that when he said he intended to go to Mayence, I at once proclaimed that I intended to stay where I was; and with Miss Minna Löwe's image in my heart, went out and selected lodgings for myself as near as possible to her father's house. Wilder said I might go to — any place I liked; he remained in his quarters at the hotel, as I found a couple of days afterwards, when I saw the fellow smoking at the gateway in the company of a score of Prussian officers, with whom he had made acquaintance.

I for my part have never been famous for that habit of extemporaneous friendship-making, which some lucky fellows possess. Like most of my countrymen, when I enter a room I always take care to look about with an air as if I heartily despised every one, and wanted to know what the d—l they did there! Among foreigners I feel this especially; for the truth is, right or wrong, I can't help despising the rogues, and feeling manifestly my own superiority. In consequence of this amiable quality, then (in this particular instance of my life), I gave up the *table d'hôte* dinner at the Star as something low and ungentlemanlike, made a point of staring and not answering when people spoke to me, and thus I have no doubt impressed all the world with a sense of my dignity. Instead of dining at the public place, then, I took my repasts alone; though, as Wilder said with some justice, though with a good deal too much *laisser-aller* of tongue, "You gweat fool, if it'th only becauth you want to be thilent, why don't you thtill dine with uth? You'll get a wegular good dinner inthtead of a bad one; and ath for *thpeaking* to you, depend on it every man in the room will thee you hanged futht!"

"Pray allow me to dine in my own way, Wilder," says I, in the most dignified way.

"Dine and be d—d!" said the lieutenant, and so I lived solitary and had my own way.

I proposed to take some German lessons; and for this purpose asked the banker, Mr. Löwe, to introduce me to a master. He procured one, a gentleman of his own persuasion; and further, had the kindness to say that his clerk, Mr. Hirsch, should come and sit with me every morning and perfect me in the tongue; so that, with the master I had and the society I kept, I might look to acquire a very decent German pronunciation.

This Hirsch was a little Albino of a creature with pinkish eyes, white hair, flame-coloured whiskers, and earrings. His eyes jutted out enormously from his countenance, as did his two large swollen red lips, which had the true Israelitish coarseness. He was always, after a short time, in and out of my apartments. He brought a dozen messages and ran as many errands for me in the course of the day. My way of addressing him was, "Hirsch, you scoundrel, get my boots!" "Hirsch, my Levite, brush my coat for me!" "Run, you stag of Israel, and put this letter in the post!" and with many similar compliments. The little rascal was, to do him justice, as willing as possible, never minded by what name I called him, and, above all,—came from Minna. He was not the rose; no, indeed, nor any thing like it; but, as the poet says, "he had lived beside it;" and was there in all Sharon such a rose as Minna Löwe?

If I did not write with a moral purpose, and because my unfortunate example may act wholesomely upon other young men of fashion, and induce them to learn wisdom, I should not say a single syllable about Minna Löwe, nor all the blunders I committed, nor the humiliation I suffered. There is about a young Englishman of twenty a degree of easy self-confidence, hardly possessed even by a Frenchman. The latter swaggers and bullies about his superiority, taking all opportunities to shriek it into your ears, and to proclaim the infinite merits of himself and his nation; but, upon my word, the bragging of the Frenchman is not so conceited or intolerable as that calm, silent, contemptuous conceit of us young Britons, who think our superiority so well established that it is really not worth arguing upon, and who take upon us to despise thoroughly the whole world through which we pass. We are hated on the Continent, they say, and no wonder. If any other nation were to attempt to domineer over us as we do over Europe, we would hate them as heartily and furiously as many a Frenchman and Italian does us.

Now when I went abroad I fancied myself one of the finest fellows under the sun. I patronised a banker's dinners as if I did him honour in eating them; I took my place before grave professors and celebrated men, and talked vapid nonsense to them in infamous French, laughing heartily in return at their own manner of pronouncing that language. I set down as a point beyond question that their customs were inferior to our own, and would not in the least scruple, in a calm way to let my opinion be known. What an agreeable young fellow I must have been!

With these opinions, and my pleasant way of expressing them, I would sit for hours by the side of lovely Minna Löwe, ridiculing, with much of that elegant satire for which the English are remarkable, every one of the customs of the country,—the dinners, with the absurd un-English pudding in the very midst of them; the dresses of the men, with their braided coats and great seal-rings. As for little Hirsch, he formed the constant subject of my raillery with Mademoiselle Minna; and I gave it as my fixed opinion, that he was only fit to sell sealing-wax and oranges to the coaches in Piccadilly.

"O fous afez tant d'esprit, fous autres jeunes Anglais," would she say; and I said, "Oui, nous avons beaucoup d'esprit, beaucoup plus que les Allemands," with the utmost simplicity; and then would half close my eyes, and give her a look that I thought must kill her.

Shall I tell the result of our conversation? In conversation 1, Minna asked me if I did not think the tea remarkably good, with which she and her sister treated me. She said it came overland from China, that her papa's correspondent at Petersburg forwarded it to them, and that no such tea was to be had in Germany. On this I seriously believed the tea to be excellent; and next morning at breakfast little Hirsch walked smirking into my room, with a parcel of six pounds of congo, for which I had the honour of paying eighteen Prussian thalers, being two pounds fourteen shillings of our money.

The next time I called, Herr Moses insisted on regaling me with a glass of Cyprus wine. His brother Löwe of Constantinople was the only person in the world who possessed this precious liquor. Four days afterwards Löwe came to know how I liked the Cyprus wine which I had ordered, and would I like another dozen? On saying that I had not ordered any, that I did not like sweet wine, he answered, "*Pardon!*" it had been in my cellar three days, and he would send some excellent Médoc at a moderate price, and would take no refusal. A basket of Médoc came that very night in my absence, with a bill directed to the "High Well-born Count von Fitz-Boodle." This excessive desire of the Löwe family to serve me made me relax my importunities somewhat. "Ah!" says Minna, with a sigh, the next time I saw her, "have we offended you, Herr George? You don't come to see us any more now!"

"I'll come to-morrow," says I; and she gave me a look and a smile which, oh!—"I am a fool, I know I am!" as the honourable member for Montrose said t'other day. And was not Samson ditto? was not Hercules another? Next day she was seated at the vine-leaves as I entered the court. She smiled, and then retreated. She had been on the look-out for me, I knew she had. She held out her little hand to me as I came into the room. Oh, how soft it was and how round! and with a little apricot-coloured glove that—that I have to this day! I had been arranging a little compliment as I came along, something quite new and killing. I had only the heart to say, "*Es ist sehr warm.*"

"Oh, Herr George!" says she; "*Lieber* Herr George,

what a progress have you made in German! You speak it like a native!"

But somehow I preferred to continue the conversation in French; and it was made up, as I am bound to say, of remarks equally brilliant and appropriate with that one above given. When old Löwe came in I was winding a skein of silk, seated in an enticing attitude, gazing with all my soul at Delilah, who held down her beautiful eyes.

That day they did not sell me any bargains at all; and the next found me, you may be very sure, in the same parlour again, where, in his *schlaf-rock*, the old Israelite was smoking his pipe.

"Get away, papa," said Minna, "English lords can't bear smoke. I'm sure Herr George dislikes it."

"Indeed, I smoke occasionally myself," answered your humble servant.

"Get his lordship a pipe, Minna, my soul's darling!" exclaimed the banker.

"O yes! the beautiful long Turkish one," cried Minna, springing up, and presently returned, bearing a long cherry-stick covered with a scarlet and gold cloth, at one end an enamelled amber mouth-piece, a gilded pipe at the other. In she came dancing, wand in hand, and looking like a fairy!

"Stop!" she said; "I must light it for Herr George." (By Jupiter! there was a way that girl had of pronouncing my name, "George," which I never heard equalled before or since.) And accordingly, bidding her sister get fire, she put herself in the prettiest attitude ever seen: with one little foot put forward, and her head thrown back, and a little hand holding the pipe-stick between finger and thumb, and a pair of red lips kissing the amber mouth-piece with the sweetest smile ever mortal saw. Her sister, giggling, lighted the tobacco, and presently you saw issuing from between those beautiful, smiling, red lips of Minna's a little curling, graceful, white smoke, which rose soaring up to the ceiling. I swear, I felt quite faint with the fragrance of it.

When the pipe was lighted, she brought it to me with quite as pretty an attitude and a glance that —— Psha! I gave old Moses Löwe fourteen pounds sterling for that pipe that very evening; and as for the mouth-piece, I would not part with it away from me, but I wrapped it up in a glove that I took from the table, and put both into my breast-pocket; and next morning, when Charley Wilder burst suddenly into my room, he found me sitting up in bed in a green silk night-cap, a little apricot-coloured glove lying on the counterpane before me, your humble servant employed in mumbling the mouth-piece as if it were a bit of barley-sugar.

He stopped, stared, burst into a shriek of laughter, and made a rush at the glove on the counterpane; but, in a fury, I sent a large single volumed Tom Moore (I am not a poetical man, but I must confess I was reading some passages in *Lalla Rookh* that I found applicable to my situation)—I sent, I say, a Tom Moore at his head, which, luckily, missed him; and to which he responded by seizing a bolster and thumping me outrageously. It was lucky that he was a good-natured fellow, and had only resorted to that harmless weapon, for I was in such a fury that I certainly would have murdered him at the least insult.

I did not murder him then; but if he peached a single word upon the subject, I swore I would, and Wilder knew I was a man of my word. He was not unaware of my *tendre* for Minna Löwe, and was for passing some of his delicate light-dragoon jokes upon it and her; but these, too, I sternly cut short.

"Why, cuth me, if I don't think you want to mawwy her!" blurted out Wilder.

"Well, sir," said I, "and suppose I do?"

"What! mawwy the daughter of that thwindling old clotheman? I tell you what, Fitth-Boodle, they alwayth thaid you were mad in the weg'ment, and run me thwough, if I don't think you are."

"The man," says I, "sir, who would address Mademoiselle Löwe in any but an honourable way is a scoundrel; and the man who says a word against her character is a liar!"

After a little further parley (which Wilder would not have continued but that he wanted to borrow money of me), that gentleman retired, declaring that "I wath ath thulky ath a bear with a thaw head," and left me to my apricot-coloured glove and my amber mouth-piece.

Wilder's assertion that I was going to act up to opinions which I had always professed, and to marry Minna Löwe, certainly astounded me, and gave me occasion for thought. Marry the daughter of a Jew banker! I, George Fitz-Boodle! That would never do; not unless she had a million to her fortune, at least, and it was not probable that a humble dealer at Bonn could give her so much. But marry her or not, I could not refrain from the sweet pleasure of falling in love with her, and shut my eyes to the morrow that I might properly enjoy the day. Shortly after Wilder's departure, little Hirsch paid his almost daily visit to me. I determined—and wondered that I had never thought of the scheme before—sagely to sound him regarding Minna's fortune, and to make use of him as my letter and message-carrier.

"Ah, Hirsch! my lion of Judah!" says I, "you have brought me the pipe-stick, have you?"

"Yes, my lord, and seven pounds of the tobacco you said you liked. 'Tis real Syrian, and a great bargain you get it, I promise."

"Egad!" replied I, affecting an air of much careless ingenuousness. "Do you know, Hirsch, my boy, that the youngest of the Miss Löwes—Miss Anna, I think you call her——"

"Minna," said Hirsch, with a grin.

"Well, Minna—Minna, Hirsch, is a devilish fine girl; upon my soul now, she is."

"Do you really think so?" says Hirsch.

"'Pon my honour, I do. And yesterday, when she was lighting the pipe-stick, she looked so confoundedly handsome that I—I quite fell in love with her; really I did."

"Ho! Vell, you do our people great honour, I'm sure," answered Hirsch.

"Father a warm man?"

"Varm! How do you mean varm?"

"Why, *rich*. We call a rich man *warm* in England; only you don't understand the language. How much will he give his daughter?"

"Oh! very little. Not a veek of your income, my lord," said Hirsch.

"Pooh, pooh! You always talk of me as if I'm rich; but I tell you I am poor—exceedingly poor."

"Go away vid you!" said Hirsch, incredulously. "*You* poor! I vish I had a year of your income; that I do" (and I have no doubt he did, or of the revenue of any one else). "I'd be a rich man, and have de best house in Bonn."

"Are you so very poor yourself, Hirsch, that you talk in this way?" asked I.

To which the young Israelite replied that he had not one dollar to rub against another; that Mr. Löwe was a close man; and finally (upon my pressing the point, like a cunning dog as I was!), that he would do anything to earn a little money.

"Hirsch," said I, like a wicked young reprobate and Don Juan, "will you carry a letter to Miss Minna Löwe?"

Now there was no earthly reason why I should have made a twopenny-postman of Mr. Hirsch. I might with just as much ease have given Minna the letter myself. I saw her daily and for hours, and it would be hard if I could not find her for a minute alone, or at least slip a note into her glove or pocket-handkerchief, if secret the note must be. But, I don't care to own it, I was as ignorant of any love-making which requires mystery as any bishop on the bench, and pitched upon Hirsch, as it were, because in comedies and romances that I had read the hero has always a go-between—a valet, or humble follower—who performs the intrigue of the piece. So I asked Hirsch the above question, "Would he carry a letter to Miss Minna Löwe?"

"Give it me," said he, with a grin.

But the deuce of it was, it wasn't written. Rosina, in the opera, has hers ready in her pocket, and says "*Eccolo qua*" when Figaro makes the same request, so I told Hirsch that I would get it ready. And a very hard task I found it too, in sitting down to compose the document. It shall be in verse, thought I, for Minna understands some English; but there is no rhyme to Minna, as every body knows, except a cockney, who might make "thinner, dinner, winner," &c., answer to it. And as for Löwe, it is just as bad. Then it became, as I thought, my painful duty to send her a note in French; and in French finally it was composed, and I blush now when I think of the nonsense and bad grammar it contained—the conceit above all. The easy vulgar assurance of victory with which I, a raw lad from the stupidest country in Europe, assailed one of the most beautiful women in the world!

Hirsch took the letter, and to bribe the fellow to silence, I agreed to purchase a great hideous amethyst brooch, which he had offered me a dozen times for sale, and which I had always refused till now. He said it had been graciously received, but as all the family were present in the evening when I called, of course no allusion could be made to the note; but I thought Minna looked particularly kind, as I sat and lost a couple of fredericks at *écarté* to a very stout Israelite lady, Madame Löwe, junior, the wife of Monsieur Solomon Löwe. I think it was on this night, or the next, that I was induced to purchase a bale of remarkably fine lawn for shirts, for old Löwe had every thing to sell, as is not uncommon with men of his profession and persuasion; and had I expressed a fancy for a coffin or a hod of mortar, I have no doubt Hirsch would have had it at my door next morning.

I went on sending letters to Minna, copying them out of a useful little work called *Le Petit Sécrétaire Français*, and easily adapting them to circumstances, by altering a phrase here and there. Day and night I used to dangle about the house. It was provoking, to be sure, that Minna was never alone now; her sister or Madam Solomon were always with her, and as they naturally spoke German, of which language I knew but few words, my evenings were passed in sighing, ogling, and saying nothing. I must have been a very charming companion. One evening was pretty much like another. Four or five times in the week old Löwe would drop in and sell me a bargain. Berlin-iron chains and trinkets for my family at home, Naples soap, a case of *eau de Cologne;* a beautiful dressing-gown, lined with fur for the winter; a rifle, one of the famous Frankfort make; a complete collection of the German classics; and finally, to my awful disgust, a set of the Byzantine historians.

I must tell you that, although my banking friend had furnished me with half a stone of Syrian tobacco from his brother at Constantinople, and though the most beautiful lips in the world had first taught me to smoke it, I discovered, after a few pipes of the weed, that it was not so much to my taste as that grown in the West Indies; and as his Havannah cigars were also not to my liking, I was compelled, not without some scruples of conscience at my infidelity, to procure my smoking supplies elsewhere.

And now I come to the fatal part of my story.

Wilder, who was likewise an amateur of the weed, once came to my lodgings in the company of a tobacconist whom he patronised, and who brought several boxes and samples for inspection. Herr Rohr, which was the gentleman's name, sat down with us, his wares were very good, and—must I own it?—I thought it would be a very clever and prudent thing on my part to exchange some of my rare Syrian against his canaster and Havannahs. I vaunted the quality of the goods to him, and, going into the inner room, returned with a packet of the real Syrian. Herr Rohr looked at the parcel rather contemptuously, I thought.

"I have plenty of these goods in my shop," said he.

"Why, you don't thay tho," says Wilder, with a grin; "it'th the weal wegular Thywian. My friend Fitth-Boodle got it from hith bankerth, and no mith-take!"

"Was it from Mr. Löwe?" says Rohr, with another provoking sneer.

"Exactly. His brother Israel sent it from Constantinople."

"Bah!" says Rohr. "I sold this very tobacco, seven pounds of it, at fourteen groschen a pound, to Miss Minna Löwe and little Mr. Hirsch, who came express to my shop for it. Here's my seal," says Mr. Rohr. And sure enough he produced, from a very fat and dirty forefinger, a seal, which bore the engraving on the packet.

"You sold that to Miss Minna Löwe?" groaned poor George Fitz-Boodle.

"Yes, and she bated me down half a gros in the price. Heaven help you, sir! she *always* makes the bargains for her father. There's something so pretty about her that we can't resist her."

"And do you thell *wineth*, too,—Thypwuth and Médoc, hay?" continued the brute Wilder, enjoying the joke.

"No," answered Mr. Rohr, with another confounded sneer. "He makes those himself; but I *have* some very fine Médoc and Greek wine, if his high well-born lordship would like a few dozen. Shall I send a pannier?"

"*Leave the room*, sir!" here shouted I, in a voice of uncontrollable ferocity, and looked so wildly that little Rohr rushed away in a fright, and Wilder burst into one of his demoniacal laughs again.

"Don't you thee, my good fwiend," continued he, "how wegularly thethe people have been doing you? I tell you their chawacterth are known all over the town. There'th not a thtudent in the place but can give you a hithtory of the family. Löwe ith an infarnal old uthuwer, and hith daughterth wegular mantwapth. At the Thtar, where I dine with the officerth of the garrithon, you and Minna are a thtandard joke. Captain Heerpauk wath caught himself for near thicth weekth; young Von Twommel wath wemoved by hith fwiends; old Colonel Blitz wath at one time tho nearly gone in love with the elder, that he would have had a divorce from hith lady. Among the thtudentth the mania hath been jutht the thame. Whenever one wath worth plucking, Löwe uthed to have him to hith houthe and wob him, until at latht the wathcal'th chawacter became tho well known that the thtudentth in a body have detherted him, and you will find that not one of them will dance with hith daughterth, handthome ath they are. Go down to Godesberg to-night and thee."

"I *am* going," answered I; "the young ladies asked me to drive down in their carriage;" and I flung myself back on the sofa and puffed away volumes of smoke, and tossed and tumbled the live-long day, with a horrible conviction that something of what Wilder had told me might be true, and with a vow to sacrifice at least one of the officers who had been laughing at me.

There they were, the scoundrels! in their cursed tight frock-coats and hay-coloured moustachios, twirling round in the waltzes with the citizens' daughters, when, according to promise, I arrived with the Israelitish ladies at the garden at Godesberg, where dancing is carried on twice or thrice in a week. There were the students, with their long pipes, and little caps, and long hair, tippling at the tables under the leaves, or dancing that absurd waltz which has always been the object of my contempt. The fact is, I am not a dancing man.

Students and officers, I thought, every eye was looking at me, as I entered the garden with Miss Minna Löwe on my arm. Wilder tells me that I looked blue with rage, and as if I should cut the throat of any man I met.

We had driven down in old Löwe's landau, the old gentleman himself acting as coachman, with Mr. Hirsch in his best clothes by his side. In the carriage came Madam Solomon, in yellow satin; Miss Löwe, in light green (it is astonishing how persons of a light complexion will wear this detestable colour); Miss Minna was in white muslin, with a pair of black knit gloves on her beautiful arms, a pink riband round her delicate waist, and a pink scarf on her shoulders, for in those days—and the fashion exists still somewhat on the Rhine—it was the custom of ladies to dress themselves in what we call an evening costume for dinner-time; and so was the lovely Minna attired. As I sat by her on the back seat, I did not say one single word, I confess, but looked unutterable things, and forgot in her beauty all the suspicions of the morning. I hadn't asked her to waltz,—for, the fact is, I didn't know how to waltz (though I learned afterwards, as you shall hear), and so only begged her hand for a quadrille.

We entered thus Mr. Blintzner's garden as I have described, the men staring at us, the lovely Minna on my arm. I ordered refreshments for the party; and we sat at a table near the boarded place where the people were dancing. No one came up to ask Minna to waltz, and I confess I was not sorry for it,—for I own to that dog-in-the-manger jealousy which is common to love,—no one came but poor little Hirsch, who had been absent to get sandwiches for the ladies, and came up making his bow just as I was asking Minna whether she would give no response to my letters. She looked surprised,—looked at Hirsch, who looked at me, and laying his hand (rather familiarly) upon my arm, put the other paw to his great, red, blubber lips, as if enjoining silence; and, before a word, carries off Minna, and began twisting her round in the waltz.

The little brute had assumed his best clothes for the occasion. He had a white hat and a pair of white gloves; a green satin stock, with profuse studs of jewèls in his shirt; a yellow waistcoat, with one of pink Cashmere underneath; very short nankeen trousers, and striped silk stockings; and a swallow-tailed, short-waisted, light-brown coat, with brass buttons; the tails whirled in the wind as he and his partner spun round to a very quick waltz,—not without agility, I confess, on the little scoundrel's part,—and oh, with what incomparable grace on Minna's! The other waltzers cleared away, doubtless to look at her performance; but though such a reptile was below my jealousy, I felt that I should have preferred to the same music to kick the little beast round the circle rather than see his hand encircling such a waist as that.

They only made one or two turns, however, and came back. Minna was blushing very red, and very much agitated.

"Will you take one turn, Fraülein Lisa?" said the active Hirsch; and after a little to-do on the part of the elder sister, she got up, and advanced to the dancing place.

What was my surprise when the people again cleared off, and left the pair to perform alone! Hirsch and his partner enjoyed their waltz, however, and returned, looking as ill-humoured as possible. The band struck up presently a quadrille tune. I would not receive any of Minna's excuses. She did not wish to dance; she was faint,—she had no *vis-à-vis*. "Hirsch," said I, with much courtesy, "take out Madam Solomon, and come and dance." We advanced,—big Mrs. Solomon and Hirsch, Minna and I,—Miss Lisa remaining with her papa over the Rhine wine and sandwiches.

There were at least twenty couple, who were mustering to make a quadrille when we advanced. Minna blushed scarlet, and I felt her trembling on my arm;

no doubt 'twas from joy at dancing with the fashionable young Englander. Hirsch, with a low bow and a scrape, led Madam Solomon opposite us, and put himself in the fifth position. It *was* rather disgusting, certainly, for George Savage Fitzboodle to be dancing *vis-à-vis* with such an animal as that!

Mr. Hirsch clapped his hands with a knowing air, to begin. I looked up from Minna (what I had been whispering to her must not be concealed,—in fact, I had said so previously, *es ist sehr warm;* but I said it with an accent that must have gone to her heart),—when I say I looked up from her lovely face, I found that every one of the other couple had retired, and that we four were left to dance the quadrille by ourselves!

Yes, by Heavens! it was so! Minna, from being scarlet, turned ghastly pale, and would have fallen back had I not encircled her with my arm. "I'm ill," said she; "let me go back to my father." "You *must dance*," said I, and held up my clenched fist to Hirsch, who I thought would have moved off too; on which the little fellow was compelled to stop. And so we four went through the quadrille.

The first figure seemed to me to last a hundred thousand years. I don't know how Minna did not fall down and faint; but gathering courage all of a sudden, and throwing a quick, fierce look round about her, as if in defiance, and a look which made my little angel for a moment look like a little demon, she went through the dance with as much gracefulness as a duchess. As for me,—at first the whole air seemed to be peopled with grinning faces, and I moved about almost choked with rage and passion. Then gradually the film of fury wore off, and I became wonderfully calm,—nay, had the leisure to look at Monsieur Hirsch, who performed all the steps with wonderful accuracy; and at every one of the faces round about us, officers, students, and citizens. None of the gentlemen, probably, liked my face,—for theirs wore, as I looked at them, a very grave and demure expression. But as Minna was dancing, I heard a voice behind her cry, sneeringly, "Brava!" I turned quickly round, and caught the speaker. He turned very red, and so betrayed himself. Our eyes met,—it was a settled thing. There was no need of any further arrangement, and it was then, as I have said, that the film cleared off; and I have to thank Capt. Heerpauk for getting through the quadrille without an apoplexy.

"Did you hear that—that voice, Herr George?" said Miss Minna, looking beseechingly in my face, and trembling on my arm, as I led her back to her father. Poor soul! I saw it all at once. She loved me,—I knew she did, and trembled lest I should run into any danger. I stuttered, stammered, vowed I did not hear it; at the same time swearing inwardly an oath of the largest dimensions, that I would cut the throat whence that "Brava!" issued. I left my lady for a moment, and finding Wilder, pointed out the man to him.

"Oh, Heerpauk," says he. "What do you want with him?"

"Charley," says I, with much heroism and ferocity, "*I want to shoot him;* just tell him so." And when, on demurring, I swore I would go and pull the captain's nose on the ground, Wilder agreed to settle the business for me; and I returned to our party.

It was quite clear that we could not stay longer in

the gardens. Löwe's carriage was not to come for an hour yet; for the banker would not expend money in stabling his horses at the inn, and had accordingly sent them back to Bonn. What should we do? There is a ruined castle at Godesberg, which looks down upon the fair green plain of the Rhine, where Mr. Blintzner's house stands (and let the reader be thankful that I don't give a description of scenery here): there is, I say, a castle at Godesberg. "*Explorons le shatto*," said I; which elegant French Hirsch translated; and this suggestion was adopted by the five Israelites, to the fairest of whom I offered my arm. The lovely Minna took it, and away we went; Wilder, who was standing at the gate, giving me a nod, to say all was right. I saw him presently strolling up the hill after me, with a Prussian officer, with whom he was talking. Old Löwe was with his daughter, and as the old banker was infirm, the pair walked but slowly. Monsieur Hirsch had given his arm to Madam Solomon. She was a fat woman; the consequence was, that Minna and I were soon considerably ahead of the rest of the party, and were ascending the hill alone. I said several things to her, such as only lovers say. "*Com il fay bo issy*," says I, in the most insinuating way. No answer. "*Es ist etwas kalt*," even I continued, admirably varying my phrase. She did not speak; she was agitated by the events of the evening, and no wonder.

That fair round arm resting on mine,—that lovely creature walking by my side in the calm moonlight,—the silver Rhine flashing before us, with Drachenfels and the Seven Mountains rising clear in the distance,—the music of the dance coming up to us from the plain below,—

the path winding every now and then into the darkest foliage, and at the next moment giving us rich views of the moonlit river and plain below. Could any man but feel the influence of a scene so exquisitely lovely?

"Minna," says I, as she wouldn't speak,—"Minna, I love you; you have known it long, long ago, I know you have. Nay, do not withdraw your hand; your heart has spoken for me. Be mine then!" and taking her hand, I kissed it rapturously, and should have proceeded to her cheek, no doubt, when——she gave me a swinging box on the ear, started back, and incontinently fell a screaming as loudly as any woman ever did.

"Minna, Minna!" I heard the voice of that accursed Hirsch shouting. "Minna, *meine gattin!*" and he rushed up the hill; and Minna flung herself into his arms, crying, "Lorenzo, my husband, save me!"

The Löwe family, Wilder, and his friend, came skurrying up the hill at the same time; and we formed what in the theatres they call a tableau.

"You coward!" says Minna, her eyes flashing fire, "who could see a woman insulted, and never defend her?"

"You coward!" roared Hirsch; "coward as well as profligate! You communicated to me your lawless love for this angel,—to me, her affianced husband; and you had the audacity to send her letters, not one of which, so help me Heaven, has been received. Yes, you will laugh at Jews,—will you, you brutal Englishman? You will insult our people,—will you, you stupid islander? Psha! I spit upon you!" and here Monsieur Hirsch snapped his fingers in my face, holding Minna at the same time round the waist, who thus became the little monster's buckler.

* * * * * *

They presently walked away, and left me in a pleasant condition. I was actually going to fight a duel on the morrow for the sake of this fury, and it appeared she had flung me off for cowardice. I had allowed myself to be swindled by her father, and insulted by her filthy little bridegroom, and for what? All the consolation I got from Wilder was,—"I told you tho, my boy, but you wouldn't lithn, you great thoopid, blundewing ignowamuth; and now I shall have to thee you shot and buwied to-morrow; and I dare thay you won't even remember me in your will. Captain Schläger," continued he, presenting me to his companion, "Mr. Fitz-Boodle; the captain acts for Heerpauk in the morning, and we were just talking matters over, when Webecca yonder quied out, and we found her in the armth of Bwian de Bois Guilbert here."

Captain Schläger was a little, social, good-humoured man, with a moustachio of a straw and silver mixed, and a brilliant purple sabre-cut across a rose-coloured nose. He had the iron-cross at his button-hole, and looked, as he was, a fierce little fighter. But he was too kind-hearted to allow of two boys needlessly cutting each other's throats; and much to the disappointment of Wilder, doubtless, who had been my second in the Martingale affair, and enjoyed no better sport, he said in English, laughing, "Vell, make your mint easy, my goot young man, I tink you af got into enough sgrabes about dis tam Shewess; and that you and Heerpauk haf no need to blow each other's brains off."

"Ath for Fitth apologithing," burst out Wilder, "that'th out of the quethtion. We gave the challenge, you know; and how the *dooth* ith we to apologithe now?"

"He gave the challenge, and you took it, and you are de greatest fool of de two. I say the two young men shall not fight;" and then the honest captain entered into a history of the worthy family of Israel, which would have saved me at least fifty pounds had I known it sooner. It did not differ in substance from what Rohr and Wilder had both told me in the morning. The venerable Löwe was a great thief and extortioner; the daughters were employed as decoy-ducks, in the first place, for the university and the garrison, and afterwards for young strangers, such as my wise self, who visited the place. There was some very sad story about the elder Miss Löwe and a tutor from St. John's College, Cambridge, who came to Bonn on a reading tour; but I am not at liberty to set down here the particulars. And with regard to Minna, there was a still more dismal history. A fine, handsome young student, the pride of the university, had first ruined himself through the offices of the father, and then shot himself for love of the daughter; from which time the whole town had put the family into Coventry; nor had they appeared for two years in public until upon the present occasion with me. As for Monsieur Hirsch, he did not care. He was of a rich Frankfort family of the people, serving his apprenticeship with Löwe, a cousin, and the destined husband of the younger daughter. He traded as much as he could on his own account, and would run upon any errand, and buy or sell any thing for a consideration. And so, instead of fighting Captain Heerpauk, I agreed willingly enough to go back to the hotel of Godesberg, and shake hands with that officer. The reconciliation, or, rather, the acquaintance between us, was effected over a bottle of wine, at Mr. Blintzner's hotel; and we rode comfortably back in a drosky together to Bonn, where the friendship was still more closely cemented by a supper. At the close of the repast, Heerpauk made a speech on England, fatherland, and German truth and love, and kindly saluted me with a kiss, which is at any lady's service who peruses this little narrative.

As for Mr. Hirsch, it must be confessed, to my shame, that the next morning a gentleman having the air of an old clothesman off duty presented me with an envelope, containing six letters of my composition addressed to Miss Minna Löwe (among them was a little poem in English, which has since called tears from the eyes of more than one lovely girl); and, furthermore, a letter from himself, in which he, Baron Hirsch, of Hirschenwald (the scoundrel, like my friend Wilder, purchased his title in the "Awthtwian Thervith")—in which he, I say, Baron Hirsch, of Hirschenwald, challenged me for insulting Miss Minna Löwe, or demanded an apology.

This, I said, Mr. Hirsch might have whenever he chose to come and fetch it, pointing to a horsewhip which lay in a corner; but that he must come early, as I proposed to quit Bonn the next morning. The baron's friend, hearing this, asked whether I would like some remarkably fine cigars for my excursion, which he could give me a great bargain? He was then shewn to the door by my body-servant; nor did Hirsch von Hirschenwald come for the apology.

Twice every year, however, I get a letter from him, dated Frankfort, and proposing to make me a present of a splendid palace in Austria or Bohemia, or 200,000 florins, should I prefer money. I saw his lady at Frankfort only last year, in a front box at the theatre, loaded with diamonds, and at least sixteen stone in weight.

Ah! Minna, Minna! thou mayest grow to be as ugly as sin, and as fat as Daniel Lambert, but I have the amber mouth-piece still, and swear that the prettiest lips in Jewry have kissed it!

The MS. here concludes with a rude design of a young lady smoking a pipe.

DOROTHEA.

THE reason why my Memoirs have not been continued with that regularity which, I believe, is considered requisite by professional persons, in order to ensure the success of their work, is a very simple one—I have been otherwise engaged; and as I do not care one straw whether the public do or do not like my speculations (heartily pitying, and at the same time despising, those poor devils who write under different circumstances)—as I say, I was in Scotland shooting grouse for some time past, coming home deucedly tired of evenings, which I devoted to a cigar and a glass of toddy, it was quite impossible to satisfy the curiosity of the public. I bagged 1114 brace of grouse in sixty days, besides dancing in kilt before her M—y at Bl—r Ath—l. By the way, when Mr. F—x M—le gives away cairngorums, he may as well say *whose property* they are. I lent the man the very stone out of a snuff-mull with which Charles Edward complimented my great-great-aunt, Flora MacWhirter.

The worthy publisher sent me down his Magazine to Dunkeld (a good deal of it will be found in wadding over the moors, and perhaps in the birds which I sent him), and, at the same time, he dispatched some critiques, both epistolary and newspaperacious, upon the former chapter of my Memoirs. The most indignant of the manuscript critiques came from a member of the Hebrew persuasion. And what do you think is the opinion of this Lion of Judah? Simply that George Savage Fitz-Boodle is a false name, assumed by some coward, whose intention it is to insult the Jewish religion! He says that my history of the Löwe family is a dastardly attack upon the people! How is it so? If I say that an individual Christian is a rogue, do I impugn the professors of the whole Christian religion? Can my Hebrew critic say that a Hebrew banker never cheated in matters of exchange, or that a Hebrew was never guilty of a roguery? If so, what was the gold-dust robbery, and why is Ikey Solomons at Botany Bay? No; the Lion of Judah may be a good lion, but he is a deucedly bad arguer,—nay, he is a bad lion, he roars before he is hurt. Be calm, thou red-maned desert-roarer, the arrows of Fitz-Boodle have no poison at their tip, and are shot only in play.

I never wished to attack the Jewish nation; far from it, I have three bills now out; nor is he right in saying that I have made a dastardly statement, which I have given under a false name; just the contrary, my name is, as everybody knows, my real name,—it is the *statement* which is false, and I confess there is not one word of truth in it—I never knew, to my knowledge, any Hirsch or Löwe in my life; I never was with Minna Löwe; the adventures never did occur at Bonn. Is my friend now satisfied? Let him remember, in the first place, that the tale is related of individuals, and not of his people at large; and in the second place, that the statement is not true. If *that* won't satisfy him, what will? Rabbi, let us part in peace! Neither thee nor thy like would George Fitz-Boodle ever willingly harm—neither thee nor any bearded nor unbearded man. If there be no worse rogues in Jewry, the people is more lucky than the rest of the world, and the fact is good to be known.

And now for the second objections. These are mainly of one kind—most of the journalists, from whose works pleasing extracts have been made, concurring in stating, that the last paper, which the Hebrew thought so dangerous, was, what is worse still, exceedingly stupid.

This disgusting unanimity of sentiment at first annoyed me a good deal, for I was pained to think that success so soon bred envy, and that the members of the British press could not bear to see an amateur enter the lists with them, and carry off laurels for which they had been striving long years in vain. Is there no honesty left in the world, I thought? And the thought gave me extreme pain, for, though (as in the Hebrew case above mentioned) I love occasionally to disport with the follies and expose the vices of individuals, to attribute envy to a whole class is extremely disagreeable to one whose feelings are more than ordinarily benevolent and pure.

An idea here struck me. I said to myself, "Fitz-Boodle! perhaps the paper *is* stupid, and the critics are right." I read the paper: I found that it *was* abominably stupid, and, as I fell asleep over it, an immense repose and calm came over my mind, and I woke reconciled with human nature.

Let authors consider the above fact well, and draw their profit from it. I have met with many men, who, like myself, fancy themselves the victims of a conspiracy—martyrs; but, in the long run, the world and the critics of nowadays are generally right; they praise too much perhaps, they puff a small reputation into a huge one, but they do not neglect much that is good; and, if literary gentlemen would but bear this truth in mind, what a deal of pain and trouble might they spare themselves! There would be no despair, ill-humour, no quarrelling with your fellow-creatures, nor jaundiced moody looks upon nature and the world. Instead of crying the world is wicked—all men are bad, is it not wiser, my brethren, to say, "I am an ass?" let me be content to know that, nor anathematise universal mankind for not believing in me. It is a well-known fact, that no natural man can see the length of his own ears; it is only the glass—the reflection that shows them to him. Let the critics be our glass, I am content to believe that they are pretty honest, that they are not actuated by personal motives of hatred in falling foul of me and others; and this being premised, I resume the narration of my adventures. If *this* chapter don't please them, they *must*, indeed, be very hard to amuse.

Beyond sparring and cricket, I do not recollect I learned any thing useful at Slaughter House School, where I was educated (according to an old family tradition, which sends particular generations of gentlemen to particular schools in the kingdom; and such is the force of habit, that, though I hate the place, I shall send my own son thither too, should I marry any day) I say I learned little that was useful at Slaughter

House, and nothing that was ornamental. I would as soon have thought of learning to dance as of learning to climb chimneys. Up to the age of seventeen, as I have shewn, I had a great contempt for the female race, and when age brought with it warmer and juster sentiments, where was I?—I could no more dance nor prattle to a young girl than a young bear could. I have seen the ugliest, little, low-bred wretches, carrying off young and lovely creatures, twirling with them in waltzes, whispering between their glossy curls in quadrilles, simpering with perfect equanimity, and cutting *pas* in that abominable cavalier seul, until my soul grew sick with fury. In a word, I determined to learn to dance.

But such things are hard to be acquired late in life, when the bones and the habits of a man are formed. Look at a man in a hunting field who has not been taught to ride as a boy. All the pluck and courage in the world will not make the man of him that I am, or as any man who has had the advantages of early education in the field.

In the same way with dancing. Though I went to work with immense energy, both in Brewer Street, Golden Square (with an advertising fellow), and afterwards with old Coulon at Paris, I never was able to be *easy* in dancing; and though little Coulon instructed me in a smile, it was a cursed forced one, that looked like the grin of a person in extreme agony. I once caught sight of it in a glass, and have hardly ever smiled since.

Most young men about London have gone through that strange secret ordeal of the dancing-school. I am given to understand, that young snobs from attorneys' offices, banks, shops, and the like, make not the least mystery of their proceedings in the saltatory line, but trip gaily, with pumps in hand, to some dancing place about Soho, waltz and quadrille it with Miss Greengrocer or Miss Butcher, and fancy they have had rather a pleasant evening. There is one house in Dover Street, where, behind a dirty curtain, such figures may be seen hopping every night, to a perpetual fiddling; and I have stood sometimes wondering in the streets, with about six blackguard boys wondering too, at the strange contortions of the figures jumping up and down to the mysterious squeaking of the kit. Have they no shame *ces gens?* are such degrading initiations to be held in public? No, the snob may, but the man of refined mind never can submit to shew himself in public labouring at the apprenticeship of this most absurd art. It is owing, perhaps, to this modesty, and the fact that I had no sisters at home, that I have never thoroughly been able to dance; for though I always arrive at the end of a quadrille (and thank Heaven for it too!) and though, I believe, I make no mistake in particular, yet I solemnly confess I have never been able thoroughly to comprehend the mysteries of it, or what I have been about from the beginning to the end of the dance. I always look at the lady opposite, and do as she does; if *she* did not know how to dance, *par hazard*, it would be all up; but if they can't do any thing else, women can dance, let us give them that praise at least.

In London, then, for a considerable time, I used to get up at eight o'clock in the morning, and pass an hour alone with Mr. Wilkinson, of the Theatres Royal, in Golden Square ;—an hour alone. It was "one, two, three ; one, two, three—now jump—right foot more out, Mr. Smith ; and if you *could*, try and look a little more cheerful ; your partner, sir, would like you hall the better." Wilkinson called me Smith, for the fact is, I did not tell him my real name, nor (thank Heaven !) does he know it to this day.

I never breathed a word of my doings to any soul among my friends ; once a pack of them met me in the strange neighbourhood, when, I am ashamed to say, I muttered something about a "little French milliner," and walked off, looking as knowing as I could.

In Paris, two Cambridge men and myself, who happened to be staying at a boarding-house together, agreed to go to Coulon, a little creature of four feet high with a pig-tail. His room was hung round with glasses. He made us take off our coats, and dance each before a mirror ; once he was standing before us playing on his kit—the sight of the little master and the pupil was so supremely ridiculous, that I burst into a yell of laughter, which so offended the old man, that he walked away abruptly, and begged me not to repeat my visits. Nor did I. I was just getting into waltzing then, but determined to drop waltzing and content myself with quadrilling for the rest of my days.

This was all very well in France and England ; but in Germany, what was I to do ? What did Hercules do when Omphale captivated him ? What did Rinaldo do when Armida fixed upon him her twinkling eyes ? Nay, to cut all historical instances short, by going at once to the earliest, what did Adam do when Eve tempted him ? he yielded and became her slave, and so do I heartily trust every honest man will yield until the end of the world—he has no heart who will not. When I was in Germany, I say, I began to learn to *waltz*. The reader from this will no doubt expect, that some new love-adventures befell me—nor will his gentle heart be disappointed. Two deep and tremendous incidents occurred which shall be notified on the present occasion.

The reader, perhaps, remembers the brief appearance of his Highness the Duke of Kalbsbraten Pumpernickel, at B—— House, in the first part of my Memoirs, at that unlucky period of my life when the Duke was led to remark the odour about my clothes, which lost me the hand of Mary M'Alister. After the upshot of the affair with Minna Löwe, (I cannot say but that for a time I was dreadfully cut up by her behaviour), I somehow found myself in his Highness's territories, of which anybody may read a description in the *Almanach de Gotha*. His Highness's father, as is well known, married Emilia Kunegunda Thomasina Charleria Emanuela Louisa Georgina, Princess of Saxe-Pumpernickel, and a cousin of his Highness the Duke. Thus the two principalities were united under one happy sovereign in the person of Philibert Sigismund Emanuel Maria, the reigning Duke, who has received from his country (on account of the celebrated pump which he erected in the market place of Kalbsbraten) the well-merited appellation of the Magnificent. The allegory which the statues round about the pump represent, is of a very mysterious and complicated sort. Minerva is observed leading up Ceres to a river god, who has his arms round the neck of Pomona; while Mars (in a full-bottomed wig) is driven away by Peace, under whose mantle two lovely children representing the Duke's two provinces, repose. The celebrated Speck is, as need scarcely be said, the author of this piece; and of other magnificent edifices in the *Residenz*, such as the guard-room, the skittle-hall (*Grossherzoglich Kalbsbraten pumpernickelisch schkil-lelspiel saal*), &c., and the superb sentry-boxes before the grand-ducal palace. He is Knight Grand Cross of the ancient Kartoffel order, as, indeed, is almost every one else in his Highness's dominions.

The town of Kalbsbraten contains a population of two thousand inhabitants, and a palace which would accommodate about six times that number. The principality sends three and a half men to the German Confederation, who are commanded by a general (excellency), two major-generals, and sixty-four officers of lower grades; all noble, all knights of the order, and almost all chamberlains to his Highness the Grand Duke. An excellent band of eighty performers is the admiration of the surrounding country, and leads the grand-ducal troops to battle in time of war. Only three of the contingent of soldiers returned from the battle of Waterloo, where they won much honour; the remainder was cut to pieces on that glorious day.

There is a chamber of representatives (which, however, nothing can induce to sit), home and foreign ministers, residents from neighbouring courts, law presidents, town councils, &c., all the adjuncts of a big or little government. The court has its chamberlains and marshals, the Grand Duchess her noble ladies in waiting and blushing maids of honour. Thou wert one, Dorothea! Dost remember the poor young Englander?

We parted in anger; but I think—I think thou hast not forgotten him.

The way in which I have Dorothea von Speck present to my mind is this,—not as I first saw her in the garden, for her hair was in bandeaux then, and a large Leghorn hat, with a deep riband, covered half her fair face,—not in a morning-dress, which, by the way, was none of the newest nor the best made—but as I saw her afterwards at a ball at the pleasant, splendid little court, where she moved the most beautiful of the beauties of Kalbsbraten. The grand saloon of the palace is lighted—the Grand Duke and his officers, the Duchess and her ladies, have passed through. I, in my uniform of the ——th, and a number of young fellows (who are evidently admiring my legs and envying my *distingué* appearance), are waiting round the entrance-door, where a huge Heyduke is standing, and announcing the titles of the guests as they arrive.

"Herr Oberhof und Bau Inspektor von Speck!" shouts the Heyduke; and the little inspector comes in. His lady is on his arm—huge, in towering plumes, and her favourite costume of light blue. Fair women always dress in light blue or light green; and Frau von Speck is very fair and stout.

But who comes behind her? Lieber Himmel! It is Dorothea! Did earth, among all the flowers which have sprung from its bosom, produce ever one more beautiful? She was none of your heavenly beauties, I tell you. She had nothing etherial about her. No, sir; she was of the earth earthy, and must have weighed ten stone four or five, if she weighed an ounce. She had none of your Chinese feet, nor waspy, unhealthy waists, which those may admire who will. No; Dora's foot was a good stout one; you could see her ankle (if her robe was short enough) without the aid of a microscope; and that envious, little, sour, skinny Amalia von Mangelwurzel, used to hold up her four fingers, and say (the two girls were most intimate friends, of course), "Dear Dorothea's vaist is so much dicker as dis;" and so I have no doubt it was.

But what then? Goethe sings in one of his divine epigrams:—

"Epicures vaunting their taste, entitle me vulgar and savage,
Give them their Brussels-sprouts, but I am contented with cabbage."

I hate your little women, that is when I am in love with a tall one; and who would not have loved Dorothea?

Fancy her, then, if you please, about five feet four inches high—fancy her in the family colour of light blue, a little scarf covering the most brilliant shoulders in the world; and a pair of gloves clinging close round an arm that may, perhaps, be somewhat too large now, but that Juno might have envied then. After the fashion of young ladies on the continent, she wears no jewels or gimcracks; her only ornament is a wreath of vine-leaves in her hair, with little clusters of artificial grapes. Down on her shoulders falls the brown hair, in rich liberal clusters; all that health, and good-humour, and beauty, can do for her face, kind Nature has done for hers. Her eyes are frank, sparkling, and kind. As for her cheeks, what paint-box or dictionary contains pigments or words to describe their red? They say she opens her mouth and smiles always to shew the dimples in her cheeks. Psha! she smiles because she is happy, and kind, and good-humoured, and not because her teeth are little pearls.

All the young fellows crowd up to ask her to dance, and taking from her waist a little mother-of-pearl remembrancer, she notes them down. Old Schnabel for the Polonaise; Klingenspohr, first waltz; Haarbart, second waltz; Count Hornpieper (the Danish envoy), third; and so on. I have said why *I* could not ask her to waltz, and turned away with a pang, and played écarté with Colonel Trumpenpack all night.

In thus introducing this lovely creature in her ball-costume, I have been somewhat premature, and had best go back to the beginning of the history of my acquaintance with her.

Dorothea, then, was the daughter of the celebrated Speck before mentioned. It is one of the oldest names in Germany, where her father's and mother's houses, those of Speck and Eyer, are loved wherever they are known. Unlike his warlike progenitor, Lorenzo Von Speck, Dorothea's father had early shewn himself a passionate admirer of art; had quitted home to study architecture in Italy, and had become celebrated throughout Europe, and Ober Hof architekt, and Kunstundbau inspektor of the united principalities. They are but four miles wide, and his genius has consequently but little room to play. What art can do, however, he does. The palace is frequently whitewashed under his eyes; the theatre painted occasionally; the noble public buildings erected, of which I have already made mention.

Smarting with recollections of Minna, I had come to Kalbsbraten, scarce knowing whither I went; and having, in about ten minutes, seen the curiosities of the place (I did not care to see the king's palace, for chairs and tables have no great charm for me), I had ordered horses, and wanted to get on I cared not whither, when Fate threw Dorothea in my way. I was yawning back to the hotel through the palace-garden, a valet-de-place at my side, when I saw a young lady seated under a tree reading a novel, her mamma on the same bench (a fat woman in light blue) knitting a stocking, and two officers, choked in their stays, with various orders on their spinach-coloured coats, standing by in first attitudes—the one was caressing the fat-lady-in-blue's little dog; the other was twirling his own moustache which was already as nearly as possible curled into his own eye.

I don't know how it is, but I hate to see men, evidently intimate with nice-looking women, and on good terms with themselves. There's something annoying in their cursed complacency—their evident sunshiny happiness. I've no woman to make sunshine for *me;* and yet my heart tells me, that not one, but several such suns, would do good to my system.

"Who are those pert-looking officers," says I, peevishly, to the guide, "who are talking to those vulgar-looking women?"

"The big one, with the epaulets, is Major von Schnabel; the little one, with the pale face, is Stiefel von Klingenspohr."

"And the big blue woman?"

"The Grand-ducal Pumpernickelian-court-architectress and Upper Palace-and-building-inspectress, Von Speck, born V. Eyer," replied the guide. "Your well-born honour has seen the pump in the market-place; that is the work of the great Von Speck."

"And yonder young person?"

"Mr. Court-architect's daughter; the Fraülein Dorothea."

* * * * * *

Dorothea looked up from her novel here, and turned her face towards the stranger who was passing, and then blushing turned it down again. Schnabel looked at me with a scowl, Klingenspohr with a simper, the dog with a yelp, the fat lady in blue just gave one glance, and seemed, I thought, rather well pleased. "Silence, Lischen!" said she to the dog. "Go on, darling Dorothea," she added, to her daughter, who continued her novel.

Her voice was a little tremulous, but very low and rich. For some reason or other, on getting back to the inn, I countermanded the horses, and said I would stay for the night.

I not only staid that night, but many, many afterwards, and as for the manner in which I became acquainted with the Speck family, why it was a good joke against me at the time, and I did not like then to have it known, but now it may as well come out at once. Speck, as every body knows, lives in the market-place, opposite his grand work of art, the town-pump, or fountain. I bought a large sheet of paper, and having a knack at drawing, sat down, with the greatest gravity, before the pump, and sketched it for several hours. I knew it would bring out old Speck to see.

At first he contented himself by flattening his nose against the window-glasses of his study, and looking what the Englander was about. Then he put on his grey cap with the huge green shade, and sauntered to the door: then he walked round me, and formed one of a band of street-idlers who were looking on: then at last he could restrain himself no more, but pulling off his cap, with a low bow, began to discourse upon arts and architecture in particular.

"It is curious," says he, "that you have taken the same view of which a print has been engraved."

"That *is* extraordinary," says I, (though it wasn't, for I had traced my drawing at a window off the very print in question.) I added that I was, like all the world, immensely struck with the beauty of the edifice; heard of it at Rome, where it was considered to be superior to any of the celebrated fountains of that capital of the fine arts; finally, that if, perhaps, the celebrated fountain of Aldgate in London might compare with it, Kalbsbraten building, *except* in that case, was incomparable.

This speech I addressed in French, of which the worthy Hof-architekt understood somewhat, and continuing to reply in German, our conversation grew pretty close. It is singular that I can talk to a man, and pay him compliments with the utmost gravity, whereas, to a woman, I at once lose all self-possession, and have never said a pretty thing in my life.

My operations on old Speck were so conducted, that in a quarter of an hour I had elicited from him an invitation to go over the town with him, and see its architectural beauties. So we walked through the huge half-furnished chambers of the palace, we panted up the copper pinnacle of the church-tower, we went to see the Museum and Gymnasium, and coming back into the market-place again, what could the Hof-architekt do but offer me a glass of wine and a seat in his house? He introduced me to his gattin, his Leocadia (the fat woman in blue), "as a young world observer, and worthy art-friend, a young scion of British Adel, who had come to refresh himself at the urquellece of his race, and see his brethren of the great family of Herrman."

I saw instantly that the old fellow was of a romantic turn, from this rhodomontade to his lady: nor was she a whit less so; nor was Dorothea less sentimental than her mamma. She knew every thing regarding the literature of Albion, as she was pleased to call it; and asked me news of all the famous writers there. I told her that Miss Edgeworth was one of the loveliest young beauties at our court; I described to her Lady Morgan, herself as beautiful as the wild Irish girl she drew; I promised to give her a signature of Mrs. Hemans (which I wrote for her that very evening); and described a fox-hunt, at which I had seen Thomas Moore and Samuel Rogers, Esquires; and a boxing-match, in which the athletic author of *Pelham* was pitched against the hardy mountain-bard, Wordsworth. You see my education was not neglected, for though I have never read the works of the above-named ladies and gentlemen, yet I knew their names well enough.

Time passed away.—I, perhaps, was never so brilliant in conversation as when excited by the Assmanshauser and the brilliant eyes of Dorothea that day. She and her parents had dined at their usual heathen hour ; but I was, I don't care to own it, so smitten, that, for the first time in my life, I did not even miss the meal, and talked on until six o'clock, when tea was served. Madame Speck said they always drunk it ; and so placing a tea-spoonful of bohea in a caldron of water, she placidly handed out this decoction, which we took with cakes and sardines. I leave you to imagine how disgusted Klingenspohr and Schnabel looked when they stepped in as usual that evening to make their party of whist with the Speck family ! Down they were obliged to sit—and the lovely Dorothea, for that night, declined to play altogether, and—sat on the sofa by me.

What we talked about, who shall tell ? I would not, for my part, break the secret of one of those delicious conversations, of which I and every man in his time have held so many. You begin, very probably, about the weather—'tis a common subject, but what sentiments the genius of Love can fling into it ! I have often, for my part, said to the girl of my heart for the time being, "It's a fine day," or, "It's a rainy morning!" in a way that has brought tears to her eyes. Something beats in your heart, and twangle ! a corresponding string thrills and echoes in hers. You offer her any thing—her knitting-needles, a slice of bread and butter—what causes the grateful blush with which she accepts the one or the other ? Why she sees your heart handed over to her upon the needles, and the bread and butter is to her a sandwich with love inside it. If you say to your grandmother, "Ma'am, it's a fine day," or what not, she would see no other meaning than their outward and visible view, but say so to the girl you love, and she understands a thousand mystic meanings in them. Thus in a word, though Dorothea and I did not, probably, on the first night of our meeting, talk of any thing more than the weather, or trumps, or some subjects which, to such listeners as Schnabel and Klingenspohr and others, might appear quite ordinary, yet to *us* they had a different signification, of which Love alone held the key.

Without further ado then, after the occurrences of that evening, I determined on staying at Kalbsbraten, and presenting my card the next day to the Hof-Marshall requesting to have the honour of being presented to his highness the prince, at one of whose court-balls my Dorothea appeared as I have described her.

It was summer when I first arrived at Kalbsbraten. The little court was removed to Siegmundslust, his highness's country-seat; no balls were taking place, and, in consequence, I held my own with Dorothea pretty well. I treated her admirer Lieutenant Klingenspohr with perfect scorn, had a manifest advantage over Major Schnabel, and used somehow to meet the fair one every day walking in company with her mamma in the palace garden, or sitting under the acacias, with Belotte in her mother's lap, and the favourite romance beside her. Dear, dear Dorothea! what a number of novels she must have read in her time! She confesses to me that she had been in love with Uncas, with Saint Preux, with Ivanhoe, and with hosts of German heroes of romance; and when I asked her, if she, whose heart was so tender towards imaginary youths, had never had a preference for any one of her living adorers, she only looked, and blushed, and sighed, and said nothing.

You see I had got on as well as man could do, until the confounded court season and the balls began, and then—why, then came my usual luck.

Waltzing is a part of a German girl's life. With the best will in the world, which, I doubt not, she entertains for me, for I never put the matter of marriage directly to her—Dorothea could not go to balls and not waltz. It was madness to me to see her whirling round the room with officers, *attachés*, prim little chamberlains with gold keys and embroidered coats, her hair floating in the wind, her hand reposing upon the abominable little dancer's epaulet, her good-humoured face lighted up with still greater satisfaction. I saw that I must learn to waltz too, and took my measures accordingly.

The leader of the ballet at the Kalbsbraten theatre in my time was Springbock, from Vienna. He had been a regular Zephyr once, 'twas said, in his younger days; and though now fifteen stone weight, I can, *hélas!* recommend him conscientiously as a master; and determined to take some lessons from him in the art which I had neglected so foolishly in early life.

It may be said, without vanity, that I was an apt pupil, and in the course of half-a-dozen lessons I had arrived at very considerable agility in the waltzing line and could twirl round the room with him at such a pace as made the old gentleman pant again, and hardly left him breath enough to puff out a compliment to his pupil. I may say, that in a single week I became an expert waltzer; but as I wished when I came out publicly in that character, to be quite sure of myself, and as I had hitherto practised not with a lady, but with a very fat old man, it was agreed that he should bring a lady of his acquaintance to perfect me, and accordingly, at my eighth lesson, Madam Springbock herself came to the dancing-room, and the old Zephyr performed on the violin.

If any man ventures the least sneer with regard to this lady, or dares to insinuate any thing disrespectful to her or myself, I say at once, that he is an impudent calumniator. Madam Springbock is old enough to be my grandmother, and as ugly a woman as I ever saw; but though old, she was *passionnée pour la danse*, and not having (on account, doubtless, of her age and unprepossessing appearance) many opportunities of indulging in her favourite pastime, made up for lost time by immense activity whenever she could get a partner. In vain, at the end of the hour, would Springbock exclaim, "Amalia, my soul's blessing, the time is up!" "Play on, dear Alphonso!" would the old lady exclaim, whisking me round: and though I had not the least pleasure in such a homely partner, yet for the sake of perfecting myself, I waltzed and waltzed with her, until we were both half dead with fatigue.

At the end of three weeks I could waltz as well as any man in Germany.

At the end of four weeks there was a grand ball at court in honour of H. H. the Prince of Dummerland aud his princess, and *then* I determined I would come out in public. I dressed myself with unusual care and splendour. My hair was curled and my moustache dyed to a nicety; and of the four hundred gentlemen present, if the girls of Kalbsbraten *did* select one who wore an English hussar uniform, why should I disguise the fact? In spite of my silence, the news had somehow got abroad, as news will in such small towns, —Herr von Fitz-Boodle was coming out in a waltz that evening. His highness the duke even made an allusion to the circumstance. When on this eventful night, I went as usual, and made him my bow in the presentation, "*Vous, Monsieur*," said he, "*vous qui êtes si jeune, devez aimer la danse.*" I blushed as red as my trousers, and bowing, went away.

I stepped up to Dorothea. Heavens! how beautiful she looked! and how archly she smiled, as, with a thumping heart, I asked her hand for a *waltz!* She took out her little mother-of-pearl dancing-book—she wrote down my name with her pencil—we were engaged for the fourth waltz, and till then I left her to other partners.

Who says that his first waltz is not a nervous moment? I vow I was more excited than by any duel I ever fought. I would not dance any contre-dance or galop. I repeatedly went to the buffet and got glasses of punch (dear simple Germany! 'tis with rum-punch and egg-flip thy children strengthen themselves for the dance!)—I went into the ball-room and looked—the couples bounded before me, the music clashed and rung in my ears—all was fiery, feverish, indistinct. The gleaming white columns, the polished oaken floors in which the innumerable tapers were reflected—all together swam before my eyes, and I was in a pitch of madness almost when the fourth waltz at length came. "*Will you dance with your sword on?*" said the sweetest voice in the world. I blushed, stammered, and trembled, as I laid down that weapon and my cap, and hark! the music began!

Oh, how my hand trembled as I placed it round the waist of Dorothea! With my left hand I took her right—did she squeeze it? I think she did—to this day I think she did. Away we went; we tripped over the polished oak floor like two young fairies. "*Courage, monsieur*," said she, with her sweet smile; then it was "*Très bien, monsieur;*" then I heard the voices humming and buzzing about. "*Il danse bien, l'Anglais:*" "*Ma foi, oui*," says another. On we went, twirling, and twisting, and turning and whirling; couple after couple dropped panting off. Little Klingenspohr himself was obliged to give in. All eyes were upon us—we were going round *alone*. Dorothea was almost exhausted, when

* * * * * * * *

I have been sitting for two hours since I marked the asterisks, thinking—thinking. I have committed crimes in my life—who hasn't? But talk of remorse, what remorse is there like *that* which rushes up in a flood to my brain sometimes when I am alone, and causes me to blush when I'm a-bed in the dark?

I fell, sir, on that infernal slippery floor. Down we came like shot; we rolled over and over in the midst of the ball-room, the music going ten miles an hour, 800 pair of eyes fixed upon us, a cursed shriek of laughter bursting out from all sides. Heavens! how clear I heard it, as we went on rolling and rolling! "My child! my Dorothea!" shrieked out Madame Speck, rushing forward, and as soon as she had breath to do so, Dorothea of course screamed too, then she fainted, then she was disentangled from out of my spurs, and borne off by a bevy of tittering women. "Clumsy brute!" said Madam Speck, turning her fat back upon me. I remained upon my *séant*, wild, ghastly, looking about. It was all up with me—I knew it was. I wished I could have died there, and I wish so still.

Klingenspohr married her, that is the long and short; but before that event I placed a sabre-cut across the young scoundrel's nose, which destroyed *his* beauty for ever.

O Dorothea! you can't forgive me—you oughtn't to forgive me; but I love you madly still.

My next flame was Ottilia; but let us keep her for another number, my feelings overpower me at present.

G. F. B.

OTTILIA.

CHAPTER I.

THE ALBUM—THE MEDITERRANEAN HEATH.

TRAVELLING some little time back in a wild part of Connamara, where I had been for fishing and seal-shooting, I had the good luck to get admission to the château of an hospitable Irish gentleman, and to procure some news of my once dear Ottilia.

Yes, of no other than Ottilia v. Schlippenschlopp, the Muse of Kalbsbraten-Pumpernickel, the friendly little town far away in Sachsenland,—where old Speck built the town-pump, where Klingenspohr was slashed across the nose,—where Dorothea rolled over and over in that horrible waltz with Fitz-Boo——. Psha!—away with the recollection: but wasn't it strange to get news of Ottilia in the wildest corner of Ireland, where I never should have thought to hear her gentle name? Walking on that very Urrisbeg mountain under whose shadow I heard Ottilia's name, Mackay, the learned author of the *Flora Patlandica*, discovered the Mediterranean heath,—such a flower as I have often plucked on the sides of Vesuvius, and as Proserpine, no doubt, amused herself in gathering as she strayed in the fields of Enna. Here it is—the self-same flower, peering out at the Atlantic from Roundstone Bay; here, too, in this wild lonely place, nestles the fragrant memory of my Ottilia!

In a word, after a day on Ballylynch Lake (where, with a brown fly and a single hair, I killed fourteen salmon, the smallest twenty-nine pounds weight, the largest somewhere about five stone ten), my young friend Blake Bodkin Lynch Browne (a fine lad who has made his Continental tour) and I, adjourned after dinner to the young gentleman's private room, for the purpose of smoking a certain cigar, which is never more pleasant than after a hard day's sport, or a day spent indoors, or after a good dinner, or a bad one, or at night when you are tired, or in the morning when you are fresh, or of a cold winter's day, or of a scorching summer's afternoon, or at any other moment you choose to fix upon.

What should I see in Blake's room but a rack of pipes, such as are to be found in almost all the bachelors' rooms in Germany, and amongst them was a porcelain pipe-head bearing the image of the Kalbsbraten pump! There it was, the old spout, the old familiar allegory of Mars, Bacchus, Apollo virorum, and the rest, that I had so often looked at from Hof-Architekt Speck's window, as I sat there by the side of Dorothea. The old gentleman had given me one of these very pipes, for he had hundreds of them painted, wherewith he used to gratify almost every stranger who came into his native town.

Any old place with which I have once been familiar (as, perhaps, I have before stated in these *Confessions* —but never mind that) is in some sort dear to me:

and were I Lord Shootingcastle or Colonel Popland, I think after a residence of six months there I should love the Fleet Prison. As I saw the old familiar pipe, I took it down, and crammed it with Cavendish tobacco, and lay down on a sofa, and puffed away for an hour well-nigh, thinking of old, old times.

"You're very entertaining to-night, Fitz," says young Blake, who had made several tumblers of punch for me, which I had gulped down without saying a word. "Don't ye think ye'd be more easy in bed than snorting and sighing there on my sofa, and groaning fit to make me go hang myself?"

"I am thinking, Blake," says I, "about Pumpernickel, where old Speck gave you this pipe."

"'Deed he did," replies the young man; "and did ye know the old Bar'n?"

"I did," said I. "My friend, I have been by the banks of the Bendemeer. Tell me, are the nightingales still singing there, and do the roses still bloom?"

"The *hwhat?*" cries Blake; "what the divvle, Fitz, are you growling about? Bendemeer's Lake's in Westmoreland, as I preshume; and as for roses and nightingales, I give ye my word it's Greek ye're talking to me." And Greek it very possibly was, for my young friend, though as good across country as any man in his county, has not that fine feeling and tender perception of beauty which may be found elsewhere, dear madam.

"Tell me about Speck, Blake, and Kalbsbraten, and Dorothea, and Klingenspohr her husband."

"He with the cut across the nose, is it?" cried Blake; "I know him well and his old wife."

"His old what, sir?" cried Fitz-Boodle, jumping up from his seat; "Klingenspohr's wife old?—Is he married again?—Is Dorothea then d-d-dead?"

"Dead!—no more dead than you are, only I take her to be five-and-thirty; and when a woman has had nine children, you know, she looks none the younger; and I can tell ye, that when she trod on my corruns at a ball at the Grand Juke's, I felt something heavier than a feather on my foot."

"Madame de Klingenspohr, then," replied I, hesitating somewhat, "has grown rather—rather st-st-out?" I could hardly get out the *out*, and trembled I don't know why as I asked the question.

"Stout, begad!—she weighs fourteen stone, saddle and bridle. That's right, down goes my pipe—flop! crash falls the tumbler into the fender! Break away, my boy, and remember, whoever breaks a glass here pays a dozen."

The fact was, that the announcement of Dorothea's changed condition caused no small disturbance within me, and I expressed it in the abrupt manner mentioned by young Blake.

Roused thus from my reverie, I questioned the young fellow about his residence at Kalbsbraten, which has been always since the war a favourite place for our young gentry, and heard with some satisfaction that Potzdorff was married to the Behrenstein, Haarbart had left the dragoons, the Crown Prince had broken with the ——; but mum! of what interest are all these details to the reader, who has never been at friendly little Kalbsbraten?

Presently Lynch reaches me down one of the three

books that formed his library (the *Racing Calendar* and a book of fishing-flies making up the remainder of the set). "And there's my album," says he; "you'll find plenty of hands in it that you'll recognise, as you are an old Pumpernickelaner." And so I did, in truth: it was a little book after the fashion of German albums, in which good simple little ledger every friend or acquaintance of the owner inscribes a poem or stanza from some favourite poet or philosopher with the transcriber's own name, as thus:—

> To the true house-friend, and beloved Irclandish youth:
> "Sera nunquam est ad bonos mores ira:"
> WACKERBART,
> Professor at the Grand-Ducal Kalbsbratenpumpernicklish Gymnasium.

Another writes:—

> "Wander on roses and forget-me-not."
> Amalia v. Nachtmutze.
> Geb: v. Schlafrock.

With a flourish, and the picture mayhap of a rose. Let the reader imagine some hundreds of these interesting inscriptions, and he will have an idea of the book.

Turning over the leaves I came presently on *Dorothea's* hand. There it was, the little, neat, pretty handwriting, the dear old up-and-down strokes that I had not looked at for many a long year,—the Mediterranean heath, which grew on the sunniest banks of Fitz-Boodle's existence, and here found, dear, dear, little sprig! in rude Galwagian bog-lands.

"Look at the other side of the page," says Lynch

rather sarcastically (for I don't care to confess that I kissed the name of "Dorothea v. Klingenspohr, born v. Speck," written under an extremely feeble passage of verse). "Look at the other side of the paper!"

I did, and what do you think I saw?

I saw the writing of five of the little Klingenspohrs, who have all sprung up since my time.

* * * * *

"Ha! ha! haw!" screamed the impertinent young Irishman, and the story was all over Connamara and Joyce's country in a day after.

CHAPTER II.

OTTILIA IN PARTICULAR.

Some kind critic who peruses these writings will, doubtless, have the goodness to point out that the simile of the Mediterranean heath is applied to two personages in this chapter—to Ottilia and Dorothea, and say, Psha! the fellow is but a poor unimaginative creature not to be able to find a simile a-piece at least for the girls; how much better would *we* have done the business!

Well, it is a very pretty simile;—the girls were rivals, were beautiful, I loved them both,—which should have the sprig of heath? Mr. Cruikshank (who has taken to serious painting) is getting ready for the Exhibition a fine piece, representing Fitz-Boodle on the Urrisbeg Mountain, County Galway, Ireland, with a sprig of heath in his hand, hesitating, like Paris, on which of the beauties he should bestow it. In the background is a certain animal between two bundles of hay, but that I take to represent the critics puzzled to which of my young beauties to assign the choice.

If Dorothea had been as rich as Miss Coutts, and had come to me the next day after the accident at the ball, and said, "George, will you marry me?" it must not be supposed I would have done any such thing. *That* dream had vanished for ever: rage and pride took the place of love; and the only chance I had of recovering from my dreadful discomfiture was by bearing it bravely, and trying, if possible, to awaken a little compassion in my favour. I limped home (arranging my scheme with great presence of mind as I actually sat spinning there on the ground), I limped home, sent for Pflastersticken, the court-surgeon, and addressed him to the following effect: "Pflastersticken," says I, "there has been an accident at court of which you will hear. You will send in leeches, pills, and the deuce knows what, and you will say that I have dislocated my leg: for some days you will state that I am in considerable danger; and you are a good fellow and a man of courage I know, for which very reason you can appreciate those qualities in another; so mind, if you breathe a word of my secret, either you or I must lose a life."

Away went the surgeon, and the next day all Kalbsbraten knew that I was on the point of death: I had been delirious all night, had had eighty leeches, besides I don't know how much medicine; but the Kalbsbrateners knew to a scruple. Whenever any body was ill, this little kind society knew what medicines were prescribed, every body in the town knew what every body had for her dinner. If Madam Rumpel had her satin dyed ever so quietly, the whole society was on the *qui vive;* if Countess Pultuski sent to Berlin for a new set of teeth, not a person in Kalbsbraten but was ready to compliment her as she put them on; if Potzdorff paid his tailor's bill, or Muffinstein bought a piece of black wax for his mustachios, it was the talk of the little city; and so, of course, was my accident. In their sorrow for my misfortune, Dorothea's was quite forgotten, and those eighty leeches saved me. I became interesting; I had cards left at my door; and I kept my room for a fortnight, during which time I read every one of M. Kotzebue's plays.

At the end of that period I was convalescent, though still a little lame. I called at old Speck's house and apologized for my clumsiness, with the most admirable coolness; I appeared at court, and stated calmly that I did not intend to dance any more; and when Klingenspohr grinned, I told that young gentleman such a piece of my mind as led to his wearing a large sticking-plaster patch on his nose, which was split as neatly down the middle as you would split an orange at dessert. In a word, what man could do to repair my defeat, I did.

There is but one thing now of which I am ashamed—of those killing epigrams which I wrote (*Mon Dieu!* must I own it?—but even the fury of my anger proves the extent of my love!) against the Speck family. They were handed about in confidence at court, and made a frightful sensation.

Is it possible?

There happened at Schloss P-mp-rn-ckel
A strange mishap our sides to tickle,
  And set the people in a roar;—
A strange caprice of Fortune fickle:
I never thought at Pumpernickel
  To see a SPECK *upon the floor!*

La Perfide Albion; or, a Caution to Waltzers.

"Come to the dance," the Briton said,
And forward D-r-th-a led,
  Fair, fresh, and three-and-twenty!
Ah, girls, beware of Britons red!
What wonder that it *turned her head!*
  SAT VERBUM SAPIENTI.

Reasons for not Marrying.

"The lovely Miss S.
Will surely say 'yes,'
You've only to ask and try;"
"That subject we'll quit,"
Says Georgy the wit,
"*I've a much better* SPEC *in my eye!*"

This last epigram especially was voted so killing that it flew like wildfire; and I know for a fact that our Chargé d'affaires at Kalbsbraten sent a courier express with it to the Foreign Office in England, whence through our amiable Foreign Secretary, Lord P-lm-rst-n, it made its way into every fashionable circle, nay, I have reason to believe caused a smile on the cheek of R-y-lty itself. Now that Time has taken away the sting of these epigrams, there can be no harm in giving them; and 'twas well enough then to endeavour to hide under the lash of wit the bitter pangs of humiliation; but my heart bleeds now to think that I should have ever brought a tear on the gentle cheek of Dorothea.

Not content with this, with humiliating her by satire, and with wounding her accepted lover across the nose, I determined to carry my revenge still farther, and to fall in love with any body else. This person was Ottilia v. Schlippenschlopp.

Otho Sigismund Freyherr Von Schlippenschlopp, Knight Grand Cross of the Ducal Order of the Two-Necked Swan of Pumpernickel, of the Porc-et-Sifflet of Kalbsbraten, Commander of the George and Blue Boar of Dummerland, Excellency, and High Chancellor of the United Duchies, lived in the second floor of a house in the Schwapsgasse, where, with his private income and his revenues as chancellor, amounting together to some 300*l.* per annum, he maintained such a state as very few other officers of the Grand-Ducal Crown could exhibit. The Baron is married to Maria Antoinetta, a countess of the house of Kartoffelstadt, branches of which have taken root all over Germany. He has no sons, and but one daughter, the Fraülein Ottilia.

The chancellor is a worthy old gentleman, too fat and wheezy to preside at the privy council, fond of his pipe, his ease, and his rubber. His lady is a very tall and pale Roman-nosed countess, who looks as gentle as Mrs. Robert Roy, where, in the novel, she is for putting Baillie Nicol Jarvie into the lake, and who keeps the honest chancellor in the greatest order. The Fraülein Ottilia had not arrived at Kalbsbraten when the little affair between me and Dorothea was going on, or rather had only just come in for the conclusion of it, being presented for the first time that year at the ball where I—where I met with my accident.

At the time when the countess was young, it was not the fashion in her country to educate the young ladies so highly as since they have been educated; and provided they could waltz, sew, and make puddings, they were thought to be decently bred; being seldom called upon for algebra or Sanscrit in the discharge of the honest duties of their lives. But Fraülein Ottilia was of the modern school in this respect, and came back from her *pension* at Strasburg speaking all the languages, dabbling in all the sciences, a historian, a poet,—a blue of the ultramarinest sort, in a word. What a difference there was, for instance, between poor, simple Dorothea's love of novel-reading, and the profound encyclopædic learning of Ottilia!

Before the latter arrived from Strasburg (where she had been under the care of her aunt the Canoness Countess Ottilia of Kartoffelstadt, to whom I here beg to offer my humblest respects), Dorothea had passed for a *bel esprit* in the little court circle, and her little simple stock of accomplishments had amused us all very well. She used to sing "Herz mein Herz" and "T'en souviens tu," in a decent manner (*once*, before Heaven, I thought her singing better than Grisi's), and then she had a little album in which she drew flowers, and used to embroider slippers wonderfully, and was very merry at a game of loto or forfeits, and had a hundred small *agrémens de société* which rendered her an acceptable member of it.

But when Ottilia arrived, poor Dolly's reputation was crushed in a month. The former wrote poems both in

French and German; she painted landscapes and portraits in real oil; and she twanged off a rattling piece of Listz or Kalkbrenner in such a brilliant way, that Dora scarcely dared to touch the instrument after her, or venture, after Ottilia had trilled and gurgled through "Una Voce," or "Di Piacer" (Rossini was in fashion then), to lift up her little modest pipe in a ballad. What was the use of the poor thing going to sit in the park, where so many of the young officers used ever to gather round her? Whirr! Ottilia went by galloping on a chestnut mare with a groom after her, and presently all the young fellows who could buy or hire horseflesh were prancing in her train.

When they met, Ottilia would bounce towards her soul's darling, and put her hands round her waist, and call her by a thousand affectionate names, and then talk of her as only ladies or authors can talk of one another, —talk of her, in a word, as Mr. Samuel Warren does of his "dear Boz," in the December number of *Blackwood's Magazine.* How tenderly she would hint at Dora's little imperfections of education!—how cleverly she would insinuate that the poor girl had no wit! and, thank God, no more she had. The fact is, that do what I will I see I'm in love with her still, and would be if she had fifty children; but my passion blinded me *then*, and every arrow that fiery Ottilia discharged I marked with savage joy. Dolly, thank Heaven, didn't mind the wit much, she was too simple for that. But still the recurrence of it would leave in her heart a vague, indefinite feeling of pain, and somehow she began to understand that her empire was passing away, and that her dear friend hated her like poison; and so she married

Klingenspohr. I have written myself almost into a reconciliation with the silly fellow, for the truth is, he has been a good, honest husband to her, and she has children, and makes puddings, and is happy.

Ottilia was pale and delicate. She wore her glistening black hair in bands, and dressed in vapoury white muslin. She sang her own words to her harp, and they commonly insinuated that she was alone in the world,—that she suffered some inexpressible and mysterious heart pangs, the lot of all finer geniuses,—that though she lived and moved in the world she was not of it,—that she was of a consumptive tendency and might look for a premature interment. She even had fixed on the spot where she should lie: the violets grew there, she said, the river went moaning by; the grey willow whispered sadly over her head, and her heart pined to be at rest. "Mother," she would say, turning to her parent, "promise me, promise me to lay me in that spot when the parting hour has come!" At which Madame de Schlippenschlopp would shriek and grasp her in her arms, and at which, I confess, I would myself blubber like a child. She had six darling friends at school, and every courier from Kalbsbraten carried off whole reams of her letter-paper.

In Kalbsbraten, as in every other German town, there are a vast number of literary characters, of whom our young friend quickly became the chief. They set up a literary journal, which appeared once a-week, upon light blue or primrose paper, and which, in compliment to the lovely Ottilia's maternal name, was called the *Kartoffelnkranz*. Here are a couple of her ballads extracted from the *Kranz*, and by far the most cheerful specimen of her style. For in her songs she never would willingly let off the heroines without a suicide or a consumption. She never would hear of such a thing as a happy marriage, and had an appetite for grief quite amazing in so young a person. As for her dying and desiring to be buried under the willow-tree, of which the first ballad is the subject, though I believed the story then, I have at present some doubts about it. For, since the publication of my memoirs, I have been thrown much into the society of literary persons (who admire my style hugely), and, egad! though some of them are dismal enough in their works, I find them in their persons the least sentimental class that ever a gentleman fell in with.

The Willow Tree.

Know ye the willow-tree
  Whose grey leaves quiver,
Whispering gloomily
  To yon pale river;
Lady, at even-tide
  Wander not near it,
They say its branches hide
  A sad, lost spirit!

Once to the willow-tree
  A maid came fearful,
Pale seemed her cheek to be,
  Her blue eye tearful;
Soon as she saw the tree,
  Her steps moved fleeter,
No one was there—ah, me!
  No one to meet her!

Quick beat her heart to hear
  The far bells' chime
Toll from the chapel-tower
  The trysting time:
But the red sun went down
  In golden flame,
And though she looked round,
  Yet no one came!

Presently came the night,
  Sadly to greet her,—
Moon in her silver light,
  Stars in their glitter;
Then sank the moon away
  Under the billow,
Still wept the maid alone—
  There by the willow!

Through the long darkness,
  By the stream rolling,
Hour after hour went on
  Tolling and tolling.
Long was the darkness,
  Lonely and stilly;
Shrill came the night-wind,
  Piercing and chilly.

Shrill blew the morning breeze
  Biting and cold,
Bleak peers the grey dawn
  Over the world.
Bleak over moor and stream
  Looks the grey dawn,
Grey, with dishevelled hair,
Still stands the willow there—
  THE MAID IS GONE!

Domine, Domine!
Sing we a litany,—
Sing for poor maiden-hearts broken and weary;
Domine, Domine!
Sing we a litany,
Wail we and weep we a wild Miserere!

One of the chief beauties of this ballad (for the translation of which I received some well-merited compliments) is the delicate way in which the suicide of the poor young woman under the willow-tree is hinted at; for that she threw herself into the water and became one among the lilies of the stream, is as clear as a pikestaff. Her suicide is committed some time in the darkness, when the slow hours move on tolling and tolling, and is hinted at darkly as befits the time and the deed.

But that romantic brute Van Cutsem, the Dutch Chargé d'affaires, sent in the *Kartoffelnkranz* of the week after a conclusion of the ballad, which shews what a poor creature he must be. His pretext for writing it was, he said, because he could not bear such melancholy endings to poems and young women, and therefore he submitted the following lines:—

I.

Long by the willow-trees
Vainly they sought her,
Wild rang the mother's screams
O'er the grey water:
"Where is my lovely one?
Where is my daughter?

II.

"Rouse thee, sir constable—
Rouse thee and look;

Fishermen, bring your net,
  Boatmen, your hook.
Beat in the lily-beds,
  Dive in the brook!"

III.

Vainly the constable
  Shouted and called her;
Vainly the fisherman
  Beat the green alder,
Vainly he flung the net,
  Never it hauled her!

IV.

Mother, beside the fire
  Sat, her nightcap in;
Father, in easy chair,
  Gloomily napping,
When at the window-sill
  Came a light tapping!

V.

And a pale countenance
  Looked through the casement.
Loud beat the mother's heart,
  Sick with amazement,
And at the vision, which
  Came to surprise her,
Shrieked in an agony—
  "Lor! it's Elizar!"

VI.

Yes, 'twas Elizabeth—
  Yes, 'twas their girl;
Pale was her cheek, and her
  Hair out of curl.

"Mother!" the loving one,
Blushing, exclaimed,
"Let not your innocent
Lizzy be blamed.

VII.

"Yesterday, going to aunt
Jones's to tea,
Mother, dear mother, I
Forgot the door-key!
And as the night was cold,
And the way steep,
Mrs. Jones kept me to
Breakfast and sleep."

VIII.

Whether her pa and ma
Fully believed her
That we shall never know,
Stern they received her;
And for the work of that
Cruel, though short, night,
Sent her to bed without
Tea for a fortnight.

IX.

MORAL.

Hey diddle diddlety,
Cat and the Fiddlety!
Maidens of England, take caution by she!
Let love and suicide
Never tempt you aside,
And always remember to take the door-key!

Some people laughed at this parody, and even preferred it to the original; but for myself I have no patience with the individual who can turn the finest sentiments of our nature into ridicule, and make every thing sacred a subject of scorn. The next ballad is less gloomy than that of the willow-tree, and in it the lovely writer expresses her longing for what has charmed us all, and, as it were, squeezes the whole spirit of the fairy-tale into a few stanzas:—

FAIRY DAYS.

Beside the old hall-fire—upon my nurse's knee,
Of happy fairy days—what tales were told to me!
I thought the world was once—all peopled with princesses,
And my heart would beat to hear—their loves and their distresses;
And many a quiet night,—in slumber sweet and deep,
The pretty fairy people—would visit me in sleep.

I saw them in my dreams—come flying east and west,
With wondrous fairy gifts—the new born babe they bless'd;
One has brought a jewel—and one a crown of gold,
And one has brought a curse—but she is wrinkled and old.
The gentle queen turns pale—to hear those words of sin,
But the king he only laughs—and bids the dance begin.

The babe has grown to be—the fairest of the land,
And rides the forest green—a hawk upon her hand,
An ambling palfrey white—a golden robe and crown;
I've seen her in my dreams—riding up and down.
And heard the ogre laugh—as she fell into his snare,
At the little tender creature—who wept and tore her hair!

But ever when it seemed—her need was at the sorest
A prince in shining mail—comes prancing through the forest,
A waving ostrich-plume—a buckler burnished bright;
I've seen him in my dreams—good sooth! a gallant knight.
His lips are coral red—beneath a dark moustache;
See how he waves his hand—and how his blue eyes flash!

"Come forth, thou Paynim knight!"—he shouts in accents
clear.
The giant and the maid—both tremble his voice to hear.
Saint Mary guard him well!—he draws his falchion keen,
The giant and the knight—are fighting on the green.
I see them in my dreams—his blade gives stroke on stroke,
The giant pants and reels—and tumbles like an oak!

With what a blushing grace—he falls upon his knee
And takes the lady's hand—and whispers "You are free!"
Ah! happy childish tales—of knight and faërie!
I waken from my dreams—but there's ne'er a knight for me;
I waken from my dreams—and wish that I could be
A child by the old hall-fire—upon my nurse's knee!

Indeed, Ottilia looked like a fairy herself: pale, small, slim, and airy. You could not see her face, as it were for her eyes, which were so wild, and so tender, and shone so that they would have dazzled an eagle, much more a poor goose of a Fitz-Boodle. In the theatre, when she sat on the opposite side of the house, those big eyes used to pursue me as I sat pretending to listen to the Zauberflöte, or to Don Carlos, or Egmont, and at the tender passages, especially, they would have such a winning, weeping, imploring look with them as flesh and blood could not bear.

Shall I tell how I became a poet for the dear girl's sake? 'Tis surely unnecessary after the reader has perused the above versions of her poems. Shall I tell what wild follies I committed in prose as well as in verse? how I used to watch under her window of icy evenings, and with chilblainy fingers sing serenades to her on the guitar? Shall I tell how, in a sledging party, I had the happiness to drive her, and of the delightful privilege which is, on these occasions, accorded to the driver?

Any reader who has spent a winter in Germany perhaps knows it. A large party of a score or more of sledges is formed. Away they go to some pleasure-house that has been previously fixed upon, where a ball and collation are prepared and where each man, as his partner descends, has the delicious privilege of saluting her. O heavens and earth! I may grow to be a thousand years old, but I can never forget the rapture of that salute.

"The keen air has given me an appetite," said the dear angel as we entered the supper-room; and to say the truth, fairy as she was, she made a remarkably good meal—consuming a couple of basins of white-soup, several kinds of German sausages, some Westphalia ham, some white puddings, an anchovy salad made with cornichons and onions, sweets innumerable, and a considerable quantity of old Stein Wein and rum-punch afterwards. Then she got up and danced as brisk as a fairy, in which operation I of course did not follow her, but had the honour at the close of the evening's amusement once more to have her by my side in the sledge, as we swept in the moonlight over the snow.

Kalbsbraten is a very hospitable place as far as tea-parties are concerned, but I never was in one where dinners were so scarce. At the palace they occurred twice or thrice in a month, but on these occasions spinsters were not invited, and I seldom had the opportunity of seeing my Ottilia except at evening parties.

Nor are these, if the truth must be told, very much to my taste. Dancing I have forsworn, whist is too severe a study for me, and I do not like to play *écarté* with old ladies, who are sure to cheat you in the course of an evening's play.

But to have an occasional glance at Ottilia was enough; and many and many a napoleon did I lose to her mamma, Madame de Schlippenschlopp, for the blest privilege of looking at her daughter. Many is the tea-party I went to, shivering into cold clothes after dinner (which is my abomination) in order to have one little look at the lady of my soul.

At these parties there were generally refreshments of a nature more substantial than mere tea—punch, both milk and rum, hot wine, *consommé*, and a peculiar and exceedingly disagreeable sandwich made of a mixture of cold white puddings and garlic, of which I have forgotten the name, and always detested the savour.

Gradually a conviction came upon me that Ottilia *ate a great deal.*

I do not dislike to see a woman eat comfortably. I even think that an agreeable woman ought to be *friande*, and should love certain little dishes and nick-nacks. I know that though at dinner they commonly take nothing, they have had roast mutton with the children at two, and laugh at their pretensions to starvation.

No! a woman who eats a grain of rice like Amina in the *Arabian Nights*, is absurd and unnatural; but there is a *modus in rebus :* there is no reason why she should be a Ghoul, a monster, an ogress, a horrid gormandiseress—faugh!

It was, then, with a rage amounting almost to agony, that I found Ottilia ate too much at every meal. She was always eating, and always eating too much. If I went there in the morning, there was the horrid familiar odour of those oniony sandwiches; if in the afternoon, dinner had been just removed, and I was choked by reeking reminiscences of roast meat. Tea we have spoken of. She gobbled up more cakes than any six people present; then came the supper and the sandwiches again, and the egg-flip and the horrible rum-punch.

She was as thin as ever, paler if possible than ever; —but, by Heavens! *her nose began to grow red!*

Mon dieu! how I used to watch and watch it! Some days it was purple, some days had more of the vermilion—I could take an affidavit that after a heavy night's supper it was more swollen, more red than before.

I recollect one night when we were playing a round game (I had been looking at her nose very eagerly and sadly for some time), she of herself brought up the conversation about eating, and confessed that she had five meals a-day.

"*That accounts for it!*" says I, flinging down the cards, and springing up and rushing like a madman out of the room. I rushed away into the night, and wrestled with my passion. "What! marry," said I, "a woman who eats meat twenty-one times in a week, besides breakfast and tea? Marry a sarcophagus, a cannibal, a butcher's shop?—Away!" I strove and strove, I drank, I groaned, I wrestled and fought with my love—but it overcame me; one look of those eyes brought me to her feet again. I yielded myself up like a slave; I fawned and whined for her; I thought her nose was not so *very* red.

Things came to this pitch that I sounded His Highness's minister to know whether he would give me service in the Duchy ; I thought of purchasing an estate there. I was given to understand that I should get a chamberlain's key and some post of honour did I choose to remain, and I even wrote home to my brother Fitz in England, hinting a change in my condition.

At this juncture the town of Hamburg sent His Highness the Grand Duke (*àpropos* of a commercial union which was pending between the two states) a singular present, no less than a certain number of barrels of oysters, which are considered extreme luxuries in Germany, especially in the inland parts of the country, where they are almost unknown.

In honour of the oysters and the new commercial treaty (which arrived in *fourgons* despatched for the purpose), His Highness announced a grand supper and ball, and invited all the quality of all the principalities round about. It was a splendid affair, the grand saloon brilliant with hundreds of uniforms and brilliant toilettes —not the least beautiful among them, I need not say, was Ottilia.

At midnight the supper-rooms were thrown open, and we formed into little parties of six, each having a table, nobly served with plate, a lackey in attendance, and a gratifying ice-pail or two of champagne to *égayer* the supper. It was no small cost to serve five hundred people on silver, and the repast was certainly a princely and magnificent one.

I had, of course, arranged with Mademoiselle de Schlippenschlopp. Captains Frumpel and Friedelberger of the Duke's Guard, Mesdames de Butterbrod and Bopp, formed our little party.

The first course, of course, consisted of *the oysters.* Ottilia's eyes gleamed with double brilliancy as the lackey opened them; there were nine a-piece for us—how well I recollect the number!

I never was much of an oyster-eater, nor can I relish them *in naturalibus* as some do, but require a quantity of sauces, lemons, cayenne peppers, bread and butter, and so forth, to render them palatable.

By the time I had made my preparations, Ottilia, the captains, and the two ladies, had well-nigh finished theirs. Indeed Ottilia had gobbled up all hers, and there were only my nine left in the dish.

I took one—IT WAS BAD. The scent of it was enough—they were all bad. Ottilia had eaten nine bad oysters.

I put down the horrid shell. Her eyes glistened more and more, she could not take them off the tray.

"Dear Herr George," she said, "*Will you give me your oysters?*"

* * * * *

* * * * *

She had them all down—before—I could say—Jack—Robinson.

* * * * *

I left Kalbsbraten that night, and have never been there since.

G. S. F. B.

SOME PASSAGES

IN THE

LIFE OF MAJOR GAHAGAN.

CHAPTER I.

"TRUTH IS STRANGE, STRANGER THAN FICTION."

I THINK it but right that in making my appearance before the public I should at once acquaint them with my titles and name. My card, as I leave it at the houses of the nobility, my friends, is as follows:—

MAJOR GOLIAH O'GRADY GAHAGAN, H.E.I.C.S.
Commanding Battalion of
Irregular Horse,
AHMEDNUGGAR.

Seeing, I say, this simple visiting-ticket, the world will avoid any of those awkward mistakes as to my person, which have been so frequent of late. There has been no end to the blunders regarding this humble title of mine, and the confusion thereby created. When I published my volume of poems, for instance, the

"Morning Post" newspaper remarked "that the Lyrics of the Heart, by Miss Gahagan, may be ranked among the sweetest flowerets of the present spring season." "The Quarterly Review," commenting upon my "Observations on the Pons Asinorum" (4to. London, 1836), called me "Doctor Gahagan," and so on. It was time to put an end to these mistakes, and I have taken the above simple remedy.

I was urged to it by a very exalted personage. Dining in August last at the Palace of the T–l–r–es at Paris, the lovely young Duch–ss of Orl—ns (who, though she does not speak English, understands it as well as I do) said to me in the softest Teutonic, "*Lieber Herr Major, haben sie den Ahmednuggarischen-jäger-battalion gelassen?*" "*Warum den?*" said I, quite astonished at her R—l H——ss's question. The P—cess then spoke of some trifle from my pen, which was simply signed Goliah Gahagan.

There was, unluckily, a dead silence as H. R. H. put this question.

"*Comment donc?*" said H. M. Lo–is Ph–l–ppe, looking gravely at Count Molé, "*le cher Major a quitté l'armée! Nicolas donc sera maître de l'Inde!*" H. M—— and the Pr— M–n–ster pursued their conversation in a low tone, and left me, as may be imagined, in a dreadful state of confusion. I blushed, and stuttered, and murmured out a few incoherent words to explain—but it would not do—I could not recover my equanimity during the course of the dinner; and while endeavouring to help an English duke, my neighbour, to *poulet à l'Austerlitz*, fairly sent seven mushrooms and three large greasy *croûtes* over his whiskers and shirt-frill. Another laugh at my expense. "*Ah! M. le Major,*" said the Q—— of the B–lg—ns, archly, "*vous n'aurez jamais votre brevet de Colonel.*" Her M——y's joke will be better understood when I state that his grace is the brother of a minister.

I am not at liberty to violate the sanctity of private life by mentioning the names of the parties concerned in this little anecdote. I only wish to have it understood that I am a gentleman, and live at least in *decent* society. *Verbum sat.*

But to be serious. I am obliged always to write the name of Goliah in full, to distinguish me from my brother, Gregory Gahagan, who was also a major (in the King's service), and whom I killed in a duel, as the public most likely knows. Poor Greg.! a very trivial dispute was the cause of our quarrel, which never would have originated but for the similarity of our names. The circumstance was this:—I had been lucky enough to render the Nawaub of Lucknow some trifling service (in the notorious affair of Choprasjee Muckjee), and his highness sent down a gold toothpick-case directed to Captain G. Gahagan, which I of course thought was for me: my brother madly claimed it; we fought, and the consequence was, that in about three minutes he received a slash in the right side (cut 6), which effectually did his business;—he was a good swordsman enough—I was THE BEST in the universe. The most ridiculous part of the affair is, that the toothpick-case was his, after all—he had left it on the Nawaub's table at tiffin. I can't conceive what madness prompted him to fight about such a paltry bauble; he had much better have yielded it at once, when he saw I was determined to have it. From this slight specimen of my adventures, the reader will perceive that my life has been one of no ordinary interest; and, in fact, I may say that I have led a more remarkable life than any man in the service—I have been at more pitched battles, led more forlorn hopes, had more success among the fair sex, drunk harder, read more, and been a handsomer man than any officer now serving her Majesty.

When I first went to India in 1802, I was a raw cornet of seventeen, with blazing red hair, six feet seven in height, athletic at all kinds of exercises, owing money to my tailor and everybody else who would trust me, possessing an Irish brogue, and my full pay of 120*l.* a-year. I need not say that with all these advantages I did that which a number of clever fellows have done before me—I fell in love, and proposed to marry immediately.

But how to overcome the difficulty?—It is true that I loved Julia Jowler—loved her to madness; but her father intended her for a member of council at least, and not for a beggarly Irish ensign. It was, however, my fate to make the passage to India (on board of the Samuel Snob East Indiaman, Captain Duffy) with this lovely creature, and my misfortune instantaneously to fall in love with her. We were not out of the Channel before I adored her, worshipped the deck which she trod upon, kissed a thousand times the cuddy-chair on which she used to sit. The same madness fell on every man in the ship. The two mates fought about her at the Cape—the surgeon, a sober, pious Scotchman, from disappointed affection, took so dreadfully to drinking as to threaten spontaneous combustion—and old Colonel Lilywhite, carrying his wife and seven daughters to Bengal, swore that he would have a divorce from Mrs. L., and made an attempt at suicide—the captain himself told me, with tears in his eyes, that he hated his hitherto-adored Mrs. Duffy, although he had had nineteen children by her.

We used to call her the witch—there was magic in her beauty and in her voice. I was spell-bound when I looked at her, and stark-staring mad when she looked at me! Oh, lustrous black eyes!—Oh, glossy night-black ringlets!—Oh, lips!—Oh, dainty frocks of white muslin!—Oh, tiny kid slippers!—though old and gouty, Gahagan sees you still! I recollect off Ascension, she looked at me in her particular way one day at dinner, just as I happened to be blowing on a piece of scalding hot green fat. I was stupefied at once—I thrust the entire morsel (about half a pound) into my mouth. I made no attempt to swallow or to masticate it, but left it there for many minutes burning, burning! I had no skin to my palate for seven weeks after, and lived on rice-water during the rest of the voyage. The anecdote is trivial, but it shows the power of Julia Jowler over me.

The writers of marine novels have so exhausted the subject of storms, shipwrecks, mutinies, engagements, sea-sickness, and so forth, that (although I have experienced each of these in many varieties) I think it quite unnecessary to recount such trifling adventures; suffice it to say, that during our five months *trajét*, my mad passion for Julia daily increased; so did the captain's and the surgeon's; so did Colonel Lilywhite's; so did the doctor's, the mate's—that of most part of the passengers, and a considerable number of the crew. For myself, I swore—ensign as I was—I would win her for my wife; I vowed that I would make her glorious with my sword—that as soon as I had made a favourable impression on my commanding officer, (which I did not doubt to create,) I would lay open to him the state of my affections, and demand his daughter's hand. With such sentimental outpourings did our voyage continue and conclude.

We landed at the Sunderbunds on a grilling hot day in December, 1802, and then for the moment Julia and I separated. She was carried off to her papa's arms in a palankeen, surrounded by at least forty Hookahbadars; whilst the poor cornet, attended but by two dandies and a solitary beasty, (by which unnatural name these blackamoors are called,) made his way humbly to join the regiment at head-quarters.

The —th regiment of Bengal Cavalry, then under the command of Lieut.-Colonel Julius Jowler, C. B., was known throughout Asia and Europe by the proud title of the Bundelcund Invincibles—so great was its character for bravery, so remarkable were its services in that delightful district of India. Major Sir George Gutch was next in command, and Tom Thrupp, as kind a fellow as ever ran a Mahratta through the body, was second major. We were on the eve of that remarkable war which was speedily to spread throughout the whole of India, to call forth the valour of a Wellesley, and the indomitable gallantry of a Gahagan; which was illustrated by our victories at Ahmednuggar, (where I was the first over the barricade at the storming of the Pettah;) at Argaum, where I slew with my own sword twenty-three matchlock-men, and cut a dromedary in two; and by that terrible day of Assaye, where Wellesley would have been beaten but for me—me alone; I headed nineteen charges of cavalry, took (aided by only four men of my own troop) seventeen field-pieces, killing the scoundrelly French artillery-men; on that day I had eleven elephants shot under me, and carried away Scindia's nose-ring with a pistol-ball. Wellesley is a duke and a marshal, I but a simple major of Irregulars; such is fortune and war! But my feelings carry me away from my narrative, which had better proceed with more order.

On arriving, I say, at our barracks at Dum Dum, I for the first time put on the beautiful uniform of the Invincibles; a light blue swallow-tailed jacket with silver lace and wings, ornamented with about 3000 sugar-loaf buttons, rhubarb-coloured leather inexpressibles, (tights,) and red morocco boots with silver spurs and tassels, set off to admiration the handsome persons of the officers of our corps. We wore powder in those days, and a regulation pig-tail of seventeen inches, a brass helmet surrounded by leopard-skin, with a bear-skin top, and a horse-tail feather, gave the head a fierce and chivalrous appearance, which is far more easily imagined than described.

Attired in this magnificent costume, I first presented myself before Colonel Jowler. He was habited in a manner precisely similar, but not being more than five feet in height, and weighing at least fifteen stone, the dress he wore did not become him quite so much as slimmer and taller men. Flanked by his tall majors,

Thrupp and Gutch, he looked like a stumpy skittle-ball between two attenuated skittles. The plump little Colonel received me with vast cordiality, and I speedily became a prime favourite with himself and the other officers of the corps. Jowler was the most hospitable of men, and, gratifying my appetite and my love together, I continually partook of his dinners, and feasted on the sweet presence of Julia.

I can see now, what I would not and could not perceive in those early days, that this Miss Jowler, on whom I had lavished my first and warmest love, whom I had endowed with all perfection and purity, was no better than a little impudent flirt, who played with my feelings, because during the monotony of a sea voyage she had no other toy to play with ; and who deserted others for me, and me for others, just as her whim or her interest might guide her. She had not been three weeks at head-quarters when half the regiment was in love with her. Each and all of the candidates had some favour to boast of, or some encouraging hopes on which to build. It was the scene of the Samuel Snob over again, only heightened in interest by a number of duels. The following list will give the reader a notion of some of them :—

1. Cornet Gahagan.	Ensign Hicks, of the Sappers and Miners. Hicks received a ball in his jaw, and was half choked by a quantity of carrotty whisker forced down his throat with the ball.
2. Capt Macgillicuddy, B. N. I.	Cornet Gahagan.—I was run through the body, but the

	sword passed between the ribs, and injured me very slightly.
3. Capt. Macgillicuddy, B. N. I.	Mr. Mulligatawney, B. C. S., Deputy - Assistant, Vice Sub-Controller of the Boggleywollah Indigo grounds, Ramgolly branch.

Macgillicuddy should have stuck to sword's play, and he might have come off in his second duel as well as in his first; as it was, the civilian placed a ball and a part of Mac's gold repeater in his stomach. A remarkable circumstance attended this shot, an account of which I sent home to the Philosophical Transactions: the surgeon had extracted the ball, and was going off, thinking that all was well, when the gold repeater struck thirteen in poor Macgillicuddy's abdomen. I suppose that the works must have been disarranged in some way by the bullet, for the repeater was one of Barraud's, never known to fail before, and the circumstance occurred at *seven* o'clock.*

I could continue, almost *ad infinitum*, an account of the wars which this Helen occasioned, but the above three specimens will, I should think, satisfy the peaceful reader. I delight not in scenes of blood, Heaven knows, but I was compelled in the course of a few weeks, and for the sake of this one woman, to fight

* So admirable are the performances of these watches, which will stand in any climate, that I repeatedly heard poor Macgillicuddy relate the following fact. The hours, as it is known, count in Italy from one to twenty-four: *the day Mac landed at Naples his repeater rung the Italian hours, from one to twenty-four:* as soon as he crossed the Alps it only sounded as usual. G. O'G. G.

nine duels myself, and I know that four times as many more took place concerning her.

I forgot to say that Jowler's wife was a half-caste woman, who had been born and bred entirely in India, and whom the Colonel had married from the house of her mother, a native. There were some singular rumours abroad regarding this latter lady's history—it was reported that she was the daughter of a native Rajah, and had been carried off by a poor English subaltern in Lord Clive's time. The young man was killed very soon after, and left his child with its mother. The black Prince forgave his daughter and bequeathed to her a handsome sum of money. I suppose that it was on this account that Jowler married Mrs. J., a creature who had not, I do believe, a Christian name, or a single Christian quality—she was a hideous, bloated, yellow creature, with a beard, black teeth, and red eyes: she was fat, lying, ugly, and stingy—she hated and was hated by all the world, and by her jolly husband as devoutly as by any other. She did not pass a month in the year with him, but spent most of her time with her native friends. I wonder how she could have given birth to so lovely a creature as her daughter. This woman was of course with the Colonel when Julia arrived, and the spice of the devil in her daughter's composition was most carefully nourished and fed by her. If Julia had been a flirt before, she was a downright jilt now; she set the whole cantonment by the ears; she made wives jealous and husbands miserable; she caused all those duels of which I have discoursed already, and yet such was the fascination of THE WITCH that I still thought her an angel. I made court to the nasty mother in order to be near the daughter ; and I listened untiringly to Jowler's interminable dull stories, because I was occupied all the time in watching the graceful movements of Miss Julia.

But the trumpet of war was soon ringing in our ears; and on the battle-field Gahagan is a man! The Bundelcund Invincibles received orders to march, and Jowler, Hector-like, donned his helmet, and prepared to part from his Andromache. And now arose his perplexity: what must be done with his daughter, his Julia? He knew his wife's peculiarities of living, and did not much care to trust his daughter to her keeping; but in vain he tried to find her an asylum among the respectable ladies of his regiment. Lady Gutch offered to receive her, but would have nothing to do with Mrs. Jowler; the surgeon's wife, Mrs. Sawbone, would have neither mother nor daughter; there was no help for it, Julia and her mother must have a house together, and Jowler knew that his wife would fill it with her odious blackamoor friends.

I could not, however, go forth satisfied to the campaign until I learned from Julia my fate. I watched twenty opportunities to see her alone, and wandered about the Colonel's bungalow as an informer does about a public-house, marking the incomings and the outgoings of the family, and longing to seize the moment when Miss Jowler, unbiassed by her mother or her papa, might listen, perhaps, to my eloquence, and melt at the tale of my love.

But it would not do—old Jowler seemed to have taken all of a sudden to such a fit of domesticity, that there was no finding him out of doors, and his rhubarb-coloured wife (I believe that her skin gave the first idea of our regimental breeches), who before had been gadding ceaselessly abroad, and poking her broad nose into every *ménage* in the cantonment, stopped faithfully at home with her spouse. My only chance was to beard the old couple in their den, and ask them at once for their *cub*.

So I called one day at tiffin:—old Jowler was always happy to have my company at this meal; it amused him, he said, to see me drink Hodgson's pale ale (I drank two hundred and thirty-four dozen the first year I was in Bengal)—and it was no small piece of fun, certainly, to see old Mrs. Jowler attack the currie-bhaut;—she was exactly the colour of it, as I have had already the honour to remark, and she swallowed the mixture with a gusto which was never equalled, except by my poor friend Dando, *à propos d'huîtres*. She consumed the first three platefuls, with a fork and spoon, like a Christian; but as she warmed to her work, the old hag would throw away her silver implements, and, dragging the dishes towards her, go to work with her hands, flip the rice into her mouth with her fingers, and stow away a quantity of eatables sufficient for a sepoy company. But why do I diverge from the main point of my story?

Julia, then, Jowler, and Mrs. J., were at luncheon: the dear girl was in the act to *sâbler* a glass of Hodgson as I entered. "How do you do, Mr. Gagin?" said the old hag, leeringly; "eat a bit o' currie-bhaut"—and she thrust the dish towards me, securing a heap as it passed. "What, Gagy, my boy, how do, how do?" said the fat colonel; "what, run through the body?—got well again

—have some Hodgson—run through your body too!" —and at this, I may say, coarse joke (alluding to the fact, that in these hot climates the ale oozes out as it were from the pores of the skin,) old Jowler laughed: a host of swarthy chobdars, kitmatgars, sices, consomers, and bobbychies laughed too, as they provided me, unasked, with the grateful fluid. Swallowing six tumblers of it, I paused nervously for a moment, and then said—

"Bobbachy, consomah, ballybaloo hoga."

The black ruffians took the hint, and retired.

"Colonel and Mrs. Jowler," said I, solemnly, "we are alone; and you, Miss Jowler, you are alone too; that is —I mean—I take this opportunity to—(another glass of ale if you please,)—to express, once for all, before departing on a dangerous campaign—(Julia turned pale)—before entering, I say, upon a war which may stretch in the dust my high-raised hopes and me, to express my hopes while life still remains to me, and to declare in the face of heaven, earth, and Colonel Jowler, that I love you, Julia!" The Colonel, astonished, let fall a steel fork, which stuck quivering for some minutes in the calf of my leg; but I heeded not the paltry interruption. "Yes, by yon bright heaven," continued I, "I love you, Julia! I respect my commander, I esteem your excellent and beauteous mother; tell me, before I leave you, if I may hope for a return of my affection. Say that you love me, and I will do such deeds in this coming war, as shall make you proud of the name of your Gahagan."

The old woman, as I delivered these touching words, stared, snapped, and ground her teeth, like an enraged monkey. Julia was now red, now white; the colonel stretched forward, took the fork out of the calf of my leg, wiped it, and then seized a bundle of letters, which I had remarked by his side.

"A cornet!" said he, in a voice choking with emotion; "a pitiful, beggarly, Irish cornet, aspire to the hand of Julia Jowler! Gag—Gahagan, are you mad, or laughing at us? Look at these letters, young man, at these letters, I say—one hundred and twenty-four epistles from every part of India (not including one from the governor-general and six from his brother, Colonel Wellesley,)—one hundred and twenty-four proposals for the hand of Miss Jowler. Cornet Gahagan," he continued, "I wish to think well of you: you are the bravest, the most modest, and, perhaps, the handsomest man in our corps, but you have not got a single rupee. You ask me for Julia, and you do not possess even an anna!—(Here the old rogue grinned, as if he had made a capital pun.) No, no," said he, waxing good-natured; "Gagy, my boy, it is nonsense! Julia, love, retire with your mamma; this silly young gentleman will remain and smoke a pipe with me."

I took one; it was the bitterest chillum I ever smoked in my life.

* * * * *

I am not going to give here an account of my military services; they will appear in my great national autobiography, in forty volumes, which I am now preparing for the press. I was with my regiment in all Wellesley's brilliant campaigns, then, taking dawk, I travelled across the country north-eastward, and had the honour of fighting by the side of Lord Lake, at Laswaree, Deeg, Furruckabad, Futtyghur, and Bhurtpore; but I will not boast of my actions—the military man knows them, MY SOVEREIGN appreciates them. If asked who was the bravest man of the Indian army, there is not an officer belonging to it who would not cry at once, GAHAGAN. The fact is, I was desperate; I cared not for life, deprived of Julia Jowler.

With Julia's stony looks ever before my eyes, her father's stern refusal in my ears, I did not care, at the close of the campaign, again to seek her company or to press my suit. We were eighteen months on service, marching and countermarching, and fighting almost every other day; to the world I did not seem altered; but the world only saw the face, and not the seared and blighted heart within me. My valour, always desperate, now reached to a pitch of cruelty; I tortured my grooms and grass-cutters for the most trifling offence or error,—I never in action spared a man,—I sheared off three hundred and nine heads in the course of that single campaign.

Some influence, equally melancholy, seemed to have fallen upon poor old Jowler. About six months after we had left Dum Dum, he received a parcel of letters from Benares (whither his wife had retired with her daughter), and so deeply did they seem to weigh upon his spirits, that he ordered eleven men of his regiment to be flogged within two days; but it was against the blacks that he chiefly turned his wrath: our fellows, in the heat and hurry of the campaign, were in the habit of dealing rather roughly with their prisoners, to extract treasure from them. They used to pull their nails out by the root, to boil them in kedgeree pots, to flog them and dress their wounds with cayenne pepper, and so on.

Jowler, when he heard of these proceedings, which before had always justly exasperated him (he was a humane and kind little man,) used now to smile fiercely, and say, "D—— the black scoundrels! Serve them right, serve them right!"

One day, about a couple of miles in advance of the column, I had been on a foraging party with a few dragoons, and was returning peaceably to camp, when of a sudden, a troop of Mahrattas burst on us from a neighbouring mango tope, in which they had been hidden: in an instant, three of my men's saddles were empty, and I was left with but seven more to make head against at least thirty of these vagabond black horsemen. I never saw, in my life, a nobler figure than the leader of the troop—mounted on a splendid black Arab: he was as tall, very nearly, as myself; he wore a steel cap, and a shirt of mail, and carried a beautiful French carbine, which had already done execution upon two of my men. I saw that our only chance of safety lay in the destruction of this man. I shouted to him in a voice of thunder (in the Hindostanee tongue of course), "Stop, dog, if you dare, and encounter a man!"

In reply his lance came whirling in the air over my head, and mortally transfixed poor Foggarty, of ours, who was behind me. Grinding my teeth, and swearing horribly, I drew that scimitar which never yet failed in its blow,* and rushed at the Indian. He came down at full gallop, his own sword making ten thousand gleaming circles in the air, shrieking his cry of battle.

* In my affair with Macgillicuddy, I was fool enough to go out with small swords:—miserable weapons, only fit for tailors.—G. O'G. G.

The contest did not last an instant. With my first blow I cut off his sword-arm at the wrist; my second I levelled at his head. I said that he wore a steel cap, with a gilt iron spike of six inches, and a hood of chain mail. I rose in my stirrups, and delivered "*St. George*;" my sword caught the spike exactly on the point, split it sheer in two, cut crashing through the steel cap and hood, and was only stopped by a ruby which he wore in his back-plate. His head, cut clean in two between the eye-brows and nostrils, even between the two front teeth, fell, one side on each shoulder, and he galloped on till his horse was stopped by my men, who were not a little amused at the feat.

As I had expected, the remaining ruffians fled on seeing their leader's fate. I took home his helmet by way of curiosity, and we made a single prisoner, who was instantly carried before old Jowler.

We asked the prisoner the name of the leader of the troop; he said it was Chowder Loll.

"CHOWDER LOLL!" shrieked Colonel Jowler. "Oh, fate! thy hand is here!" He rushed wildly into his tent—the next day applied for leave of absence. Gutch took the command of the regiment, and I saw him no more for some time.

* * * * * *

As I had distinguished myself not a little during the war, General Lake sent me up with dispatches to Calcutta, where Lord Wellesley received me with the greatest distinction. Fancy my surprise, on going to a ball at Government-house, to meet my old friend Jowler; my trembling, blushing, thrilling delight, when I saw Julia by his side!

Jowler seemed to blush too when he beheld me. I thought of my former passages with his daughter. "Gagy, my boy," says he, shaking hands, "glad to see you, old friend, Julia—come to tiffin—Hodgson's pale—brave fellow Gagy." Julia did not speak, but she turned ashy pale and fixed upon me with her awful eyes! I fainted almost, and uttered some incoherent words. Julia took my hand, gazed at me still, and said "Come!" Need I say I went?

I will not go over the pale ale and currie-bhaut again, but this I know, that in half an hour I was as much in love as I ever had been; and that in three weeks—I, yes, I—was the accepted lover of Julia! I did not pause to ask, where were the one hundred and twenty-four offers? why I, refused before, should be accepted now? I only felt that I loved her, and was happy!

* * * * * *

One night, one memorable night, I could not sleep, and, with a lover's pardonable passion, wandered solitary through the city of palaces until I came to the house which contained my Julia. I peeped into the compound—all was still;—I looked into the verandah—all was dark, except a light—yes, one light—and it was in Julia's chamber! My heart throbbed almost to stifling. I would—I *would* advance, if but to gaze upon her for a moment, and to bless her as she slept. I *did* look, I *did* advance; and, oh Heaven! I saw a lamp burning, Mrs. Jow. in a night-dress, with a very dark baby in her arms, and Julia, looking tenderly at an Ayah, who was nursing another.

"O, mamma," said Julia, "what would that fool Gahagan say, if he knew all?"

"*He does know all!*" shouted I, springing forward, and tearing down the tatties from the window. Mrs. Jow. ran shrieking out of the room, Julia fainted, the cursed black children squalled, and their d—d nurse fell on her knees, gabbling some infernal jargon of Hindostanee. Old Jowler at this juncture entered with a candle and a drawn sword.

"Liar! scoundrel! deceiver!" shouted I. "Turn, ruffian, and defend yourself!" But old Jowler, when he saw me, only whistled, looked at his lifeless daughter, and slowly left the room.

Why continue the tale? I need not now account for Jowler's gloom on receiving his letters from Benares—for his exclamation upon the death of the Indian chief—for his desire to marry his daughter: the woman I was wooing was no longer Miss Julia Jowler, she was Mrs. CHOWDER LOLL!

CHAPTER II.

ALLYGHUR AND LASWAREE.

I SAT down to write gravely and sadly, for (since the appearance of some of my adventures in a monthly magazine) unprincipled men have endeavoured to rob me of the only good I possess, to question the statements that I make, and themselves, without a spark of honour or good feeling, to steal from me that which is my sole wealth—my character as a teller of THE TRUTH.

The reader will understand that it is to the illiberal strictures of a profligate press I now allude; among the London journalists, none (luckily for themselves) have dared to question the veracity of my statements; they know me, and they know that I am *in London.* If I can use the pen, I can also wield a more manly and terrible weapon, and would answer their contradictions with my sword! No gold or gems adorn the hilt of that war-worn scimetar, but there is blood upon the blade—the blood of the enemies of my country, and the maligners of my honest fame. There are others, however—the disgrace of a disgraceful trade—who borrowing from distance a despicable courage, have ventured to assail me. The infamous editors of the "Kelso Champion," the "Bungay Beacon," the "Tipperary Argus," and the "Stoke Pogis Sentinel," and other dastardly organs of the provincial press, have, although differing in politics, agreed upon this one point, and with a scoundrelly unanimity, vented a flood of abuse upon the revelations made by me.

They say that I have assailed private characters, and wilfully perverted history to blacken the reputation of public men. I ask, was any one of these men in Bengal in the year 1803? Was any single conductor of any one of these paltry prints ever in Bundelcund or the Rohilla country? Does this *exquisite* Tipperary scribe know the difference between Hurrygurrybang and Burrumtollah? Not he! and because, forsooth, in those strange and distant lands strange circumstances have taken place, it is insinuated that the relator is a liar, nay, that the very places themselves have no existence but in my imagination. Fools!—but I will not waste my anger upon them, and proceed to recount some other portions of my personal history.

It is, I presume, a fact which even *these* scribbling assassins will not venture to deny, that before the commencement of the campaign against Scindiah, the English general formed a camp at Kanouge on the Jumna, where he exercised that brilliant little army which was speedily to perform such wonders in the Dooab. It will be as well to give a slight account of the causes of a war which was speedily to rage through some of the fairest portions of the Indian continent.

Shah Allum, the son of Shah Lollum, the descendant by the female line of Nadir Shah (that celebrated Toorkomaun adventurer, who had well-nigh hurled Bajazet and Selim the Second from the throne of Bagdad); Shah Allum, I say, although nominally the Emperor of Delhi, was, in reality, the slave of the various warlike chieftains who lorded it by turns over the country and the sovereign, until conquered and slain by some more successful rebel. Chowder Loll Masolgee, Zubberdust Khan, Dowsunt Row Scindiah, and the celebrated Bobbachy Jung Bahawder, had held for a time complete mastery in Delhi. The second of these, a ruthless Afghaun soldier, had abruptly entered the capital, nor was he ejected from it until he had seized upon the principal jewels, and likewise put out the eyes of the last of the unfortunate family of Afrasiâb. Scindiah came to the rescue of the sightless Shah Allum, and though he destroyed his oppressor, only increased his slavery, holding him in as painful a bondage as he had suffered under the tyrannous Afghaun.

As long as these heroes were battling among themselves, or as long rather as it appeared that they had any strength to fight a battle, the British government, ever anxious to see its enemies by the ears, by no means interfered in the contest. But the French Revolution broke out, and a host of starving sans-culottes appeared among the various Indian states, seeking for military service, and inflaming the minds of the various native princes against the British East India Company. A number of these entered into Scindiah's ranks—one of them, Perron, was commander of his army; and though that chief was as yet quite engaged in his hereditary quarrel with Jeswunt Row Holkar, and never thought of an invasion of the British territory, the Company all of a sudden discovered that Shah Allum, his sovereign, was shamefully ill-used, and determined to re-establish the ancient splendour of his throne.

Of course it was sheer benevolence for poor Shah Allum that prompted our governors to take these kindly measures in his favour. I don't know how it happened that, at the end of the war, the poor Shah was not a whit better off than at the beginning; and that though Holkar was beaten, and Scindiah annihilated, Shah Allum was much such a puppet as before. Somehow, in the hurry and confusion of this struggle, the oyster remained with the British government, who had so kindly offered to dress it for the emperor, while his majesty was obliged to be contented with the shell.

The force encamped at Kanouge bore the title of the Grand Army of the Ganges and the Jumna; it consisted of eleven regiments of cavalry and twelve battalions of infantry, and was commanded by General Lake in person.

Well, on the 1st of September we stormed Perron's

camp at Allyghur; on the 4th we took that fortress by assault; and as my name was mentioned in general orders, I may as well quote the commander-in-chief's words regarding me—they will spare me the trouble of composing my own eulogium.

"The commander-in-chief is proud thus publicly to declare his high sense of the gallantry of Lieutenant Gahagan, of the —— cavalry. In the storming of the fortress, although unprovided with a single ladder, and accompanied but by a few brave men, Lieutenant Gahagan succeeded in escalading the inner and fourteenth wall of the place. Fourteen ditches, lined with sword blades and poisoned chevaux-de-frise, fourteen walls bristling with innumerable artillery, and as smooth as looking-glasses, were in turns triumphantly passed by that enterprising officer. His course was to be traced by the heaps of slaughtered enemies lying thick upon the platforms; and, alas! by the corpses of most of the gallant men who followed him!—when at length he effected his lodgment, and the dastardly enemy, who dared not to confront him with arms, let loose upon him the tigers and lions of Scindiah's menagerie:—this meritorious officer destroyed, with his own hand, four of the largest and most ferocious animals, and the rest, awed by the indomitable majesty of British valour, shrunk back to their dens. Thomas Higgory, a private, and Runty Goss, Havildar, were the only two who remained out of the nine hundred who followed Lieutenant Gahagan. Honour to them! Honour and tears for the brave men who perished on that awful day!"

* * * * *

I have copied this, word for word, from the Bengal

Hurkaru of September 24, 1803; and anybody who has the slightest doubt as to the statement, may refer to the paper itself.

And here I must pause to give thanks to fortune, which so marvellously preserved me, Sergeant-Major Higgory, and Runty Goss. Were I to say that any valour of ours had carried us unhurt through this tremendous combat, the reader would laugh me to scorn. No: though my narrative is extraordinary, it is nevertheless authentic; and never, never would I sacrifice truth for the mere sake of effect. The fact is this:—the citadel of Allyghur is situated upon a rock, about a thousand feet above the level of the sea, and is surrounded by fourteen walls, as his excellency was good enough to remark in his dispatch. A man who would mount these without scaling-ladders, is an ass; he who would *say* he mounted them without such assistance, is a liar and a knave. We *had* scaling-ladders at the commencement of the assault, although it was quite impossible to carry them beyond the first line of batteries. Mounted on them, however, as our troops were falling thick about me, I saw that we must ignominiously retreat, unless some other help could be found for our brave fellows to escalade the next wall. It was about seventy feet high—I instantly turned the guns of wall A. on wall B., and peppered the latter so as to make not a breach, but a scaling-place, the men mounting in the holes made by the shot. By this simple stratagem, I managed to pass each successive barrier—for to ascend a wall, which the General was pleased to call "as smooth as glass," is an absurd impossibility. I seek to achieve none such:—

"I dare do all that may become a man,
Who dares do more, is neither more nor less."

Of course, had the enemy's guns been commonly well served, not one of us would ever have been alive out of the three; but whether it was owing to fright, or to the excessive smoke caused by so many pieces of artillery, arrive we did. On the platforms, too, our work was not quite so difficult as might be imagined—killing these fellows was sheer butchery. As soon as we appeared, they all turned and fled, helter-skelter, and the reader may judge of their courage by the fact that out of about seven hundred men killed by us, only forty had wounds in front, the rest being bayoneted as they ran.

And beyond all other pieces of good fortune was the very letting out of these tigers, which was the *dernier ressort* of Bournonville, the second commandant of the fort. I had observed this man (conspicuous for a tricoloured scarf which he wore,) upon every one of the walls as we stormed them, and running away the very first among the fugitives. He had all the keys of the gates; and in his tremor, as he opened the menagerie portal, left the whole bunch in the door, which I seized when the animals were overcome. Runty Goss then opened them by one, our troops entered, and the victorious standard of my country floated on the walls of Allyghur!

When the general, accompanied by his staff, entered the last line of fortifications, the brave old man raised me from the dead rhinoceros on which I was seated, and pressed me to his breast. But the excitement which had borne me through the fatigues and perils of that fearful day failed all of a sudden, and I wept like a child upon his shoulder.

Promotion, in our army, goes unluckily by seniority; nor is it in the power of the general-in-chief to advance a Cæsar, if he finds him in the capacity of a subaltern: *my* reward for the above exploit was, therefore, not very rich. His excellency had a favourite horn snuff-box (for though exalted in station he was in his habits most simple): of this, and about a quarter of an ounce of high-dried Welsh, which he always took, he made me a present, saying, in front of the line, "Accept this, Mr. Gahagan, as a token of respect from the first, to the bravest officer in the army."

Calculating the snuff to be worth a halfpenny, I should say that four-pence was about the value of this gift; but it has at least this good effect—it serves to convince any person who doubts my story, that the facts of it are really true. I have left it at the office of my publisher, along with the extract from the Bengal Hurkaru, and any body may examine both by applying in the counting-house of Mr. Cunningham.* That once popular expression, or proverb, "Are you up to snuff?" arose out of the above circumstance; for the officers of my corps, none of whom, except myself, had ventured on the storming party, used to twit me about this modest reward for my labours. Never mind;

* The major certainly offered to leave an old snuff-box at Mr. Cunningham's office; but it contained no extract from a newspaper, and does not *quite* prove that he killed a rhinoceros, and stormed fourteen intrenchments at the siege of Allyghur.—M. A. T.

when they want me to storm a fort *again*, I shall know better.

Well, immediately after the capture of this important fortress, Perron, who had been the life and soul of Scindiah's army, came in to us, with his family and treasure, and was passed over to the French settlements at Chandernagur. Bourquien took his command, and against him we now moved. The morning of the 11th of September found us upon the plains of Delhi.

It was a burning hot day, and we were all refreshing ourselves after the morning's march, when I, who was on the advanced piquet along with O'Gawler of the king's dragoons, was made aware of the enemy's neighbourhood in a very singular manner. O'Gawler and I were seated under a little canopy of horse-cloths, which we had formed to shelter us from the intolerable heat of the sun, and were discussing with great delight a few Manilla cheroots, and a stone jar of the most exquisite, cool, weak, refreshing sangaree. We had been playing cards the night before, and O'Gawler had lost to me seven hundred rupees. I emptied the last of the sangaree into the two pint tumblers out of which we were drinking, and holding mine up, said, "Here's better luck to you next time, O'Gawler!"

As I spoke the words—whish!—a cannon-ball cut the tumbler clean out of my hand, and plumped into poor O'Gawler's stomach. It settled him completely, and of course I never got my seven hundred rupees. Such are the uncertainties of war!

To strap on my sabre and my accoutrements—to mount my Arab charger—to drink off what O'Gawler had left of the sangaree—and to gallop to the general, was a work of a moment. I found him as comfortably at tiffin, as if he were at his own house in London.

"General," said I, as soon as I got into his paijamahs (or tent), "you must leave your lunch if you want to fight the enemy."

"The enemy—psha! Mr. Gahagan, the enemy is on the other side of the river."

"I can only tell your excellency, that the enemy's guns will hardly carry five miles; and that Cornet O'Gawler was this moment shot dead at my side with a cannon ball."

"Ha! is it so?" said his excellency, rising, and laying down the drum-stick of a grilled chicken. "Gentlemen, remember that the eyes of Europe are upon us, and follow me!"

Each aide-de-camp started from table and seized his cocked hat; each British heart beat high at the thoughts of the coming *mêlée.* We mounted our horses, and galloped swiftly after the brave old general; I not the last in the train, upon my famous black charger.

It was perfectly true, the enemy were posted in force within three miles of our camp, and from a hillock in the advance to which we galloped, we were enabled with our telescopes to see the whole of his imposing line. Nothing can better describe it than this:—

—A is the enemy, and the dots represent the hundred

and twenty pieces of artillery which defended his line. He was, moreover, entrenched; and a wide morass in his front gave him an additional security.

His excellency for a moment surveyed the line, and then said, turning round to one of his aides-de-camp, "Order up Major-General Tinkler and the cavalry."

"*Here*, does your excellency mean?" said the aide-de-camp, surprised, for the enemy had perceived us, and the cannon-balls were flying about as thick as peas.

"*Here, Sir*," said the old general, stamping with his foot in a passion, and the A.D.C. shrugged his shoulders and galloped away. In five minutes we heard the trumpets in our camp, and in twenty more the greater part of the cavalry had joined us.

Up they came, five thousand men, their standards flapping in the air, their long line of polished jack-boots gleaming in the golden sun-light. "And now we are here," said Major-General Sir Theophilus Tinkler, "what next?" "O d—— it," said the commander-in-chief, "charge, charge—nothing like charging—galloping—guns—rascally black scoundrels—charge, charge!" and then, turning round to me, (perhaps he was glad to change the conversation,) he said, "Lieutenant Gahagan, you will stay with me."

And well for him I did, for I do not hesitate to say, that the battle *was gained by me*. I do not mean to insult the reader by pretending that any personal exertions of mine turned the day,—that I killed, for instance, a regiment of cavalry, or swallowed a battery of guns,—such absurd tales would disgrace both the hearer and the teller. I, as is well known, never say a single word which cannot be proved, and hate more than all other vices the absurd sin of egotism ; I simply mean that my *advice* to the general, at a quarter past two o'clock in the afternoon of that day, won this great triumph for the British army.

Gleig, Mill, and Thorn have all told the tale of this war, though somehow they have omitted all mention of the hero of it. General Lake, for the victory of that day, became Lord Lake, of Laswaree. Laswaree! and who forsooth was the real conqueror of Laswaree? I can lay my hand upon my heart, and say that *I* was. If any proof is wanting of the fact, let me give it at once, and from the highest military testimony in the world, I mean that of the EMPEROR NAPOLEON.

In the month of March, 1817, I was passenger on board the Prince Regent, Captain Harris, which touched at St. Helena on its passage from Calcutta to England. In company with the other officers on board the ship, I paid my respects to the illustrious exile of Longwood, who received us in his garden, where he was walking about in a nankeen dress and a large broad-brimmed straw-hat, with General Montholon, Count Las Cases, and his son Emanuel, then a little boy, who I dare say does not recollect me, but who nevertheless played with my sword-knot and the tassels of my Hessian boots during the whole of our interview with his Imperial Majesty.

Our names were read out (in a pretty accent, by the way!) by General Montholon, and the Emperor, as each was pronounced, made a bow to the owner of it, but did not vouchsafe a word. At last Montholon came to mine. The Emperor looked me at once in the face, took his hands out of his pockets, put them behind his back, and coming up to me smiling, pronounced the following words :—

"*Assye, Delhi, Deeg, Futtyghur.*"

I blushed, and taking off my hat with a bow, said—"*Sire, c'est moi.*"

"*Parbleu! je le savais bien,*" said the Emperor, holding out his snuff-box. "*En usez vous, Major?*" I took a large pinch (which, with the honour of speaking to so great a man, brought the tears into my eyes), and he continued as nearly as possible in the following words :—

"Sir, you are known; you come of an heroic nation. Your third brother, the Chef de Bataillon, Count Godfrey Gahagan, was in my Irish brigade."

Gahagan.—"Sire, it is true. He and my countrymen in your Majesty's service stood under the green flag in the breach of Burgos, and beat Wellington back. It was the only time, as your Majesty knows, that Irishmen and Englishmen were beaten in that war."

Napoleon (looking as if he would say "D— your candour, Major Gahagan.")—"Well, well; it was so. Your brother was a Count, and died a General in my service."

Gahagan.—"He was found lying upon the bodies of nine-and-twenty Cossacks at Borodino. They were all dead, and bore the Gahagan mark."

Napoleon (to Montholon).—"C'est vrai, Montholon, je vous donne ma parole d'honneur la plus sacrée, que c'est vrai. Ils ne font pas d'autres, ces terribles Ga'gans. You must know that Monsieur gained the battle of Delhi as certainly as I did that of Austerlitz. In this way :—*Ce belître de Lor Lake,* after calling up his cavalry, and placing them in front of Holkar's batteries, *qui balayaient la plaine*, was for charging the enemy's batteries with his horse, who would have been *écrasés, mitraillés, foudroyés* to a man, but for the cunning of *cc grand rouge que vous voyez.*"

Montholon.—"*Coquin de Major, va!*"

Napoleon.—"Montholon! tais-toi. When Lord Lake, with his great bull-headed English obstinacy, saw the *fâcheuse* position into which he had brought his troops, he was for dying on the spot, and would infallibly have done so—and the loss of his army would have been the ruin of the East India Company—and the ruin of the English East India Company would have established my empire (bah! it was a republic then!) in the East; but that the man before us, Lieutenant Goliah Gahagan, was riding at the side of General Lake."

Montholon (with an accent of despair and fury).—"*Gredin! cent mille tonnerres de Dieu!*"

Napoleon (benignantly).—"*Calme-toi, mon fidèle ami.* What will you? It was fate. Gahagan, at the critical period of the battle, or rather slaughter (for the English had not slain a man of the enemy), advised a retreat."

Montholon—"*Le lâche! Un Français meurt, mais il ne recule jamais.*"

Napoleon.—"*Stupide!* Don't you see *why* the retreat was ordered?—don't you know that it was a feint on the part of Gahagan to draw Holkar from his impregnable retrenchments? Don't you know that the ignorant Indian fell into the snare, and issuing from behind the cover of his guns, came down with his cavalry on the plains in pursuit of Lake and his dragoons? Then it was that the Englishmen turned upon him; the hardy children of the north swept down his feeble horsemen, bore them back to their guns, which were useless, entered Holkar's entrenchments along with his troops, sabred the artillerymen at their pieces, and won the battle of Delhi!"

As the Emperor spoke, his pale cheek glowed red, his eye flashed fire, his deep clear voice rung as of old, when he pointed out the enemy from beneath the shadow of the Pyramids, or rallied his regiments to the charge upon the death-strewn plain of Wagram. I have had many a proud moment in my life, but never such a proud one as this; and I would readily pardon the word "coward," as applied to me by Montholon, in consideration of the testimony which his master bore in my favour.

"Major," said the Emperor to me in conclusion, "why had I not such a man as you in my service? I would have made you a Prince and a Marshal!" and here he fell into a reverie, of which I knew and respected the purport. He was thinking doubtless, that I might have retrieved his fortunes, and indeed I have very little doubt that I might.

Very soon after, coffee was brought by Monsieur Marchand, Napoleon's valet-de-chambre, and after partaking of that beverage and talking upon the politics of the day, the Emperor withdrew, leaving me deeply impressed by the condescension he had shewn in this remarkable interview.

CHAPTER III.

A PEEP INTO SPAIN—ACCOUNT OF THE ORIGIN AND SERVICES OF THE AHMEDNUGGAR IRREGULARS.

Head Quarters, Morella, Sept. 15, 1838.

I HAVE been here for some months, along with my young friend Cabrera; and in the hurry and bustle of war—daily on guard and in the batteries for sixteen hours out of the twenty-four, with fourteen severe wounds, and seven musket-balls in my body—it may be imagined that I have had little time to think about the publication of my memoirs. *Inter arma silent leges* —in the midst of fighting be hanged to writing! as the poet says; and I never would have bothered myself with a pen, had not common gratitude incited me to throw off a few pages. The publisher and editor of "The New Monthly Magazine" little know what service has been done to me by that miscellany.

Along with Oraa's troops, who have of late been beleaguering this place, there was a young Milesian gentleman, Mr. Toone O'Connor Emmett Fitzgerald Sheeny, by name, a law student, and member of Gray's Inn, and what he called *Bay Ah* of Trinity College, Dublin. Mr. Sheeny was with the Queen's people not in a military capacity, but as representative of an English journal, to which, for a trifling weekly remuneration, he was in the habit of transmitting accounts of the movements of the belligerents, and his own opinion of the politics of Spain. Receiving, for the discharge of this duty, a couple of guineas a-week from the proprietors of the journal in question, he was enabled, as I need scarcely say, to make such a show in Oraa's camp as only a Christino general officer, or at the very least a colonel of a regiment, can afford to keep up.

In the famous sortie which we made upon the twenty-third, I was of course among the foremost in the *melée*, and found myself, after a good deal of slaughtering (which it would be as disagreeable as useless to describe here), in the court of a small inn or podesta, which had been made the headquarters of several queenite officers during the siege. The pesatero or landlord of the inn had been despatched by my brave chapel-churies, with his fine family of children—the officers quartered in the podesta had of course bolted; but one man remained, and my fellows were on the point of cutting him into ten thousand pieces with their borachios, when I arrived in the room time enough to prevent the catastrophe. Seeing before me an individual in the costume of a civilian—a white hat, a light-blue satin cravat, embroidered with butterflies and other quadrupeds, a green coat and brass buttons, and a pair of blue plaid trousers, I recognised at once a countryman, and interposed to save his life.

In an agonized brogue the unhappy young man was saying all that he could to induce the chapel-churies to give up their intention of slaughtering him; but it is very little likely that his protestations would have had any effect upon them, had not I appeared in the room, and shouted to the ruffians to hold their hand.

Seeing a general officer before them (I have the

honour to hold that rank in the service of his Catholic Majesty), and moreover one six feet four in height, and armed with that terrible *cabecilla* (a sword, so called, because it is five feet long) which is so well known among the Spanish armies—seeing, I say, this figure, the fellows retired, exclaiming, "*Adios, corpo di bacco, nosotros*," and so on, clearly proving (by their words) that they would, if they dared, have immolated the victim whom I had thus rescued from their fury. "Villains!" shouted I, hearing them grumble, "away! quit the apartment!" Each man, sulkily sheathing his sombrero, obeyed, and quitted the camarilla.

It was then that Mr. Sheeny detailed to me the particulars to which I have briefly adverted; and, informing me at the same time that he had a family in England who would feel obliged to me for his release, and that his most intimate friend the English ambassador would move heaven and earth to revenge his fall, he directed my attention to a portmanteau passably well filled, which he hoped would satisfy the cupidity of my troops. I said, though with much regret, that I must subject his person to a search; and hence arose the circumstance which has called for what I fear you will consider a somewhat tedious explanation. I found upon Mr. Sheeny's person three sovereigns in English money (which I have to this day), and singularly enough a copy of "The New Monthly Magazine" for March, which contained my article. It was a toss-up whether I should let the poor young man be shot or no, but this little circumstance saved his life. The gratified vanity of authorship induced me to accept his portmanteau and valuables, and to allow the poor wretch to go free.

I put the Magazine in my coat-pocket, and left him and the podesta.

The men, to my surprise, had quitted the building, and it was full time for me to follow, for I found our sallying-party, after committing dreadful ravages in Oraa's lines, were in full retreat upon the fort, hotly pressed by a superior force of the enemy. I am pretty well known and respected by the men of both parties in Spain (indeed I served for some months on the Queen's side before I came over to Don Carlos); and, as it is my maxim never to give quarter, I never expect to receive it when taken myself. On issuing from the podesta, with Sheeny's portmanteau and my sword in my hand, I was a little disgusted and annoyed to see our own men in a pretty good column retreating at double-quick, and about four hundred yards beyond me up the hill leading to the fort, while on my left hand, and at only a hundred yards, a troop of the queenite lancers were clattering along the road.

I had got into the very middle of the road before I made this discovery, so that the fellows had a full sight of me, and, whizz! came a bullet by my left whisker before I could say Jack Robinson. I looked round—there were seventy of the accursed *malvados* at the least, and within, as I said, a hundred yards. Were I to say that I stopped to fight seventy men, you would write me down a fool or a liar: no, Sir, I did not fight, I ran away.

I am six feet four—my figure is as well known in the Spanish army as that of the Count de Luchana, or my fierce little friend Cabrera himself. "GAHAGAN!" shouted out half-a-dozen scoundrelly voices, and fifty more shots came rattling after me. I was running, running as the brave stag before the hounds—running as I have done a great number of times before in my life, when there was no help for it but a race.

After I had run about five hundred yards, I saw that I had gained nearly three upon our column in front, and that likewise the Christino horsemen were left behind some hundred yards more, with the exception of three, who were fearfully near me. The first was an officer without a lance; he had fired both his pistols at me, and was twenty yards in advance of his comrades; there was a similar distance between the two lancers who rode behind him. I determined then to wait for No. 1, and as he came up delivered cut 3 at his horse's near leg—off it flew, and down, as I expected, went horse and man. I had hardly time to pass my sword through my prostrate enemy, when No. 2 was upon me. If I could but get that fellow's horse, thought I, I am safe, and I executed at once the plan which I hoped was to effect my rescue.

I had, as I said, left the podesta with Sheeny's portmanteau, and, unwilling to part with some of the articles it contained—some shirts, a bottle of whiskey, a few cakes of Windsor soap, &c., &c.,—I had carried it thus far on my shoulders, but now was compelled to sacrifice it *malgré moi*. As the lancer came up, I dropped my sword from my right hand, and hurled the portmanteau at his head with aim so true, that he fell back on his saddle like a sack, and thus when the horse gallopped up to me, I had no difficulty in dismounting the rider—the whiskey bottle struck him over his right eye, and he was completely stunned. To dash him from the saddle and spring myself into it, was the work of a moment; indeed, the two combats had taken place in about a fifth part of the time which it has taken the reader to peruse the description. But in the rapidity of the last encounter, and the mounting of my enemy's horse, I had committed a very absurd oversight—I was scampering away *without my sword!* What was I to do?—to scamper on, to be sure, and trust to the legs of my horse for safety!

The lancer behind me gained on me every moment, and I could hear his horrid laugh as he neared me. I leaned forward jockey-fashion in my saddle, and kicked, and urged, and flogged with my hand, but all in vain. Closer—closer—the point of his lance was within two feet of my back. Ah! ah! he delivered the point, and fancy my agony when I felt it enter——through exactly fifty-nine pages of the "New Monthly Magazine." Had it not been for "The New Monthly Magazine and Humourist," I should have been impaled without a shadow of a doubt. Am I wrong in feeling gratitude? Have I not cause to continue my contributions?

When I got safe into Morella, along with the tail of the sallying party, I was for the first time made acquainted with the ridiculous result of the lancer's thrust (as he delivered his lance, I must tell you that a ball came whiz over my head from our fellows, and, entering at his nose, put a stop to *his* lancing for the future). I hastened to Cabrera's quarter, and related to him some of my adventures during the day.

"But, General," said he, "you are standing. I beg you '*chiudete l'uscio*' (take a chair)."

I did so, and then for the first time was aware that

there was some foreign substance in the tail of my coat, which prevented my sitting at ease. I drew out the Magazine which I had seized, and there, to my wonder, *discovered the Christino lance* twisted up like a fish-hook, or a pastoral crook.

"Ha! ha! ha!" said Cabrera (who is a notorious wag).

"Valdepeñas madrileños," growled out Tristany.

"By my cachuca di caballero" (upon my honour as a gentleman), shrieked out Ros d'Eroles, convulsed with laughter, "I will send it to the Bishop of Leon for a crozier."

"Gahagan has *consecrated* it," giggled out Ramon Cabrera; and so they went on with their muchacas for an hour or more. But, when they heard that the means of my salvation from the lance of the scoundrelly Christino had been the Magazine containing my own history, their laugh was changed into wonder. I read them (speaking Spanish more fluently than English) every word of my story. "But how is this?" said Cabrera. "You surely have other adventures to relate?"

"Excellent Sir," said I, "I have;" and that very evening, as we sat over our cups of tertullia (sangaree), I continued my narrative in nearly the following words:—

"I left off in the very middle of the battle of Delhi, which ended, as everybody knows, in the complete triumph of the British arms. But who gained the battle? Lord Lake is called Viscount Lake of Delhi and Laswaree, while Major Gaha—nonsense, never mind *him*, never mind the charge he executed when, sabre in hand, he leaped the six-foot wall in the mouth of the roaring cannon, over the heads of the gleaming pikes, when, with one hand seizing the sacred peish-cush, or fish—which was the banner always borne before Scindiah,—he, with his good sword, cut off the trunk of the famous white elephant, which, shrieking with agony, plunged madly into the Mahratta ranks, followed by his giant brethren, tossing, like chaff before the wind, the affrighted kitmatgars. He, meanwhile, now plunging into the midst of a battalion of consumahs, now cleaving to the chine a screaming and ferocious bobbachee,* rushed on, like the simoom across the red Zaharan plain, killing, with his own hand, a hundred and forty-thr—but never mind—'*alone he did it*;' sufficient be it for him, however, that the victory was won; he cares not for the empty honours which were awarded to more fortunate men!

"We marched after the battle to Delhi, where poor blind old Shah Allum received us, and bestowed all kinds of honours and titles on our general. As each of the officers passed before him, the shah did not fail to remark my person,† and was told my name.

"Lord Lake whispered to him my exploits, and the old man was so delighted with the account of my victory over the elephant (whose trunk I use to this day), that he said, 'Let him be called GUJPUTI,' or the lord of elephants, and Gujputi was the name by which I

* The double-jointed camel of Bactria, which the classic reader may recollect is mentioned by Suidas (in his Commentary on the Flight of Darius), is so called by the Mahrattas.

† There is some trifling inconsistency on the Major's part. Shah Allum was notoriously blind: how, then, could he have seen Gahagan? The thing is manifestly impossible.

was afterwards familiarly known among the natives—the men, that is. The women had a softer appellation for me, and called me 'Mushook,' or charmer.

"Well, I shall not describe Delhi, which is doubtless well known to the reader; nor the siege of Agra, to which place we went from Delhi; nor the terrible day at Laswaree, which went nigh to finish the war. Suffice it to say that we were victorious, and that I was wounded, as I have invariably been in the two hundred and four occasions when I have found myself in action. One point, however, became in the course of this campaign *quite* evident—*that something must be done for Gahagan.* The country cried shame, the king's troops grumbled, the sepoys openly murmured that their Gujputi was only a lieutenant, when he had performed such signal services. What was to be done? Lord Wellesley was in an evident quandary. 'Gahagan,' wrote he, 'to be a subaltern is evidently not your fate—*you were born for command;* but Lake and General Wellesley are good officers, they cannot be turned out—I must make a post for you. What say you, my dear fellow, to a corps of *irregular horse!*'

"It was thus that the famous corps of AHMEDNUGGAR IRREGULARS had its origin; a guerilla force, it is true, but one which will long be remembered in the annals of our Indian campaigns.

* * * * * * * *

"As the commander of this regiment, I was allowed to settle the uniform of the corps, as well as to select recruits. These were not wanting as soon as my appointment was made known, but came flocking to my standard a great deal faster than to the regular corps in the Company's service. I had European officers, of course, to command them, and a few of my countrymen as sergeants; the rest were all natives, whom I chose of the strongest and bravest men in India, chiefly Pitans, Afghans, Hurrumzadehs, and Calliawns, for these are well known to be the most warlike districts of our Indian territory.

"When on parade and in full uniform we made a singular and noble appearance. I was always fond of dress; and, in this instance, gave a *carte-blanche* to my taste, and invented the most splendid costume that ever perhaps decorated a soldier. I am, as I have stated already, six feet four inches in height, and of matchless symmetry and proportion. My hair and beard are of the most brilliant auburn, so bright as scarcely to be distinguished at a distance from scarlet. My eyes are bright blue, overshadowed by bushy eyebrows of the colour of my hair, and a terrific gash of the deepest purple, which goes over the forehead, the eyelid, and the cheek, and finishes at the ear, gives my face a more strictly military appearance than can be conceived. When I have been drinking (as is pretty often the case) this gash becomes ruby bright, and as I have another which took off a piece of my under lip, and shows five of my front teeth, I leave you to imagine that 'seldom lighted on the earth,' (as the monster Burke remarked of one of his unhappy victims,) 'a more extraordinary vision.' I improved these natural advantages; and, while in cantonment during the hot winds at Chitty-bobbary, allowed my hair to grow very long, as did my beard, which reached to my waist. It took me two hours daily to curl my hair in ten thousand little corkscrew ringlets, which waved over my shoulders, and to get my mustachios well round to the corners of my eyelids. I dressed in loose scarlet trousers and red morocco boots, a scarlet jacket, and a shawl of the same colour round my waist; a scarlet turban three feet high, and decorated with a tuft of the scarlet feathers of the flamingo, formed my headdress, and I did not allow myself a single ornament, except a small silver skull and cross-bones in front of my turban. Two brace of pistols, a Malay creese, and a tulwar, sharp on both sides, and very nearly six feet in length, completed this elegant costume. My two flags were each surmounted with a real skull and cross-bones, and ornamented one with a black, and the other with a red beard, (of enormous length, taken from men slain in battle by me.) On one flag were of course the arms of John Company; on the other, an image of myself bestriding a prostrate elephant, with the simple word 'GUJPUTI' written underneath in the Nagaree, Persian, and Sanscrit character. I rode my black horse, and looked, by the immortal gods, like Mars! To me might be applied the words which were written concerning handsome General Webb, in Marlborough's time:

"'To noble danger he conducts the way,
His great example all his troop obey,
Before the front the MAJOR sternly rides,
With such an air as Mars to battle strides.
Propitious heaven must sure a hero save
Like Paris handsome, and like Hector brave!'

"My officers (Captains Biggs and Mackanulty, Lieutenants Glogger, Pappendick, Stuffle, &c. &c.) were dressed exactly in the same way, but in yellow, and the men were similarly equipped, but in black. I have seen many regiments since, and many ferocious-looking men, but the Ahmednuggar Irregulars were more dreadful to the view than any set of ruffians on which I ever set eyes. I would to heaven that the Czar of Muscovy had passed through Caubul and Lahore, and that I with my old Ahmednuggars stood on a fair field to meet him! Bless you, bless you, my swart companions in victory! through the mist of twenty years I hear the booming of your war-cry, and mark the glitter of your scimetars as ye rage in the thickest of the battle!*

"But away with melancholy reminiscences. You may fancy what a figure the Irregulars cut on a field-day—a line of five hundred black-faced, black-dressed, black-horsed, black-bearded men—Biggs, Glogger, and the other officers in yellow, galloping about the field like flashes of lightning: myself enlightening them, red, solitary, and majestic, like yon glorious orb in heaven.

"There are very few men, I presume, who have not heard of Holkar's sudden and gallant incursion into the Dooâb, in the year 1804, when we thought that the victory of Laswaree and the brilliant success at Deeg had completely finished him. Taking ten thousand horse, he broke up his camp at Palimbang; and the first thing General Lake heard of him was, that he was at Putna, then at Rumpooge, then at Doncaradam—he was, in fact, in the very heart of our territory.

* I do not wish to brag of my style of writing, or to pretend that my genius as a writer has not been equalled in former times; but if, in the works of Byron, Scott, Goethe, or Victor Hugo, the reader can find a more beautiful sentence than the above, I will be obliged to him, that is all—I simply say, *I will be obliged to him.*—G. O'G. G., M. H. E. I. C. S., C. I. H. A.

"The unfortunate part of the affair was this:—His excellency, despising the Mahratta chieftain, had allowed him to advance about two thousand miles in his front, and knew not in the slightest degree where to lay hold on him. Was he at Hazarubaug? was he at Bogly Gunge? nobody knew, and for a considerable period the movements of Lake's cavalry were quite ambiguous, uncertain, promiscuous, and undetermined.

"Such briefly was the state of affairs in October, 1804. At the beginning of that month I had been wounded (a trifling scratch cutting off my left upper eyelid, a bit of my cheek, and my under-lip), and I was obliged to leave Biggs in command of my Irregulars, whilst I retired for my wounds to an English station at Furruckabad, *alias* Futtyghur—it is, as every two-penny postman knows, at the apex of the Dooâb. We have there a cantonment, and thither I went for the mere sake of the surgeon and the sticking-plaster.

"Furruckabad, then, is divided into two districts or towns; the lower Cotwal, inhabited by the natives, and the upper (which is fortified slightly, and has all along been called Futtyghur, meaning in Hindostanee, 'the-favourite-resort-of-the-white-faced-Feringhees-near-the-mangoe-tope-consecrated-to-Ram') occupied by Europeans. (It is astonishing, by the way, how comprehensive that language is, and how much can be conveyed in one or two of the commonest phrases.)

"Biggs, then, and my men were playing all sorts of wondrous pranks with Lord Lake's army, whilst I was detained an unwilling prisoner of health at Futtyghur.

"An unwilling prisoner, however, I should not say. The cantonment at Futtyghur contained that which would have made *any* man a happy slave. Woman, lovely woman, was there in abundance and variety! The fact is, that, when the campaign commenced in 1803, the ladies of the army all congregated to this place, where they were left, as it was supposed, in safety. I might, like Homer, relate the names and qualities of all. I may at least mention *some* whose memory is still most dear to me. There was—

"Mrs. Major General Bulcher, wife of Bulcher of the infantry.

"Miss Bulcher.

"MISS BELINDA BULCHER (whose name I beg the printer to place in large capitals).

"Mrs. Colonel Vandegobbleschroy.

"Mrs. Major Macan and the four Misses Macan.

"The Honourable Mrs. Burgoo, Mrs. Flix, Hicks, Wicks, and many more too numerous to mention. The flower of our camp was, however, collected there, and the last words of Lord Lake to me, as I left him, were 'Gahagan, I commit those women to your charge. Guard them with your life, watch over them with your honour, defend them with the matchless power of your indomitable arm.'

"Futtyghur is, as I have said, an European station, and the pretty air of the bungalows, amid the clustering topes of mangoe-trees, has often ere this excited the admiration of the tourist and sketcher. On the brow of a hill, the Burrumpooter river rolls majestically at its base, and no spot, in a word, can be conceived more exquisitely arranged, both by art and nature, as a favourite residence of the British fair. Mrs. Bulcher, Mrs. Vandegobbleschroy, and the other married ladies above-mentioned, had each of them delightful bungalows and gardens in the place, and between one cottage and another my time passed as delightfully as can the hours of any man who is away from his darling occupation of war.

"I was the commandant of the fort. It is a little insignificant pettah, defended simply by a couple of gabions, a very ordinary counterscarp, and a bomb-proof embrasure; on the top of this my flag was planted, and the small garrison of forty men only were comfortably barracked off in the casemates within. A surgeon and two chaplains (there were besides three reverend gentlemen, of amateur missions, who lived in the town) completed, as I may say, the garrison of our little fortalice, which I was left to defend and to command.

"On the night of the 1st of November, in the year 1804, I had invited Mrs. Major-General Bulcher and her daughters, Mrs. Vandegobbleschroy, and, indeed, all the ladies in the cantonment, to a little festival in honour of the recovery of my health, of the commencement of the shooting-season, and indeed as a farewell visit, for it was my intention to take dawk the very next morning and return to my regiment. The three amateur missionaries whom I have mentioned, and some ladies in the cantonment of very rigid religious principles, refused to appear at my little party. They had better never have been born than have done as they did, as you shall hear.

"We had been dancing merrily all night, and the supper (chiefly of the delicate condor, the luscious adjutant, and other birds of a similar kind, which I had shot in the course of the day) had been duly *fêted* by every lady and gentleman present; when I took an opportunity to retire on the ramparts, with the interesting and lovely Belinda Bulcher. I was occupied, as the French say, in *conter*-ing *fleurettes* to this sweet young creature, when, all of a sudden, a rocket was seen whizzing through the air, and a strong light was visible in the valley below the little fort.

"'What, fire-works! Captain Gahagan,' said Belinda, 'this is too gallant.'

"'Indeed, my dear Miss Bulcher,' said I, 'they are fire-works of which I have no idea: perhaps our friends the missionaries——'

"'Look, look!' said Belinda, trembling, and clutching tightly hold of my arm; 'what do I see? yes—no—yes! it is—*our bungalow is in flames!*'

"It was true the spacious bungalow occupied by Mrs. Major-General was at that moment seen a prey to the devouring element—another and another succeeded it—seven bungalows, before I could almost ejaculate the name of Jack Robinson, were seen blazing brightly in the black midnight air!

"I seized my night-glass, and looking towards the spot where the conflagration raged, what was my astonishment to see thousands of black forms dancing round the fires; whilst by their lights I could observe columns after columns of Indian horse, arriving and taking up their ground in the very middle of the open square or tank, round which the bungalows were built!

"'Ho, warder!' shouted I (while the frightened and trembling Belinda clung closer to my side, and pressed the stalwart arm that encircled her waist), 'down with the drawbridge! see that your masolgees (small tumbrils which are used in place of large artillery) be well loaded; you sepoys, hasten and man the ravelin! you choprasees, put out the lights in the embrasures! we shall have warm work of it to-night, or my name is not Goliah Gahagan.'

"The ladies, the guests (to the number of eighty-three), the sepoys, choprasees, masolgees, and so on, had all crowded on the platform at the sound of my shouting, and dreadful was the consternation, shrill the screaming, occasioned by my words. The men stood irresolute and mute with terror; the women trembling, knew scarcely whither to fly for refuge. 'Who are yonder ruffians?' said I; a hundred voices yelped in reply—some said the Pindarees, some said the Maharattas, some vowed it was Scindiah, and others declared it was Holkar—no one knew.

"'Is there any one here,' said I, 'who will venture to reconnoitre yonder troops?' There was a dead pause.

"'A thousand tomauns to the man who will bring me news of yonder army!' again I repeated. Still a dead silence. The fact was that Scindiah and Holkar both were so notorious for their cruelty, that no one dared venture to face the danger. 'Oh for fifty of my brave Ahmednuggarees!' thought I.

"'Gentlemen,' said I, 'I see it—you are cowards—none of you dare encounter the chance even of death. It is an encouraging prospect—know you not that the ruffian Holkar, if it be he, will with the morrow's dawn beleaguer our little fort, and throw thousands of men against our walls? know you not that, if we are taken, there is no quarter, no hope; death for us—and worse than death for these lovely ones assembled here?' Here the ladies shrieked and raised a howl as I have heard the jackalls on a summer's evening. Belinda, my dear Belinda! flung both her arms round me, and sobbed on my shoulder, (or in my waistcoat-pocket rather, for the little witch could reach no higher.)

"'Captain Gahagan,' sobbed she, '*Go—Go—Goggle—iah!*'

"'My soul's adored!' replied I.

"'Swear to me one thing.'

"'I swear.'

"'That if—that if—the nasty, horrid, odious black Mah-ra-a-a-attahs take the fort, you will put me out of their power.'

"I clasped the dear girl to my heart, and swore upon my sword that, rather than she should incur the risk of dishonour, she should perish by my own hand. This comforted her; and her mother, Mrs. Major-General Bulcher, and her elder sister, who had not until now known a word of our attachment (indeed, but for these extraordinary circumstances, it is probable that we ourselves should never have discovered it), were under these painful circumstances made aware of my beloved Belinda's partiality for me. Having communicated thus her wish of self-destruction, I thought her example a touching and excellent one, and proposed to all the ladies that they should follow it, and that at the entry of the enemy into the fort, and at a signal given by me, they should one and all make away with themselves. Fancy my disgust when, after making this proposition, not one of the ladies chose to accede to it, and received it with the same chilling denial that my former proposal to the garrison had met with.

"In the midst of this hurry and confusion, as if purposely to add to it, a trumpet was heard at the gate of the fort, and one of the sentinels came running to me, saying that a Mahratta soldier was before the gate with a flag of truce!

"I went down, rightly conjecturing, as it turned out, that the party, whoever they might be, had no artillery; and received at the point of my sword a scroll, of which the following is a translation:—

"'TO GOLIAH GAHAGAN GUJPUTI.

"'Lord of Elephants, Sir,—I have the honour to inform you that I arrived before this place at eight o'clock P.M. with ten thousand cavalry under my orders. I have burned since my arrival, seventeen bungalows in Furruckabad and Futtyghur, and have likewise been under the painful necessity of putting to death three clergymen (mollahs), and seven English officers whom I found in the village; the women have been transferred to safe keeping in the harems of my officers and myself.

"'As I know your courage and talents, I shall be very happy if you will surrender the fortress, and take service as a major-general (hookabadar) in my army. Should my proposal not meet with your assent, I beg leave to state that to-morrow I shall storm the fort, and on taking it, shall put to death every male in the garrison, and every female above twenty years of age. For yourself I shall reserve a punishment, which for novelty and exquisite torture, has, I flatter myself, hardly ever been exceeded. Awaiting the favour of a reply, I am, Sir,

"'Your very obedient servant,

"'JASWUNT ROW HOLKAR.

"'*Camp before Futtyghur, Sept.* 1, 1804.

"'R. S. V. P'"

"The officer who had brought this precious epistle (it is astonishing how Holkar had aped the forms of English correspondence), an enormous Pitan soldier, with a shirt of mail, and a steel cap and cape round which his turban wound, was leaning against the gate on his matchlock, and whistling a national melody. I read the letter, and saw at once there was no time to be lost. That man, thought I, must never go back to Holkar. Were he to attack us now before we were prepared, the fort would be his in half an hour.

"Tying my white pocket-handkerchief to a stick, I flung open the gate and advanced to the officer; he was standing, I said, on the little bridge across the moat. I made him a low salaam, after the fashion of the country, and, as he bent forward to return the compliment, I am sorry to say, I plunged forward, gave him a violent blow on the head which deprived him of all sensation, and then dragged him within the wall, raising the drawbridge after me.

"I bore the body into my own apartment; there, swift as thought, I stripped him of his turban, cammerbund, peijammahs, and papooshes, and, putting them on myself, determined to go forth and reconnoitre the enemy."

* * * * *

Here I was obliged to stop, for Cabrera, Ros d'Eroles, and the rest of the staff, were sound asleep! What I did in my reconnaissance, and how I defended the fort of Futtyghur, I shall have the honour of telling on another occasion.

CHAPTER IV.

THE INDIAN CAMP—THE SORTIE FROM THE FORT.

Head Quarters, Morella, October 3, 1838.

It is a balmy night. I hear the merry jingle of the tambourine, and the cheery voices of the girls and peasants, as they dance beneath my casement, under the shadow of the clustering vines. The laugh and song pass gaily round, and even at this distance I can distinguish the elegant form of Ramon Cabrera, as he whispers gay nothings in the ears of the Andalusian girls, or joins in the thrilling chorus of Riego's hymn, which is ever and anon vociferated by the enthusiastic soldiery of Carlos Quinto. I am alone, in the most inaccessible and most bomb-proof tower of our little fortalice; the large casements are open—the wind, as it enters, whispers in my ear its odorous recollections of the orange grove and the myrtle bower. My torch (a branch of the fragrant cedar tree) flares and flickers in the midnight breeze, and disperses its scent and burning splinters on my scroll and the desk where I write—meet implements for a soldier's authorship!—it is *cartridge* paper over which my pen runs so glibly, and a yawning barrel of gunpowder forms my rough writing-table. Around me, below me, above me, all—all is peace! I think, as I sit here so lonely, on my country, England! and muse over the sweet and bitter recollections of my early days! Let me resume my narrative, at the point where (interrupted by the authoritative summons of war) I paused on the last occasion.

I left off, I think (for I am a thousand miles away from proof-sheets as I write—and, were I not writing the simple TRUTH, must contradict myself a thousand times in the course of my tale,) I think, I say, that I left off at that period of my story, when, Holkar being before Futtyghur, and I in command of that fortress, I had just been compelled to make away with his messenger; and, dressed in the fallen Indian's accoutrements, went forth to reconnoitre the force, and, if possible, to learn the intentions of the enemy. However much my figure might have resembled that of the Pitan, and, disguised in his armour, might have deceived the lynx-eyed Mahrattas, into whose camp I was about to plunge, it was evident that a single glance at my fair face and auburn beard would have undeceived the dullest blockhead in Holkar's army. Seizing, then, a bottle of Burgess's walnut catsup, I dyed my face and my hands, and, with the simple aid of a flask of Warren's jet, I made my hair and beard as black as ebony. The Indian's helmet and chain hood covered likewise a great part of my face, and I hoped thus, with luck, impudence, and a complete command of all the Eastern dialects and languages, from Burmah to Afghanistan, to pass scot-free through this somewhat dangerous ordeal.

I had not the word of the night it is true—but I

trusted to good fortune for that, and passed boldly out of the fortress, bearing the flag of truce as before; I had scarcely passed on a couple of hundred yards, when, lo! a party of Indian horsemen, armed like him I had just overcome, trotted towards me. One was leading a noble white charger, and no sooner did he see me than, dismounting from his own horse, and giving the rein to a companion, he advanced to meet me with the charger; a second fellow likewise dismounted and followed the first; one held the bridle of the horse, while the other (with a multitude of salaams, aleikums, and other genuflexions,) held the jewelled stirrup, and kneeling, waited until I should mount.

I took the hint at once: the Indian who had come up to the fort was a great man—that was evident; I walked on with a majestic air, gathered up the velvet reins, and sprung into the magnificent high-peaked saddle. "Buk, buk," said I, "It is good—in the name of the forty-nine Imaums, let us ride on;" and the whole party set off at a brisk trot, I keeping silence, and thinking with no little trepidation of what I was about to encounter.

As we rode along, I heard two of the men commenting upon my unusual silence (for I suppose, I—that is, the Indian—was a talkative officer.) "The lips of the Bahawder are closed," said one—"where are those birds of Paradise, his long-tailed words? they are imprisoned between the golden bars of his teeth!"

"Kush," said his companion, "be quiet! Bobbachy Bahawder has seen the dreadful Feringhee, Gahagan Khan Gujputi, the elephant-lord, whose sword reaps the harvest of death; there is but one champion who can wear the papooshes of the elephant-slayer—it is Bobbachy Bahawder!"

"You speak truly, Puneeree Muckun, the Bahawder ruminates on the words of the unbeliever; he is an ostrich, and hatches the eggs of his thoughts."

"Bekhusm! on my nose be it! May the young birds, his actions, be strong, and swift in flight."

"May they *digest iron!*" said Puneeree Muckun, who was evidently a wag in his way.

O, ho! thought I, as suddenly the light flashed upon me. It was, then, the famous Bobbachy Bahawder, whom I overcame just now! and he is the man destined to stand in *my* slippers, is he? and I was at that very moment standing in his own! Such are the chances and changes that fall to the lot of the soldier!

I suppose everybody—everybody who has been in India, at least,—has heard the name of Bobbachy Bahawder; it is derived from the two Hindoostanee words—bobbachy, general; bahawder, artilleryman. He had entered into Holkar's service in the latter capacity, and had, by his merit and his undaunted bravery in action, attained the dignity of the peacock's feather, which is only granted to noblemen of the first class; he was married, moreover, to one of Holkar's innumerable daughters; a match which, according to the *Chronique Scandaleuse*, brought more of honour than of pleasure to the poor Bobbachy. Gallant as he was in the field, it was said that in the harem he was the veriest craven alive—completely subjugated by his ugly and odious wife. In all matters of importance the late Bahawder had been consulted by his prince, who had, as it appears (knowing my character, and not caring to do anything rash in his attack upon so formidable an enemy), sent forward the unfortunate Pitan to reconnoitre the fort; he was to have done yet more, as I learned from the attendant Puneeree Muckun, who was, I soon found out, an old favourite with the Bobbachy—doubtless on account of his honesty and love of repartee.

"The Bahawder's lips are closed," said he, at last, trotting up to me; "has he not a word for old Puneeree Muckun?"

"Bismillah, mashallah, barikillah," said I; which means, "my good friend, what I have seen is not worth the trouble of relation, and fills my bosom with the darkest forebodings."

"You could not then see the Gujputi alone, and stab him with your dagger?"

[Here was a pretty conspiracy!] "No, I saw him, but not alone; his people were always with him."

"Hurrumzadeh! it is a pity; we waited but the sound of your jogree (whistle), and straightway would have galloped up, and seized upon every man, woman, and child in the fort: however, there are but a dozen men in the garrison, and they have not provision for two days—they must yield; and then, hurrah for the moon-faces! Mashallah! I am told the soldiers who first get in are to have their pick. How my old woman, Rotee Muckun, will be surprised, when I bring home a couple of Feringhee wives,—ha! ha!"

"Fool!" said I, "be still!—twelve men in the garrison! there are twelve hundred! Gahagan himself is as good as a thousand men; and as for food, I saw, with my own eyes, five hundred bullocks grazing in the court-yard as I entered." This *was* a bouncer, I confess; but my object was to deceive Puneeree Muckun, and give him as high a notion as possible of the capabilities of defence which the besieged had.

"Pooch, pooch," murmured the men; "it is a wonder of a fortress, we shall never be able to take it until our guns come up."

There was hope, then! they had no battering train. Ere this arrived, I trusted that Lord Lake would hear of our plight, and march down to rescue us. Thus occupied in thought and conversation, we rode on until the advanced sentinel challenged us, when old Puneeree gave the word, and we passed on into the centre of Holkar's camp.

It was a strange—a stirring sight! The camp-fires were lighted; and round them—eating, reposing, talking, looking at the merry steps of the dancing-girls, or listening to the stories of some Dhol Baut (or Indian improvvisatore)—were thousands of dusky soldiery. The camels and horses were picketed under the banyan trees, on which the ripe mangoe fruit was growing, and offered them an excellent food. Towards the spot which the golden fish and royal purdahs, floating in the wind, designated as the tent of Holkar, led an immense avenue—of elephants! the finest street, indeed, I ever saw. Each of the monstrous animals had a castle on its back, armed with Mauritanian archers and the celebrated Persian matchlock-men; it was the feeding-time of these royal brutes, and the grooms were observed bringing immense toffungs or baskets, filled with pineapples, plantains, bandannas, Indian corn, and cocoa-nuts, which grow luxuriantly at all seasons of the year. We passed down this extraordinary avenue—no less than three hundred and eighty-eight tails did I count on each side—each tail appertaining to an elephant twenty-five feet high—each elephant having a two-storied castle on its back—each castle containing sleeping and eating-rooms for the twelve men that formed its garrison, and were keeping watch on the roof—each roof bearing a flag-staff twenty feet long on its top, the crescent glittering with a thousand gems, and round it the imperial standard,—each standard, of silk velvet, and cloth of gold, bearing the well-known device of Holkar, argent an or gules, between a sinople of the first, a chevron, truncated, wavy. I took nine of these myself in the course of a very short time after, and shall be happy, when I come to England, to shew them to any gentleman who has a curiosity that way. Through this gorgeous scene our little cavalcade passed, and at last we arrived at the quarters occupied by Holkar.

That celebrated chieftain's tents and followers were gathered round one of the British bungalows which had escaped the flames, and which he occupied during the siege. When I entered the large room where he sate, I found him in the midst of a council of war; his chief generals and viziers seated round him, each smoking his hookah, as is the common way with these black fellows, before, at, and after breakfast, dinner, supper, and bedtime. There was such a cloud raised by their smoke you could hardly see a yard before you—another piece of good luck for me—as it diminished the chances of my detection. When, with the ordinary ceremonies, the kitmutgars and consomahs had explained to the prince that Bobbachy Bahawder, the right eye of the Sun of the universe (as the ignorant heathens called me), had arrived from his mission, Holkar immediately summoned me to the maidaun, or elevated platform, on which he was seated in a luxurious easy chair, and I, instantly taking off my slippers, falling on my knees, and beating my head against the ground ninety-nine times, proceeded, still on my knees, a hundred and twenty feet through the room, and then up the twenty steps which led to his maidaun—a silly, painful, and disgusting ceremony, which can only be considered as a relic of barbarian darkness, which tears the knees and shins to pieces, let alone the pantaloons. I recommend anybody who goes to India, with the prospect of entering the service of the native rajahs, to recollect my advice, and have them *well wadded.*

Well, the right eye of the Sun of the universe scrambled as well as he could up the steps of the maidaun (on which, in rows, smoking as I have said, the musnuds or general officers were seated), and I arrived within speaking-distance of Holkar, who instantly asked me the success of my mission. The impetuous old man thereon poured out a multitude of questions: "How many men are there in the fort?" said he; "how many women? Is it victualled? have they ammunition? Did you see Gahagan Sahib, the commander? did you kill him?" All these questions Jeswunt Row Holkar puffed out with so many whiffs of tobacco.

Taking a chillum myself, and raising about me such a cloud, that, upon my honour as a gentleman, no man at three yards' distance could perceive anything of me except the pillar of smoke in which I was encompassed,

I told Holkar, in Oriental language, of course, the best tale I could with regard to the fort.

"Sir," said I, "to answer your last question first—that dreadful Gujputi I have seen—and he is alive; he is eight feet, nearly, in height; he can eat a bullock daily (of which he has seven hundred at present in the compound, and swears that during the siege he will content himself with only three a-week): he has lost, in battle, his left eye; and what is the consequence? O Ram Gunge (O thou-with-the-eye-as-bright-as-morning and-with-beard-as-black-as-night), Goliah Gujputi—NEVER SLEEPS!"

"Ah, you Ghorumsaug" (you thief of the world), said the Prince Vizier, Saadut Allee Beg Bimbukchee—"it's joking you are;"—and there was a universal buzz through the room at the announcement of this bouncer.

"By the hundred and eleven incarnations of Vishnou," said I, solemnly (an oath which no Indian was ever known to break), "I swear that so it is; so at least he told me, and I have good cause to know his power. Gujputi is an enchanter, he is leagued with devils, he is invulnerable. "Look," said I, unsheathing my dagger, and every eye turned instantly towards me—"thrice did I stab him with this steel—in the back, once—twice right through the heart; but he only laughed me to scorn, and bade me tell Holkar that the steel was not yet forged which was to inflict an injury upon him."

I never saw a man in such a rage as Holkar was when I gave him this somewhat imprudent message.

"Ah, lily-livered rogue!" shouted he out to me, "milk-blooded unbeliever! pale-faced miscreant! lives be after insulting thy master in thy presence? In the name of the Prophet, I spit on thee, defy thee, abhor thee, degrade thee! Take that, thou liar of the universe! and that—and that—and that!"

Such are the frightful excesses of barbaric minds! every time this old man said "Take that," he flung some article near him at the head of the undaunted Gahagan—his dagger, his sword, his carbine, his richly ornamented pistols, his turban covered with jewels, worth a hundred thousand crores of rupees—finally, his hookah, snake, mouth-piece, silver bell, chillum and all —which went hissing over my head, and flattening into a jelly the nose of the grand vizier.

"Yock muzzee!" "my nose is off," said the old man, mildly; "will you have my life, O Holkar? it is thine likewise!" and no other word of complaint escaped his lips.

Of all these missiles, though a pistol and carbine had gone off as the ferocious Indian flung them at my head, and the naked scimitar, fiercely but unadroitly thrown, had lopped off the limbs of one or two of the musnuds as they sat trembling on their omrahs, yet, strange to say, not a single weapon had hurt me. When the hubbub ceased, and the unlucky wretches who had been the victims of this fit of rage had been removed, Holkar's good-humour somewhat returned, and he allowed me to continue my account of the fort; which I did, not taking the slightest notice of his burst of impatience, as indeed it would have been the height of impoliteness to have done, for such accidents happened many times in the day.

"It is well that the Bobbachy has returned," snuffled

out the poor Grand Vizier, after I had explained to the council the extraordinary means of defence possessed by the garrison. "Your star is bright, O Bahawder! for this very night we had resolved upon an escalade of the fort, and we had sworn to put every one of the infidel garrison to the edge of the sword."

"But you have no battering train," said I.

"Bah! we have a couple of ninety-six pounders, quite sufficient to blow the gates open; and then, hey for a charge!" said Loll Mahommed, a general of cavalry, who was a rival of Bobbachy's, and contradicted, therefore, every word I said. "In the name of Juggernaut, why wait for the heavy artillery? Have we not swords? have we not hearts? Mashallah! Let cravens stay with Bobbachy, all true men will follow Loll Mahommed! Allahhumdillah, Bismillah, Barikallah?"* and drawing his scimitar, he waved it over his head, and shouted out his cry of battle. It was repeated by many of the other omrahs; the sound of their cheers was carried into the camp, and caught up by the men; the camels began to cry, the horses to prance and neigh, the eight hundred elephants set up a scream, the trumpeters and drummers clanged away at their instruments. I never heard such a din before or after. How I trembled for my little garrison when I heard the enthusiastic cries of this innumerable host!

There was but one way for it. "Sir," said I, addressing Holkar, "go out to-night, and you go to certain death. Loll Mahommed has not seen the fort as I

* The Major has put the most approved language into the mouths of his Indian characters. Bismillah, Barikallah, and so on, according to the novelists, form the very essence of Eastern conversation.

have. Pass the gate if you please, and for what? to fall before the fire of a hundred pieces of artillery; to storm another gate, and then another, and then to be blown up, with Gahagan's garrison, in the citadel. Who talks of courage? Were I not in your august presence, O star of the faithful, I would crop Loll Mahommed's nose from his face, and wear his ears as an ornament in my own pugree! Who is there here that knows not the difference between yonder yellow-skinned coward and Gahagan Khan Guj—I mean Bobbachy Bahawder? I am ready to fight one, two, three, or twenty of them, at broad-sword, small-sword, single-stick, with fists, if you please; by the holy piper, fighting is like mate and dthrink to Ga—to Bobbachy, I mane—whoop! come on, you divvle, and I'll bate the skin off your ugly bones."

This speech had very nearly proved fatal to me, for, when I am agitated, I involuntarily adopt some of the phraseology peculiar to my own country; which is so uneastern, that, had there been any suspicion as to my real character, detection must indubitably have ensued. As it was, Holkar perceived nothing, but instantaneously stopped the dispute. Loll Mahommed, however, evidently suspected something, for, as Holkar, with a voice of thunder, shouted out, "Tomasha," "silence," Loll sprung forward and gasped out—

"My Lord! my Lord; this is not Bob——"

But he could say no more. "Gag the slave!" screamed out Holkar, stamping with fury; and a turban was instantly twisted round the poor devil's jaws. "Ho, Furoshes! carry out Loll Mahommed Khan, give him a hundred dozen on the soles of his feet, set him upon a white donkey, and carry him round the camp, with an inscription before him—'This is the way that Holkar rewards the talkative.'"

I breathed again; and ever as I heard each whack of the bamboo, falling on Loll Mahommed's feet, I felt peace returning to my mind, and thanked my stars that I was delivered of this danger.

"Vizier," said Holkar, who enjoyed Loll's roars amazingly, "I owe you a reparation for your nose: kiss the hand of your prince, O Saadat Allee Beg Bimbukchee! be from this day forth Zoheir u Dowlut!"

The good old man's eyes filled with tears. "I can bear thy severity, O Prince," said he, "I cannot bear thy love. Was it not an honour that your highness did me just now, when you condescended to pass over the bridge of your slave's nose?"

The phrase was by all voices pronounced to be very poetical. The vizier retired, crowned with his new honours, to bed. Holkar was in high good-humour.

"Bobbachy," said he, "thou, too, must pardon me;—àpropos—I have news for thee. Your wife, the incomparable Puttee-Rooge, (white and red rose,) has arrived in camp."

"My wife, my Lord!" said I, aghast.

"Our daughter, the light of thine eyes! Go, my son; I see thou art wild with joy. The princess's tents are set up close by mine, and I know thou longest to join her."

My wife! here was a complication truly!

CHAPTER V.

THE ISSUE OF MY INTERVIEW WITH MY WIFE.

I FOUND Puneeree Muckun, with the rest of my attendants, waiting at the gate, and they immediately conducted me to my own tents in the neighbourhood. I have been in many dangerous predicaments before that time and since, but I don't care to deny that I felt in the present instance such a throbbing of the heart as I never have experienced when leading a forlorn hope, or marching up to a battery.

As soon as I entered the tents a host of menials sprung forward, some to ease me of my armour, some to offer me refreshments, some with hookahs, attar of roses (in great quart bottles), and the thousand delicacies of Eastern life. I motioned them away. "I will wear my armour," said I; "I shall go forth to-night: carry my duty to the princess, and say I grieve that to-night I have not the time to see her. Spread me a couch here, and bring me supper here; a jar of Persian wine well cooled, a lamb stuffed with pistachio-nuts, a pillaw of a couple of turkeys, a curried kid—anything. Begone! Give me a pipe; leave me alone, and tell me when the meal is ready."

I thought by these means to put off the fair Puttee Rooge, and hoped to be able to escape without subjecting myself to the examination of her curious eyes. After smoking for a while, an attendant came to tell me that my supper was prepared in the inner apartment of the tent (I suppose that the reader, if he be possessed of the commonest intelligence, knows that the tents of the Indian grandees are made of the finest Cashmere shawls, and contain a dozen rooms at least, with carpets, chimneys, and sash windows complete). I entered, I say, into an inner chamber, and there began with my fingers to devour my meal in the oriental fashion, taking, every now and then, a pull from the wine-jar which was cooling deliciously in another jar of snow.

I was just in the act of despatching the last morsel of a most savoury stewed lamb and rice, which had formed my meal, when I heard a scuffle of feet, a shrill clatter of female voices, and, the curtain being flung open, in marched a lady accompanied by twelve slaves, with moon-faces and slim waists, lovely as the houris in Paradise.

The lady herself, to do her justice, was as great a contrast to her attendants as could possibly be; she was crooked, old, of the complexion of molasses, and rendered a thousand times more ugly by the tawdry dress and the blazing jewels with which she was covered. A line of yellow chalk drawn from her forehead to the tip of her nose (which was further ornamented by an immense glittering nose-ring), her eye-lids painted bright red, and a large dab of the same colour on her chin, showed she was not of the Mussulman, but the Brahmin faith—and of a very high caste; you could see that by her eyes. My mind was instantaneously made up as to my line of action.

The male attendants had of course quitted the apartment, as they heard the well-known sound of her voice. It would have been death to them to have remained and looked in her face. The females ranged themselves round their mistress, as she squatted down opposite to me.

"And is this," said she, "a welcome, O Khan! after six months' absence, for the most unfortunate and loving wife in all the world—is this lamb, O glutton! half so tender as thy spouse? Is this wine, O sot! half so sweet as her looks?"

I saw the storm was brewing—her slaves to whom she turned, kept up a kind of chorus;—

"O, the faithless one!" cried they; "O, the rascal, the false one, who has no eye for beauty, and no heart for love, like the Khanum's!"

"A lamb is not so sweet as love," said I, gravely: "but a lamb has a good temper; a wine-cup is not so intoxicating as a woman—but a wine-cup has *no tongue*, O Khanum Gee!" and again I dipped my nose in the soul-refreshing jar.

The sweet Puttee Rooge was not, however, to be put off by my repartees; she and her maidens recommenced their chorus, and chattered and stormed until I lost all patience.

"Retire, friends," said I, "and leave me in peace."

"Stir, on your peril!" cried the Khanum.

So, seeing there was no help for it but violence, I drew out my pistols, cocked them, and said, "O houris! these pistols contain each two balls: the daughter of Holkar bears a sacred life for me—but for you!—by all the saints of Hindoostan, four of ye shall die if ye stay a moment longer in my presence!" This was enough; the ladies gave a shriek, and skurried out of the apartment like a covey of partridges on the wing.

Now, then, was the time for action. My wife, or rather Bobbachy's wife, sate still, a little flurried by the unusual ferocity which her lord had displayed in her presence. I seized her hand, and, gripping it close, whispered in her ear, to which I put the other pistol, "O Khanum, listen and scream not; the moment you scream, you die!" She was completely beaten: she turned as pale as a woman could in her situation, and said, "Speak, Bobbachy Bahawder, I am dumb."

"Woman," said I, taking off my helmet, and removing the chain cape which had covered almost the whole of my face—"*I am not thy husband*—I am the slayer of elephants, the world-renowned GAHAGAN!"

As I said this, and as the long ringlets of red hair fell over my shoulders (contrasting strangely with my dyed face and beard), I formed one of the finest pictures that can possibly be conceived, and I recommend it as a subject to Mr. Heath, for the next "Book of Beauty."

"Wretch!" said she, "what wouldst thou?"

"You black faced fiend," said I, "raise but your voice, and you are dead!"

"And afterwards," said she, "do you suppose that *you* can escape? The torments of hell are not so terrible as the tortures that Holkar will invent for thee."

"Tortures, madam," answered I, coolly, "fiddlesticks! You will neither betray me, nor will I be put to the torture: on the contrary, you will give me your best jewels and facilitate my escape to the fort. Don't grind your teeth and swear at me. Listen, madam; you know this dress and these arms, they are the arms of your husband, Bobbachy Bahawder—*my prisoner*. He now lies in yonder fort, and, if I do not return before daylight, *at sunrise he dies:* and then, when they send his corpse back to Holkar, what will you, *his widow*, do?"

"O!" said she, shuddering, "spare me, spare me!"

"I'll tell you what you will do. You will have the pleasure of dying along with him—of *being roasted*, madam, an agonizing death, from which your father cannot save you, to which he will be the first man to condemn and conduct you. Ha! I see we understand each other, and you will give me over the cash-box and jewels." And so saying I threw myself back with the calmest air imaginable, flinging the pistols over to her. "Light me a pipe, my love," said I, "and then go and hand me over the dollars; do you hear?" You see I had her in my power—up a tree, as the Americans say, and she very humbly lighted my pipe for me, and then departed for the goods I spoke about.

What a thing is luck! If Loll Mahommed had not been made to take that ride round the camp, I should infallibly have been lost.

My supper, my quarrel with the princess, and my pipe afterwards, had occupied a couple of hours of my time. The princess returned from her quest, and brought with her the box, containing valuables to the amount of about three millions sterling. (I was cheated of them afterwards, but have the box still, a plain deal one.) I was just about to take my departure, when a tremendous knocking, shouting, and screaming was heard at the entrance of the tent. It was Holkar himself, accompanied by that cursed Loll Mahommed, who, after his punishment, found his master restored to good-humour, and had communicated to him his firm conviction that I was an impostor.

"Ho, Begum!" shouted he, in the ante-room (for he and his people could not enter the women's apartments), "speak, O my daughter! is your husband returned?"

"Speak, madam," said I, "or *remember the roasting*."

"He is, papa," said the Begum.

"Are you sure? Ho! ho! ho!" (the old ruffian was laughing outside)—"are you sure it is?—Ha! ha! ha! —*he-e-e!*"

"Indeed it is he, and no other. I pray you, father, to go, and to pass no more such shameless jests on your daughter. Have I ever seen the face of any other man?" And hereat she began to weep as if her heart would break—the deceitful minx!

Holkar's laugh was instantly turned to fury. "O, you liar and eternal thief!" said he, turning round (as I presume, for I could only hear,) to Loll Mahommed, "to make your prince eat such monstrous dirt as this! Furoshes, seize this man. I dismiss him from my service, I degrade him from his rank, I appropriate to myself all his property; and, hark ye, Furoshes, GIVE HIM A HUNDRED DOZEN MORE!"

Again I heard the whacks of the bamboos, and peace flowed into my soul.

* * * * * *

Just as morn began to break, two figures were seen to approach the little fortress of Futtyghur; one was a woman wrapped closely in a veil, the other a warrior, remarkable for the size and manly beauty of his form, who carried in his hand a deal box of considerable size. The warrior at the gate gave the word and was admitted; the woman returned slowly to the Indian camp. Her name was Puttee Rooge; his was—

G. O'G. G., M. H. E. I. C. S. C. I. H. A.

CHAPTER VI.

FAMINE IN THE GARRISON.

Thus my dangers for the night being overcome, I hastened with my precious box into my own apartment, which communicated with another, where I had left my prisoner, with a guard to report if he should recover, and to prevent his escape. My servant, Ghorumsaug, was one of the guard. I called him and the fellow came, looking very much confused and frightened, as it seemed, at my appearance.

"Why, Ghorumsaug," said I, "what makes thee look so pale, fellow?" (He was as white as a sheet.) "It is thy master, dost thou not remember him?" The man had seen me dress myself in the Pitan's clothes, but was not present when I had blacked my face and beard in the manner I have described.

"O Bramah, Vishnou, and Mahomet!" cried the faithful fellow, "and do I see my dear master disguised in this way? For heaven's sake let me rid you of this odious black paint; for what will the ladies say in the ball-room, if the beautiful Feringhee should appear amongst them with his roses turned into coal?"

I am still one of the finest men in Europe, and at the

time of which I write, when only two-and-twenty, I confess I *was* a little vain of my personal appearance, and not very willing to appear before my dear Belinda disguised like a blackamoor. I allowed Ghorumsaug to divest me of the heathenish armour and habiliments which I wore; and having, with a world of scrubbing and trouble, divested my face and beard of their black tinge, I put on my own becoming uniform, and hastened to wait on the ladies; hastened, I say,—although delayed would have been the better word, for the operation of bleaching lasted at least two hours.

"How is the prisoner, Ghorumsaug?" said I, before leaving my apartment.

"He has recovered from the blow which the Lion dealt him: two men and myself watch over him; and Macgillicuddy Sahib (the second in command) has just been the rounds, and has seen that all was secure."

I bade Ghorumsaug help me to put away my chest of treasure (my exultation in taking it was so great, that I could not help informing him of its contents); and this done I despatched him to his post near the prisoner, while I prepared to sally forth and pay my respects to the fair creatures under my protection. What good after all have I done, thought I to myself, in this expedition which I had so rashly undertaken? I had seen the renowned Holker, I had been in the heart of his camp; I knew the disposition of his troops, that there were eleven thousand of them, and that he only waited for his guns to make a regular attack on the fort. I had seen Puttee Rooge; I had robbed her (I say *robbed* her, and I don't care what the reader or any other man may think of the act,) of a deal box, containing jewels to the amount of three millions sterling, the property of herself and husband.

Three millions in money and jewels! And what the deuce were money and jewels to me or to my poor garrison? Could my adorable Miss Bulcher eat a fricasee of diamonds, or, Cleopatra-like, melt down pearls to her tea? Could I, careless as I am about food, with a stomach that would digest anything—(once, in Spain, I ate the leg of a horse during a famine, and was so eager to swallow this morsel that I bolted the shoe, as well as the hoof, and never felt the slightest inconvenience from either)—could I, I say, expect to live long and well upon a ragout of rupees, or a dish of stewed emeralds and rubies? With all the wealth of Crœsus before me I felt melancholy; and would have paid cheerfully its weight in carats for a good honest round of boiled beef. Wealth, wealth, what art thou? What is gold?—Soft metal. What are diamonds?—Shining tinsel. The great wealth-winners, the only fame achievers, the sole objects worthy of a soldier's consideration, are beef-steaks, gunpowder, and cold iron.

The two latter means of competency we possessed; I had in my own apartments a small store of gunpowder (keeping it under my own bed, with a candle burning for fear of accidents); I had 14 pieces of artillery (4 long 48's and 4 carronades, 5 howitzers, and a long brass mortar, for grape, which I had taken myself at the battle of Assye), and muskets for ten times my force. My garrison, as I have told the reader in a previous number, consisted of 40 men, two chaplains, and a surgeon; add to these my guests, 83 in number, of whom nine only were gentlemen (in tights, powder, pigtails, and silk stockings, who had come out merely for a dance, and found themselves in for a siege). Such were our numbers:—

Troops and artillerymen . . .	40
Ladies	74
Other noncombatants	11
MAJOR G. O'G. GAHAGAN . .	1000
	1125

I count myself good for a thousand, for so I was regularly rated in the army: with this great benefit to it, that I only consumed as much as an ordinary mortal. We were then, as far as the victuals went, 126 mouths; as combatants we numbered 1040 gallant men, with 12 guns and a fort, against Holkar and his 12,000. No such alarming odds, if—

If!—ay, there was the rub—*if* we had *shot*, as well as powder, for our guns; *if* we had not only *men* but *meat*. Of the former commodity we had only three rounds for each piece. Of the latter, upon my sacred honour, to feed 126 souls, we had but

Two drumsticks of fowls, and a bone of ham.
Fourteen bottles of ginger-beer.
Of soda-water, four do. do.
Two bottles fine Spanish olives.
Raspberry cream—the remainder of two dishes.
Seven macaroons lying in the puddle of a demolished trifle.
Half a drum of best Turkey figs.
Some bits of broken bread; two Dutch cheeses (whole);

the crust of an old Stilton; and about an ounce of almonds and raisins.

Three ham-sandwiches, and a pot of currant-jelly, and 197 bottles of brandy, rum, madeira, pale ale (my private stock); a couple of hard eggs for a salad, and a flask of Florence oil.

This was the provision for the whole garrison! The men after supper had seized upon the relics of the repast, as they were carried off from the table; and these were the miserable remnants I found and counted on my return: taking good care to lock the door of the supper-room, and treasure what little sustenance still remained in it.

When I appeared in the saloon, now lighted up by the morning sun, I not only caused a sensation myself, but felt one in my own bosom, which was of the most painful description. O, my reader! may you never behold such a sight as that which presented itself: eighty-three men and women in ball dresses; the former with their lank powdered locks streaming over their faces; the latter with faded flowers, uncurled wigs, smudged rouge, blear eyes, draggling feathers, rumpled satins—each more desperately melancholy and hideous than the other—each, except my beloved Belinda Bulcher, whose raven ringlets never having been in curl could of course never go *out* of curl; whose cheek, pale as the lily, could, as it may naturally be supposed, grow no paler; whose neck and beauteous arms, dazzling as alabaster, needed no pearl-powder, and therefore, as I need not state, did not suffer because the pearl-powder had come off. Joy (deft link-boy!) lit his lamps in each of her eyes as I entered. As if I had been her sun, her spring, lo! blushing roses mantled in her cheek! Seventy-three ladies, as I entered, opened their fire upon me, and stunned me with cross-questions, regarding my adventures in the camp—*she*, as she saw me, gave a faint scream (the sweetest, sure, that ever gurgled through the throat of a woman!) then started up—then made as if she would sit down—then moved backwards—then tottered forwards—then tumbled into my—Psha! why recal, why attempt to describe that delicious—that passionate greeting of two young hearts? What was the surrounding crowd to *us?* What cared we for the sneers of the men, the titters of the jealous women, the shrill "Upon my word," of the elder Miss Bulcher, and the loud expostulations of Belinda's mamma? The brave girl loved me, and wept in my arms. "Goliah! my Goliah!" said she, "my brave, my beautiful, *thou* art returned, and hope comes back with thee. Oh! who can tell the anguish of my soul, during this dreadful, dreadful night!" Other similar ejaculations of love and joy she uttered; and if I *had* perilled life in her service, if I *did* believe that hope of escape there was none, so exquisite was the moment of our meeting, that I forgot all else in this overwhelming joy! * * * * *

[The major's description of this meeting, which lasted at the very most not ten seconds, occupies thirteen pages of writing. We have been compelled to dock off twelve-and-a-half; for the whole passage, though highly creditable to his feelings, might possibly be tedious to the reader.]

* * * * *

As I said, the ladies and gentlemen were inclined to sneer, and were giggling audibly. I led the dear girl to a chair, and, scowling round with a tremendous fierceness, which those who know me know I can sometimes put on, I shouted out, "Hark ye! men and women —I am this lady's truest knight—her husband I hope one day to be. I am commander, too, in this fort—the enemy is without it; another word of mockery—another glance of scorn—and, by Heaven, I will hurl every man and woman from the battlements, a prey to the ruffianly Holkar!" This quieted them. I am a man of my word, and none of them stirred or looked disrespectfully from that moment.

It was now *my* turn to make *them* look foolish. Mrs. Vandegobbleschroy (whose unfailing appetite is pretty well known to every person who has been in India) cried, "Well, Captain Gahagan, your ball has been so pleasant, and the supper was despatched so long ago, that myself and the ladies would be very glad of a little breakfast." And Mrs. Van giggled as if she had made a very witty and reasonable speech. "Oh! breakfast, breakfast by all means," said the rest; "we really are dying for a warm cup of tea."

"Is it bohay tay or souchong tay that you'd like, ladies?" says I.

"Nonsense, you silly man; any tea you like," said fat Mrs. Van.

"What do you say, then, to some prime GUNPOWDER?" Of course they said it was the very thing.

"And do you like hot rowls or cowld—muffins or crumpets—fresh butter or salt? And you, gentlemen, what do you say to some ilegant divvled-kidneys for yourselves, and just a trifle of grilled turkeys, and a couple of hundthred new-laid eggs for the ladies?"

"Pooh, pooh! be it as you will, my dear fellow," answered they all.

"But stop," says I. "O ladies, O ladies; O gentlemen, gentlemen, that you should ever have come to the quarters of Goliah Gahagan, and he been without—"

"What?" said they, in a breath.

"Alas! alas! I have not got a single stick of chocolate in the whole house."

"Well, well, we can do without it."

"Or a single pound of coffee."

"Never mind; let that pass too." (Mrs. Van and the rest were beginning to look alarmed.)

"And about the kidneys—now I remember, the black divvles outside the fort have seized upon all the sheep; and how are we to have kidneys without them?" (Here there was a slight o—o—o!)

"And with regard to the milk and crame, it may be remarked that the cows are likewise in pawn, and not a single drop can be had for money or love: but we can beat up eggs, you know, in the tay, which will be just as good."

"Oh! just as good."

"Only the divvle's in the luck, there's not a fresh egg to be had—no, nor a fresh chicken," continued I, "nor a stale one either; nor a tayspoonful of souchong, nor a thimbleful of bohay; nor the laste taste in life of butther, salt or fresh; nor hot rowls or cowld!"

"In the name of Heaven!" said Mrs. Van, growing very pale, "what is there, then?"

"Ladies and gentlemen, I'll tell you what there is, now," shouted I. "There's

Two drumsticks of fowls, and a bone of ham.
Fourteen bottles of ginger-beer," &c. &c. &c.

And I went through the whole list of eatables as before, ending with the ham-sandwiches and the pot of jelly.

"Law! Mr. Gahagan," said Mrs. Colonel Vandegobbleschroy, "give me the ham-sandwiches—I must manage to breakfast off them."

And you should have heard the pretty to-do there was at this modest proposition! Of course I did not accede to it—why should I? I was the commander of the fort, and intended to keep these three very sandwiches for the use of myself and my dear Belinda. "Ladies," said I, "there are in this fort one hundred and twenty-six souls, and this is all the food which is to last us during the siege. Meat there is none—of drink there is a tolerable quantity; and, at one o'clock punctually, a glass of wine and one olive shall be served out to each woman: the men will receive two glasses, and an olive and a fig—and this must be your food during the siege. Lord Lake cannot be absent more than three days; and, if he be, why still there is a chance—why do I say a chance?—*a certainty* of escaping from the hands of these ruffians."

"Oh, name it, name it, dear Captain Gahagan!" screeched the whole covey at a breath.

"It lies," answered I, "in the *powder magazine*. I

will blow this fort, and all it contains, to atoms, ere it becomes the prey of Holkar."

The women, at this, raised a squeal that might have been heard in Holkar's camp, and fainted in different directions; but my dear Belinda whispered in my ear, "Well done, thou noble knight! bravely said, my heart's Goliah!" I felt I was right: I could have blown her up twenty times for the luxury of that single moment! "And now, ladies," said I, "I must leave you. The two chaplains will remain with you to administer professional consolation—the other gentlemen will follow me up stairs to the ramparts, where I shall find plenty of work for them."

CHAPTER VII.

THE ESCAPE.

Loth as they were, these gentlemen had nothing for it but to obey, and they accordingly followed me to the ramparts, where I proceeded to review my men. The fort, in my absence, had been left in command of Lieutenant Macgillicuddy, a countryman of my own (with whom, as may be seen in an early chapter of my memoirs, I had an affair of honour); and the prisoner Bobbachy Bahawder, whom I had only stunned, never wishing to kill him, had been left in charge of that officer. Three of the garrison (one of them a man of the Ahmednuggar Irregulars, my own body-servant, Ghorumsaug above-named) were appointed to watch the captive by turns, and never leave him out of their sight. The lieutenant was instructed to look to them and to their prisoner, and as Bobbachy was severely injured by the blow which I had given him, and was moreover, bound hand and foot, and gagged smartly with cords, I considered myself sure of his person.

Macgillicuddy did not make his appearance when I reviewed my little force, and the three havildars were likewise absent—this did not surprise me, as I had told them not to leave their prisoner; but, desirous to speak with the lieutenant, I despatched a messenger to him, and ordered him to appear immediately.

The messenger came back; he was looking ghastly pale: he whispered some information into my ear, which instantly caused me to hasten to the apartments, where I had caused Bobbachy Bahawder to be confined.

The men had fled;—Bobbachy had fled; and in his place, fancy my astonishment when I found—with a rope, cutting his naturally wide mouth almost into his ears—with a dreadful sabre-cut across his forehead—with his legs tied over his head, and his arms tied between his legs—my unhappy, my attached friend—Mortimer Macgillicuddy!

He had been in this position for about three hours—it was the very position in which I had caused Bobbachy Bahawder to be placed—an attitude uncomfortable, it is true, but one which renders escape impossible, unless treason aid the prisoner.

I restored the lieutenant to his natural erect position: I poured half-a-bottle of whiskey down the immensely enlarged orifice of his mouth, and when he had been released, he informed me of the circumstances that had taken place.

Fool that I was! idiot!—upon my return to the fort, to have been anxious about my personal appearance, and to have spent a couple of hours, in removing the artificial blackening from my beard and complexion, instead of going to examine my prisoner; when his escape would have been prevented—O foppery, foppery! —it was that cursed love of personal appearance, which had led me to forget my duty to my general, my country, my monarch, and my own honour!

Thus it was that the escape took place. My own fellow of the Irregulars, whom I had summoned to dress me, performed the operation to my satisfaction, invested me with the elegant uniform of my corps, and removed the Pitan's disguise which I had taken from the back of the prostrate Bobbachy Bahawder. What did the rogue do next?—Why, he carried back the dress to the Bobbachy—he put it, once more, on its right owner, he and his infernal black companions (who had been so won over by the Bobbachy, with promises of enormous reward), gagged Macgillicuddy, who was going the rounds, and then marched with the Indian coolly up to the outer gate, and gave the word. The sentinel, thinking it was myself, who had first come in, and was as likely to go out again (indeed, my rascally valet said, that Gahagan Saib was about to go out with him and his two companions to reconnoitre)—opened the gates, and off they went!

This accounted for the confusion of my valet when I entered!—and for the scoundrel's speech, that the lieutenant had *just been the rounds;*—he *had*, poor fellow, and had been seized and bound in this cruel way. The three men, with their liberated prisoner, had just been on the point of escape, when my arrival disconcerted them: I had changed the guard at the gate (whom they had won over likewise); and yet, although they had overcome poor Mac, and although they were ready for the start, they had positively no means for effecting their escape, until I was ass enough to put means in their way. Fool! fool! thrice besotted fool that I was, to think of my own silly person when I should have been occupied solely with my public duty.

From Macgillicuddy's incoherent accounts, as he was gasping from the effects of the gag, and the whiskey he had taken to revive him, and from my own subsequent observations, I learned this sad story. A sudden and painful thought struck me—my precious box!—I rushed back, I found that box—I have it still—opening it, there where I had left ingots, sacks of bright tomauns, kopeks, and rupees, strings of diamonds as big as ducks' eggs, rubies as red as the lips of my Belinda, countless strings of pearls, amethysts, emeralds, piles upon piles of bank notes—I found—a piece of paper! with a few lines in the Sanscrit language, which are thus, word for word, translated:—

EPIGRAM.

(*On disappointing a certain Major.*)

The conquering lion return'd with his prey,
And safe in his cavern he set it,
The sly little fox stole the booty away;
And, as he escaped, to the lion did say,
"*Aha*, don't you wish you may get it?"

Confusion! Oh, how my blood boiled as I read these

cutting lines. I stamped,—I swore,—I don't know to what insane lengths my rage might have carried me, had not at this moment a soldier rushed in, screaming, " The enemy, the enemy!"

CHAPTER VIII.

THE CAPTIVE.

It was high time, indeed, that I should make my appearance. Waving my sword with one hand, and seizing my telescope with the other, I at once frightened and examined the enemy. Well they knew when they saw that flamingo-plume floating in the breeze—that awful figure standing in the breach—that waving war-sword sparkling in the sky—well, I say, they knew the name of the humble individual who owned the sword, the plume, and the figure. The ruffians were mustered in front, the cavalry behind. The flags were flying, the drums, gongs, tambourines, violoncellos, and other instruments of eastern music, raised in the air a strange, barbaric melody; the officers (yatabals), mounted on white dromedaries, were seen galloping to and fro, carrying to the advancing hosts the orders of Holkar.

You see that two sides of the fort of Futtyghur (rising as it does on a rock that is almost perpendicular), are defended by the Burrumpooter river, two hundred feet deep at this point, and a thousand yards wide, so that I had no fear about them attacking me in *that* quarter. My guns, therefore, (with their six-and-thirty miserable charges of shot,) were dragged round to the point at which I conceived Holkar would be most likely to attack me. I was in a situation that I did not dare to fire, except at such times as I could kill a hundred men by a single discharge of a cannon; so the attacking party marched and marched, very strongly, about a mile and a half off, the elephants marching without receiving the slightest damage from us, until they had come to within four hundred yards of our walls, (the rogues knew all the secrets of our weakness, through the betrayal of the dastardly Ghorumsaug, or they never would have ventured so near). At that distance—it was about the spot where the Futtyghur hill began gradually to rise—the invading force stopped; the elephants drew up in a line, right angles with our wall (the fools! they thought they should expose themselves too much by taking a position parallel to it!) the cavalry halted too, and—after the deuce's own flourish of trumpets, and banging of gongs, to be sure,—somebody, in a flame-coloured satin dress, with an immense jewel blazing in his pugree (that looked through my telescope like a small but very bright planet), got up from the back of one of the very biggest elephants, and began a speech.

The elephants were, as I said, in a line formed with admirable precision, about three hundred of them. The following little diagram will explain matters:—

E, is the line of elephants. F is the wall of the fort. G a gun in the fort. *Now* the reader will see what I did.

The elephants were standing, their trunks waggling to and fro gracefully before them; and I, with superhuman skill and activity, brought the gun G (a devilish long brass gun) to bear upon them. I pointed it myself; bang it went, and what was the consequence? Why this:—

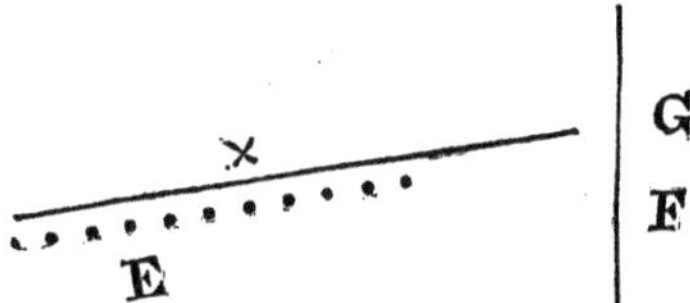

F is the fort, as before. G is the gun, as before. E, the elephants, as we have previously seen them. What then is + ? + *is the line taken by the ball fired from* G, which took off *one hundred and thirty-four elephants'* trunks, and only spent itself in the tusk of a very old animal, that stood the hundred and thirty-fifth!

I say that such a shot was never fired before or since; that a gun was never pointed in such a way. Suppose I had been a common man, and contented myself with firing bang at the head of the first animal? An ass would have done it, prided himself had he hit his mark,—and what would have been the consequence? Why, that the ball might have killed two elephants and wounded a third; but here, probably, it would have stopped, and done no further mischief. The *trunk* was the place at which to aim; there are no bones there; and away, consequently, went the bullet, shearing, as I have said, through one hundred and thirty-five probosces. Heavens! what a howl there was when the shot took effect! What a sudden stoppage of Holkar's speech! What a hideous snorting of elephants! What a rush backwards was made by the whole army, as if some-demon was pursuing them!

Away they went. No sooner did I see them in full retreat, than, rushing forward myself, I shouted to my men," My friends, yonder lies your dinner!" We flung open the gates—we tore down to the spot where the elephants had fallen; seven of them were killed; and of those that escaped to die of their hideous wounds elsewhere, most had left their tusks behind them. A great quantity of them we seized; and I myself, cutting up with my scimetar a couple of the fallen animals, as a butcher would a calf, motioned to the men to take the pieces back to the fort, where barbacued elephant was served round for dinner, instead of the miserable allowance of an olive and a glass of wine, which I had promised to my female friends, in my speech to them. The animal reserved for the ladies was a young white one—the fattest and tenderest I ever ate in my life: they are very fair eating, but the flesh has an India-rubber flavour, which, until one is accustomed to it, is unpalatable.

It was well that I had obtained this supply, for, during my absence on the works, Mrs. Vandegobbleschroy and one or two others, had forced their way into the supper-room, and devoured every morsel of the garrison larder, with the exception of the cheeses, the olives, and the wine, which were locked up in my own apartment, before which stood a sentinel. Disgusting Mrs. Van! When I heard of her gluttony, I had almost a mind to eat *her*. However, we made a very comfortable dinner off the barbacued steaks, and when every body had done, had the comfort of knowing that there was enough for one meal more.

The next day, as I expected, the enemy attacked us in great force, attempting to escalade the fort; but by the help of my guns, and my good sword, by the distinguished bravery of Lieutenant Macgillicuddy and the rest of the garrison, we beat this attack off completely, the enemy sustaining a loss of seven hundred men. We were victorious; but when another attack was made, what were we to do? We had still a little powder left, but had fired off all the shot, stones, iron bars, &c., in the garrison! On this day, too, we devoured the last morsel of our food; I shall never forget Mrs. Vandegobbleschroy's despairing look, as I saw her sitting alone, attempting to make some impression on the little white elephant's roasted tail.

The third day the attack was repeated. The resources of genius are never at an end. Yesterday, I had no ammunition; to-day, I had discovered charges sufficient for two guns, and two swivels, which were much longer, but had bores of about blunderbuss size.

This time my friend Loll Mahommed, who had received, as the reader may remember, such a bastinadoing for my sake, headed the attack. The poor wretch could not walk, but he was carried in an open palanquin, and came on waving his sword, and cursing horribly in his Hindoostan jargon. Behind him came troops of matchlock men, who picked off every one of our men who showed their noses above the ramparts; and a great host of blackamoors with scaling ladders, bundles to fill the ditch, fascines, gabions, culverins, demilunes, counterscarps, and all the other appurtenances of offensive war.

On they came; my guns and men were ready for them. You will ask how my pieces were loaded? I answer, that though my garrison were without food, I knew my duty as an officer, and *had put the two Dutch cheeses into the two guns, and had crammed the contents of a bottle of olives into each swivel.*

They advanced,—whish! went one of the Dutch cheeses,—bang! went the other. Alas! they did little execution. In their first contact with an opposing body, they certainly floored it; but they became at once like so much Welsh-rabbit, and did no execution beyond the man whom they struck down.

"Hogree, pogree, wongree-fum;" (praise to Allah, and the forty-nine Imaums!) shouted out the ferocious Loll Mahommed, when he saw the failure of my shot. "Onward, sons of the Prophet! the infidel has no more ammunition—a hundred thousand lakhs of rupees to the man who brings me Gahagan's head!"

His men set up a shout, and rushed forward—he, to do him justice, was at the very head, urging on his own palanquin bearers, and poking them with the tip of his scimetar. They came panting up the hill: I was black with rage, but it was the cold, concentrated rage of despair. "Macgillicuddy," said I, calling that faithful officer, "you know where the barrels of powder are?" He did. "You know the use to make of them?" He did. He grasped my hand. "Goliah," said he, "farewell! I swear that the fort shall be in atoms, as soon as yonder unbelievers have carried it. Oh, my poor mother!" added the gallant youth, as sighing, yet fearless, he retired to his post.

I gave one thought to my blessed, my beautiful Belinda, and then, stepping into the front, took down one of the swivels;—a shower of matchlock balls came whizzing round my head. I did not heed them.

I took the swivel, and aimed coolly. Loll Mahommed, his palanquin, and his men, were now not above two hundred yards from the fort. Loll was straight before me, gesticulating and shouting to his men. I fired—bang!!!

I aimed so true, that *one hundred and seventeen best Spanish olives were lodged in a lump in the face of the unhappy Loll Mahommed.* The wretch, uttering a yell the most hideous and unearthly I ever heard, fell back dead—the frightened bearers flung down the palanquin and ran—the whole host ran as one man; their screams might be heard for leagues. "Tomasha, tomasha," they cried, "it is enchantment!" Away they fled, and the victory a third time was ours. Soon as the fight was done, I flew back to my Belinda—we had eaten nothing for twenty-four hours, but I forgot hunger in the thought of once more beholding *her!*

The sweet soul turned towards me with a sickly smile as I entered, and almost fainted in my arms; but, alas! it was not love which caused in her bosom an emotion so strong—it was hunger! "Oh! my Goliah," whispered she, "for three days I have not tasted food—I could not eat that horrid elephant yesterday; but now—oh! heaven!" She could say no more, but sunk almost lifeless on my shoulder. I administered to her a trifling dram of rum, which revived her for a moment, and then rushed down stairs, determined that if it were a piece of my own leg, she should still have something to satisfy her hunger. Luckily I remembered that three or four elephants were still lying in the field, having been killed by us in the first action, two days before. Necessity, thought I, has no law; my adorable girl must eat elephant, until she can get something better.

I rushed into the court where the men were, for the most part, assembled. "Men," said I, "our larder is empty; we must fill it as we did the day before yesterday; who will follow Gahagan on a foraging party?" I expected that, as on former occasions, every man would offer to accompany me.

To my astonishment, not a soul moved—a murmur arose among the troops; and at last, one of the oldest and bravest came forward.

"Captain," he said, "it is of no use; we cannot feed upon elephants for ever; we have not a grain of powder left, and must give up the fort when the attack is made to-morrow. We may as well be prisoners now as then, and we won't go elephant-hunting any more."

"Ruffian!" I said, "he who first talks of surrender, dies!" and I cut him down. "Is there any one else who wishes to speak?"

No one stirred.

"Cowards! miserable cowards!" shouted I; "what, you dare not move for fear of death, at the hands of those wretches who even now fled before your arms—what, do I say *your* arms?—before *mine!*—alone I did it; and as alone I routed the foe, alone I will victual the fortress! Ho! open the gate!"

I rushed out; not a single man would follow. The bodies of the elephants that we had killed still lay on the ground where they had fallen, about four hundred yards from the fort. I descended calmly the hill, a very steep one, and coming to the spot, took my pick of the animals, choosing a tolerably small and plump one, of about thirteen feet high, which the vultures had respected. I threw this animal over my shoulders, and made for the fort.

As I marched up the acclivity, whizz—piff—whirr! came the balls over my head; and pitter-patter, pitter-patter! they fell on the body of the elephant like drops of rain. The enemy were behind me; I knew it, and quickened my pace. I heard the gallop of their horse: they came nearer, nearer; I was within a hundred yards of the fort—seventy—fifty! I strained every nerve; I panted with the superhuman exertion—I ran, —could a man run very fast with such a tremendous weight on his shoulders?

Up came the enemy; fifty horsemen were shouting and screaming at my tail. Oh, heaven! five yards more—one moment—and I am saved!—It is done—I strain the last strain—I make the last step—I fling forward my precious burden into the gate opened wide to receive me and it, and—I fall! The gate thunders to, and I am left *on the outside!* Fifty knives are gleaming before my bloodshot eyes—fifty black hands are at my throat, when a voice exclaims, "Stop!—kill him not, it is Gujputi!" A film came over my eyes—exhausted nature would bear no more.

CHAPTER IX.

SURPRISE OF FUTTYGHUR.

When I awoke from the trance into which I had fallen, I found myself in a bath, surrounded by innumerable black faces; and a Hindoo pothukoor (whence our word apothecary) feeling my pulse, and looking at me with an air of sagacity.

"Where am I?" I exclaimed, looking round and examining the strange faces, and the strange apartment which met my view. "Bekhusm!" said the apothecary. "Silence! Gahagan Saib is in the hands of those who know his valour, and will save his life."

"Know my valour, slave? Of course you do," said I; "but the fort—the garrison—the elephant—Belinda, my love—my darling—Macgillicuddy—the scoundrelly mutineers—the deal bo—" * * *

I could say no more; the painful recollections pressed so heavily upon my poor shattered mind and frame, that both failed once more. I fainted again, and I know not how long I lay insensible.

Again, however, I came to my senses; the pothukoor applied restoratives, and after a slumber of some hours, I awoke, much refreshed. I had no wound; my repeated swoons had been brought on (as indeed well they might) by my gigantic efforts in carrying the elephant up a steep hill a quarter of a mile in length. Walking, the task is bad enough, but running, it is the deuce; and I would recommend any of my readers who may be disposed to try and carry a dead elephant, never, on any account, to go a pace of more than five miles an hour.

Scarcely was I awake, when I heard the clash of arms at my door (plainly indicating that sentinels were posted there), and a single old gentleman, richly habited, entered the room. Did my eyes deceive me? I had surely seen him before. No—yes—no—yes—it *was* he—the snowy white beard, the mild eyes, the nose flattened to a jelly, and level with the rest of the venerable face, proclaimed him at once to be—Saadut Allee Beg Bimbukchee, Holkar's prime vizier, whose nose, as the reader may recollect, his highness had flattened with his kaleawn, during my interview with him in the Pitan's disguise.—I now knew my fate but too well—I was in the hands of Holkar.

Saadut Allee Beg Bimbukchee slowly advanced towards me, and with a mild air of benevolence, which distinguished that excellent man (he was torn to pieces by wild horses the year after, on account of a difference with Holkar), he came to my bedside, and taking gently my hand, said, "Life and death, my son, are not ours. Strength is deceitful, valour is unavailing, fame is only wind—the nightingale sings of the rose all night—where is the rose in the morning? Booch, booch! it is withered by a frost. The rose makes remarks regarding the nightingale, and where is that delightful song-bird? Pena-bekhoda, he is netted, plucked, spitted, and roasted! Who knows how misfortune comes? It has come to Gahagan Gujputi!"

"It is well," said I, stoutly, and in the Malay language. "Gahagan Gujputi will bear it like a man."

"No doubt—like a wise man and a brave one; but there is no lane so long to which there is not a turning, no night so black to which there comes not a morning. Icy winter is followed by merry spring time—grief is often succeeded by joy."

"Interpret, oh riddler!" said I; "Gahagan Khan is no reader of puzzles—no prating Mollah. Gujputi loves not words, but swords."

"Listen, then, oh, Gujputi: you are in Holkar's power."

"I know it."

"You will die by the most horrible tortures to-morrow morning?"

"I dare say."

"They will tear your teeth from your jaws, your nails from your fingers, and your eyes from your head."

"Very possibly."

"They will flay you alive, and then burn you."

"Well; they can't do any more."

"They will seize upon every man and woman in yonder fort"—it was not then taken!—"and repeat upon them the same tortures."

"Ha! Belinda! Speak—how can all this be avoided?"

"Listen. Gahagan loves the moon-face, called Belinda."

"He does, Vizier, to distraction."

"Of what rank is he in the Koompani's army?"

"A captain."

"A miserable captain—oh, shame! Of what creed is he?"

"I am an Irishman, and a Catholic."

"But he has not been very particular about his religious duties?"

"Alas, no."

"He has not been to his mosque for these twelve years?"

"'Tis too true."

"Hearken, now, Gahagan Khan. His Highness Prince Holkar has sent me to thee. You shall have the moon-face for your wife—your second wife, that is; —the first shall be the incomparable Puttee Rooge, who loves you to madness;—with Puttee Rooge, who is the wife, you shall have the wealth and rank, of Bobbachy Bahawder, of whom his highness intends to get rid. You shall be second in command of his highness's forces. Look, here is his commission signed with the celestial seal, and attested by the sacred names of the forty-nine Imaums. You have but to renounce your religion and your service, and all these rewards are yours."

He produced a parchment, signed as he said, and gave it to me (it was beautifully written in Indian ink —I had it for fourteen years, but a rascally valet, seeing it very dirty, *washed* it, forsooth, and washed off every bit of the writing)—I took it calmly, and said, "This is a tempting offer; oh, Vizier, how long wilt thou give me to consider of it?"

After a long parley, he allowed me six hours, when I promised to give him an answer. My mind, however, was made up—as soon as he was gone, I threw myself on the sofa and fell asleep.

* * * * *

At the end of the six hours the Vizier came back: two people were with him; one, by his martial appearance, I knew to be Holkar, the other I did not recognise. It was about midnight.

"Have you considered?" said the Vizier, as he came to my couch.

"I have," said I, sitting up,—I could not stand, for my legs were tied, and my arms fixed in a neat pair of steel handcuffs. "I have," said I, "unbelieving dogs! I have. Do you think to pervert a Christian gentleman from his faith and honour? Ruffian blackamoors! do your worst; heap tortures on this body, they cannot last long—tear me to pieces—after you have torn me into a certain number of pieces, I shall not feel it—and if I did, if each torture could last a life—if each limb were to feel the agonies of a whole body, what then? I would bear all—all—all—all—all—ALL!"—My breast heaved—my form dilated—my eye flashed as I spoke these words. "Tyrants!" said I, "Dulce et decorum est pro patriâ mori." Having thus clinched the argument, I was silent.

The venerable Grand Vizier turned away, I saw a tear trickling down his cheeks.

"What a constancy," said he; "oh, that such beauty and such bravery should be doomed so soon to quit the earth!"

His tall companion only sneered and said, "*and Belinda*—"

"Ha!" said I; "ruffian, be still!—Heaven will protect her spotless innocence. Holkar, I know thee, and thou knowest *me*, too! Who with his single sword destroyed thy armies?—Who, with his pistol, cleft in twain thy nose-ring? Who slew thy generals? Who slew thy elephants? Three hundred mighty beasts went forth to battle: of these, *I* slew one hundred and thirty-five!—Dog, coward, ruffian, tyrant, unbeliever! Gahagan hates thee, spurns thee, spits on thee!"

Holkar, as I made these uncomplimentary remarks, gave a scream of rage, and, drawing his scimetar, rushed on to despatch me at once (it was the very thing I wished for), when the third person sprang forward, and seizing his arm, cried—

"Papa; oh, save him!" It was Puttee Rooge! "Remember," continued she, "his misfortunes—remember, oh, remember my—love!"—and here she blushed, and putting one finger into her mouth and hanging down her head, looked the very picture of modest affection.

Holkar sulkily sheathed his scimetar, and muttered, "'Tis better as it is; had I killed him now, I had spared him the torture. None of this shameless fooling, Puttee Rooge," continued the tyrant, dragging her away. "Captain Gahagan dies three hours from hence"—Puttee Rooge gave one scream and fainted—her father and the Vizier carried her off between them; nor was I loath to part with her, for, with all her love, she was as ugly as the deuce.

They were gone—my fate was decided. I had but three hours more of life: so I flung myself again on the sofa, and fell profoundly asleep. As it may happen to any of my readers to be in the same situation, and to be hanged themselves, let me earnestly entreat them to adopt this plan of going to sleep, which I for my part have repeatedly found to be successful.—It saves unnecessary annoyance, it passes away a great deal of unpleasant time, and it prepares one to meet like a man the coming catastrophe.

* * * * *

Three o'clock came: the sun was at this time making his appearance in the heavens, and with it came the guards, who were appointed to conduct me to the torture. I woke, rose, was carried out, and was set on the very white donkey on which Loll Mahommed was conducted through the camp, after he was bastinadoed. Bobbachy Bahawder rode behind me, restored to his rank and state; troops of cavalry hemmed us in on all sides; my ass was conducted by the common executioner: a crier went forward, shouting out, "Make way for the destroyer of the faithful—he goes to bear the punishment of his crimes." We came to the fatal plain: it was the very spot whence I had borne away the elephant, and in full sight of the fort. I looked towards it. Thank Heaven! King George's banner waved on it still—a crowd were gathered on the walls—the men, the dastards who had deserted me—and women, too. Among the latter I thought I distinguished *one* who—Oh, gods! the thought turned me sick—I trembled and looked pale for the first time.

"He trembles! he turns pale," shouted out Bobbachy Bahawder, ferociously exulting over his conquered enemy.

"Dog!" shouted I—(I was sitting with my head to the donkey's tail, and so looked the Bobbachy full in the face)—"not so pale as you looked, when I felled you with this arm—not so pale as your women looked, when I entered your harem!" Completely chop-fallen, the Indian ruffian was silent: at any rate, I had done for *him*.

We arrived at the place of execution—a stake, a couple of feet thick and eight high, was driven in the grass; round the stake, about seven feet from the ground, was an iron ring, to which were attached two fetters; in these my wrists were placed—two or three executioners stood near with strange-looking instruments: others were blowing at a fire, over which was a cauldron, and in the embers were stuck other prongs and instruments of iron.

The crier came forward and read my sentence. It was the same in effect as that which had been hinted to me the day previous by the Grand Vizier. I confess I was too agitated exactly to catch every word that was spoken.

Holkar himself, on a tall dromedary, was at a little distance. The Grand Vizier came up to me—it was his duty to stand by, and see the punishment performed. "It is yet time," said he.

I nodded my head, but did not answer.

The Vizier cast up to heaven a look of inexpressible anguish, and with a voice choking with emotion, said, "*Executioner—do—your—duty!*"

The horrid man advanced—he whispered sulkily in the ears of the Grand Vizier, "*Guggly ka ghee, hum khedgeree*," said he, "*the oil does not boil yet*—wait one minute." The assistants blew, the fire blazed, the oil was heated. The Vizier drew a few feet aside, taking a large ladle full of the boiling liquid, he advanced, and—

* * * * * *
* * * * * *

Whish! bang, bang! pop! the executioner was dead at my feet, shot through the head; the ladle of scalding oil had been dashed in the face of the unhappy Grand Vizier, who lay on the plain, howling. "Whish! bang! pop! Hurrah!—charge!—forwards!—cut them down!—no quarter!"

I saw—yes, no, yes, no, yes!—I saw regiment upon regiment of galloping British horsemen, riding over the ranks of the flying natives! First of the host, I recognised, oh, Heaven! my AHMEDNUGGAR IRREGULARS! On came the gallant line of black steeds and horsemen; swift, swift before them rode my officers in yellow—Glogger, Pappendick, and Stuffle; their sabres gleamed in the sun, their voices rung in the air. "D— them!" they cried, "give it them, boys!" A strength supernatural thrilled through my veins at that delicious music; by one tremendous effort, I wrenched the post from its foundation, five feet in the ground. I could not release my hands from the fetters, it is true; but, grasping the beam tightly, I sprung forward—with one blow, I levelled the five executioners in the midst of the fire, their fall upsetting the scalding oil-can; with the next, I swept the bearers of Bobbachy's palanquin off their legs; with the third, I caught that chief himself in the small of the back, and sent him flying on to the sabres of my advancing soldiers!

The next minute, Glogger and Stuffle were in my arms, Pappendick leading on the Irregulars. Friend and foe in that wild chase had swept far away. We were alone, I was freed from my immense bar; and ten minutes afterwards, when Lord Lake trotted up with his staff, he found me sitting on it.

"Look at Gahagan," said his lordship. "Gentlemen, did I not tell you we should be sure to find him *at his post?*"

The gallant old nobleman rode on: and this was the famous BATTLE OF FURRUCKABAD, OR SURPRISE OF FUTTYGHUR, fought on the 17th of November, 1804.

* * * * *

About a month afterwards, the following announcement appeared in *Boggleywallah Hurkaru*, and other Indian papers:—"Married, on the 25th of December, at Futtyghur, by the Rev. Dr. Snorter, Captain Goliah O'Grady Gahagan, Commanding Irregular Horse Ahmednuggar, to Belinda, second daughter of Major-General Bulcher, C. B. His Excellency the Commander-in-Chief gave away the bride; and after a splendid *déjeuné*, the happy pair set off to pass the Mango season at Hurrygurrybang. Venus must recollect, however, that Mars must not *always* be at her side. The Irregulars are nothing without their leader."

Such was the paragraph—such the event—the happiest in the existence of

G. O' G. M. H. E. I. C. S. C. I. H. A.

THE END.

THACKERAY (the author of "Vanity Fair"), the late ROBERT SOUTHEY, JOHN FORSTER, SIR HUMPHREY DAVY, JOHN WILSON ("Christopher North" of Blackwood), WALTER SAVAGE LANDOR, the Writers for the LONDON TIMES, the leading QUARTERLY REVIEWS, LEIGH HUNT, the late WILLIAM HAZLITT, the authors of the "Rejected Addresses," BARHAM (author of the "Ingoldsby Legends"), SIR FRANCIS HEAD, JAMES MONTGOMERY, &c., &c., comprising generally the most brilliant authors of the Nineteenth Century.

APPLETONS' POPULAR LIBRARY will be printed uniformly in a very elegant and convenient 16mo. form, in volumes of from 250 to 400 pages each, from new type and on superior paper, and will be *bound* in a novel and attractive style for preservation, in fancy cloth, and will be sold at the average price of fifty cents per volume.

The following books, indicating the variety of the series, are preparing for immediate publication; and orders of the Trade are solicited:—

ESSAYS: A SERIES OF PERSONAL AND HISTORICAL SKETCHES FROM THE LONDON TIMES.

LIFE AND MISCELLANIES OF THEODORE HOOK.

JOHN FORSTER'S LIFE OF GOLDSMITH.

THE YELLOWPLUSH PAPERS AND OTHER VOLUMES, BY WILLIAM M. THACKERAY, AUTHOR OF "VANITY FAIR."

JEREMY TAYLOR; A BIOGRAPHY, BY ROBERT ARIS WILLMOTT.

LEIGH HUNT'S BOOK FOR A CORNER.

THE MISCELLANEOUS WRITINGS OF JAMES AND HORACE SMITH, THE AUTHORS OF THE "REJECTED ADDRESSES."

THE INGOLDSBY LEGENDS, BY BARHAM.

LITTLE PEDLINGTON AND THE PEDLINGTONIANS BY JOHN POOLE, AUTHOR OF "PAUL PRY."

&c., &c., &c.

APPLETONS' POPULAR LIBRARY.

THE MAIDEN AND MARRIED LIFE OF MARY POWELL,

AFTERWARDS MISTRESS MILTON.

Price Fifty Cents

"A reproduction "in their manners as they lived" of John Milton and his young bride, of whom the anecdote of their separation and reconciliation is told in Dr. Johnson's biography of the poet. The narrative is in the style of the period as the Diary of Lady Willoughby is written, and is remarkable for its feminine grace and character—and the interest of real life artistically disposed: a book for the selected shelf of the lady's boudoir in its touches of nature and sentiment no less than as a study of one of England's greatest poets "at home."

ENGLISH NOTICES.

"This is a charming book; and whether we regard its subject, cleverness or delicacy of sentiment and expression, it is likely to be a most acceptable present to young or old, be their peculiar taste for religion, morals, poetry, history, or romance."—*Christian Observer.*

"Unquestionably the production of an able hand, and a refined mind. We recommend it to all who love pure, healthy literary fare."—*Church and State Gazette.*

"Full of incident and character, and exceedingly delightful in its happy sketching and freshness of feeling. It is by far the best work of the small and novel class to which it belongs, a mixture of truth and fiction in a form which belongs to the fictitious more than to the substantial contents."—*Nonconformist.*

"The odd history of Milton's first marriage—the desertion of his wife, and her subsequent terror when she heard that he was just the man to put in practice his own opinions respecting divorce—forms one of those chapters, peculiarly open to illustration and fancy."—*Atlas.*

MINIATURE CLASSICAL LIBRARY.

Published in Elegant Form, with Frontispieces.

POETIC LACON; or, Aphorisms from the Poets. 38 cents.

BOND'S Golden Maxims. 31 cents.

CLARKE'S Scripture Promises. Complete. 38 cents.

ELIZABETH; or, The Exiles of Siberia. 31 cents.

GOLDSMITH'S Vicar of Wakefield. 38 cents.

——— Essays. 38 cents.

GEMS FROM AMERICAN POETS. 38 cents.

HANNAH MORE'S Private Devotions. 31 cents.

——— Practical Piety. 2 vols. 75 cents.

HEMANS' Domestic Affections. 31 cents.

HOFFMAN'S Lays of the Hudson, &c. 38 cents.

JOHNSON'S History of Rasselas. 38 cents.

MANUAL OF MATRIMONY. 31 cents.

MOORE'S Lallah Rookh. 38 cents.

——— Melodies. Complete. 38 cents.

PAUL AND VIRGINIA. 31 cts.

POLLOK'S Course of Time. 38 cts.

PURE GOLD FROM THE RIVERS OF WISDOM. 38 cents.

THOMSON'S Seasons. 38 cents.

TOKEN OF THE HEART. DO. OF AFFECTION. DO. OF REMEMBRANCE. DO. OF FRIENDSHIP. DO. OF LOVE. Each 31 cents.

USEFUL LETTER-WRITER. 38 cents.

WILSON'S Sacra Privata. 31 cents.

YOUNG'S Night Thoughts. 38 cts.

JUVENILE.

AUNT FANNY'S Christmas Stories. Illustrated. Boards, 31 cents; cloth, 50 cts.

AUNT KITTY'S Tales. By Maria J. McIntosh. 12mo. 75 cts.

AMERICAN Historical Tales. 16mo. 75 cents.

BOYS' MANUAL. Containing the Principle of Conduct, &c. 18mo. 50 cts.

——— STORY BOOK. 16mo. 75 c.

CARAVAN (The). A collection of Popular Eastern Tales. 16mo. Illustrated. 62 cents.

FIRESIDE FAIRIES; or, Evenings at Aunt Elsie's. Beautifully Illustrated. 16mo. 75 cts.

FRIDAY CHRISTIAN; or, The First-Born on Pitcairn's Island. 16mo. 50 cents.

GIRLS' MANUAL. Containing the Principle of Conduct. 50 cents.

——— STORY BOOK. 16mo. 75 c.

GUIZOT'S Young Student. 3 vols. in 1. 75 cents.

HOWITT, MARY. Picture and Verse Book. Commonly called Otto Specter's Fable Book. Illustrated with 100 Plates. Cheap Edition, 50 cents; cloth, 63 cents; gilt leaves, 75 cents.

HOME RECREATIONS. Edited by Grandfather Merryman. Colored Plates. 16mo. 75 cents.

INNOCENCE OF CHILDHOOD. By Mrs. Colman. 16mo. Illus. 50 cts.

JOAN OF ARC, Story of. By R. M. Evans. With 24 Illus. 16mo. 75 cts.

LOUIS' SCHOOL DAYS. By E. J. May. Illustrated. 16mo. 75 cts.

LEGENDS OF THE FLOWERS. By Susan Pindar. Illus. 16mo. 75 cts.

LIVES AND ANECDOTES OF ILLUSTRIOUS MEN. 16mo. 75 cts.

LOUISE; or, The Beauty of Integrity; and other Tales. 16mo. Boards, 31 cents; cloth, 38 cents.

MARRYATT'S Settlers in Canada. 2 vols. in 1. 62 cts.

——— Scenes in Africa. 2 vols. in 1. 62 cents.

——— Masterman Ready. 3 vols. in 1. 62 cents.

MIDSUMMER FAYS; or, The Holidays at Woodleigh. By Susan Pindar. 1 vol., 16mo. Cloth, 75 cents; cloth, gilt, $1.

NO SUCH WORD AS FAIL. By Cousin Alice. 16mo. Illus. 62 cents.

HANNAH MORE'S Village Tales. 18mo. 75 cents.

WILLIAM TELL, the Patriot of Switzerland. To which is added, Andreas Hofer, the "Tell" of the Tyrol. Cloth, 50 cents; half cloth, 38 cents.

YOUTH'S CORONAL. By H. F. Gould. 16mo. 63 cents.

PICTURE STORY BOOKS. By Great Authors and Great Painters. Four parts in 1 vol. Cloth, 75 cts; gilt edg., $1.

PUSS IN BOOTS. Finely Illustrated by Otto Specter. Square 18mo. Bds., 25 cts.; cloth, 38 cts.; extra gilt, 63 cts.

ROBINSON CRUSOE. Pictorial Edition. 3[illegible] Plates. 8vo. $1 50.

STORY OF LITTLE JOHN. Illustrated. 16mo. 63 cents.

——— OF A GENIUS. 38 cts.

YOUTH'S BOOK OF NATURE. Illustrated. 16mo. 75 cts.

——— STORY BOOK. 16mo. 75 cents.

JUVENILE.

Uncle Amerel's Story Books.

THE LITTLE GIFT BOOK. 18mo. Cloth, 25 cents.

THE CHILD'S STORY BOOK. Illustrated. 18mo. Cloth, 25 cents.

SUMMER HOLIDAYS. 18mo. Cloth, 25 cents.

WINTER HOLIDAYS. Illustrated. 18mo. Cloth, 25 cents.

GEORGE'S ADVENTURES IN THE COUNTRY. Illus. 18mo. Cloth, 25 c.

CHRISTMAS STORIES. Illustrated. 18mo Cloth, 25 cents.

Mary Howitt's Juvenile Tales.

New Editions bound together, entitled:

POPULAR MORAL TALES. 16mo. 75 cents.

JUVENILE TALES AND STORIES. 16mo. 75 cents.

MY JUVENILE DAYS, and other Tales. 16mo. 75 cents.

TALES AND STORIES FOR BOYS AND GIRLS. 75 cents.

Library for My Young Countrymen.

This Series is edited by the popular author of "Uncle Philip's Tales." The volumes are uniform in size and style.

ADVENTURES OF CAPT. JOHN SMITH. By the Author of "Uncle Philip." 38 cents.

ADVENTURES OF DANIEL BOONE. By do. 38 cents.

DAWNINGS OF GENIUS. By Anne Pratt. 38 cents.

LIFE AND ADVENTURES OF HENRY HUDSON. By the Author of "Uncle Philip." 38 cents.

LIFE AND ADVENTURES OF HERNAN CORTEZ. By the Author of "Uncle Philip." 38 cents.

PHILIP RANDOLPH. A Tale of Virginia. By Mary Gertrude. 38 cents.

ROWAN'S HISTORY OF THE FRENCH REVOLUTION. 2 volumes. 75 cents.

SOUTHEY'S LIFE OF OLIVER CROMWELL. 38 cents.

Tales for the People and their Children.

ALICE FRANKLIN By Mary Howitt. 38 cents.

CROFTON BOYS (The) By Harriet Martineau. 38 cents.

DANGERS OF DINING OUT. By Mrs. Ellis. 38 cents.

DOMESTIC TALES. By Hannah More. 2 vols. 75 cents.

EARLY FRIENDSHIP. By Mrs. Copley. 38 cents.

FARMER'S DAUGHTER (The). By Mrs. Cameron. 38 cents.

FIRST IMPRESSIONS. By Mrs. Ellis. 38 cents.

HOPE ON, HOPE EVER! By Mary Howitt. 38 cents.

LITTLE COIN, MUCH CARE. By do. 38 cents.

LOOKING - GLASS FOR THE MIND. Many Plates. 38 cents.

LOVE AND MONEY. By Mary Howitt. 88 cents.

MINISTER'S FAMILY. By Mrs. Ellis. 38 cents.

MY OWN STORY. By Mary Howitt. 38 cents.

MY UNCLE, THE CLOCK-MAKER. By Mary Howitt. 38 cents.

NO SENSE LIKE COMMON SENSE. By do. 38 cents.

PEASANT AND THE PRINCE. By H. Martineau. 28 cents.

POPLAR GROVE. By Mrs. Copley. 38 cents.

SOMERVILLE HALL. By Mrs. Ellis. 38 cents.

SOWING AND REAPING. By Mary Howitt. 38 cents.

STRIVE AND THRIVE. By do. 38 cents.

THE TWO APPRENTICES. By do. 38 cents.

TIRED OF HOUSEKEEPING. By T. S. Arthur. 38 cents.

TWIN SISTERS (The). By Mrs. Sandham. 38 cents.

WHICH IS THE WISER? By Mary Howitt. 38 cents.

WHO SHALL BE GREATEST? By do. 38 cts.

WORK AND WAGES. By do. 38 cents.

SECOND SERIES.

ANCES AND CHANGES. By arles Burdett. 38 cents.

DMAKER'S VILLAGE. By chokke. 38 cents.

NEVER TOO LATE. By Charles Burdett. 38 cents.

OCEAN WORK, Ancient and Modern. By J. H. Wright.

www.ingramcontent.com/pod-product-compliance
Lightning Source LLC
LaVergne TN
LVHW010221110826
845151LV00004B/1168